The Development and Impact of St. Andrew's Parish Church, Barbados

The Development and Impact of St. Andrew's Parish Church, Barbados

Dr. Sylvan R. Catwell, J.P.

2014

Copyright © 2014 by Dr. Sylvan R. Catwell, J.P.

The Development and Impact of St. Andrew's Parish Church, Barbados
by Dr. Sylvan R. Catwell, J.P.

Printed in the United States of America

ISBN 9781629524238

All rights reserved solely by the author. The author guarantees all contents are original and do not infringe upon the legal rights of any other person or work. No part of this book may be reproduced in any form without the permission of the author. The views expressed in this book are not necessarily those of the publisher.

Unless otherwise indicated, Bible quotations are taken from English Standard Version. Copyright © 2001 by Crossway. Bible quotations also taken from the New International Version. Copyright © 1973, 1978, 1984 by International Bible Society.

www.xulonpress.com

Dedication

This book is dedicated to my grandparents Deacon George and Dorcas Catwell, my wife Dolores, my daughters Joyann, Cheriann and Alala, and Fr. Gatherer.

Abstract

This work arose out of observation of the unique position occupied—among Barbados's 11 Anglican parish churches—by the St. Andrews Parish Church. Situated in one of the most inhospitable areas of the land in terms of a harsh environment, and subject to severe financial strictures, the Church under its now retired Rector of 52 years engaged in a never-ending struggle to combine its traditional ongoing pastoral and social work with a need to maintain a perpetually eroding physical structure. Research centred on uncovering and recording techniques employed, attitudes adopted or encountered, and the spiritual force at work which eventually led to an outcome that attracted the island-wide and overseas interest of even those not within the denominational ambit of the Church. In the course of the unfolding events, its indomitable leader engaged in a legal contest with Church authorities which eventually led to the validation of the Constitution, Canons and Regulations and rewriting of Church history of the 300-year-old Anglican Church of the Diocese of Barbados.

Some folklore of the parish, along with questions the general church is asking, will be noted, as well as how the Anglican Church braved the challenges of disestablishment and kept its doors opened.

Interviews to record the oral history and reminiscences of parishioners and clergy, visits to England to search out original resources, internet searches, publications and in-person visitations in the district to gain a "feel" for the life of the parish, were among the tools employed to ferret out the Church's history and the lessons to be learned therefrom by both clergy and laymen. It was noteworthy that, as is so often the case, some personal characteristics, normally highly commended, could contribute to placing a restraint on easy relationships within the church family. Leaders have to be aware that overstaying their years of effective ministry (usefulness) can be detrimental to their congregations. Ongoing training and retraining is in order if a ministry is to meet the ever-changing needs of parishioners, and sound advice must be considered, if not heeded in its entirety, if difficulties are to be minimised.

A prime lesson emerging is the fact that the Church is not above the law. The clergy must appreciate that Church laws and constitutions need to be grounded in sound theology and civil law, and appropriately revised and upgraded to remain relevant and effective.

Acknowledgement

The readiness of Father Gatherer, Rector of St. Andrew's Parish Church, to approve and support the writing of this book is lauded. He willingly made some prized pictures and one of his cherished personal small diaries available to me. During the last two years of this work, it became more difficult for him to consistently recall information. It is regrettable that Father Gatherer's story and thoughts had not been carefully sought and chronicled at an earlier moment in time.

This book is partly dedicated to 1) my grandparents, Deacon George and Dorcas Catwell, who raised me, while never ceasing to encourage me to become a church leader (Reverend) and a doctor, 2) Father Gatherer whom my wife and her family informed me, was very kind to them. They "ate out of his pot"—not after, but with him; and nothing was too good for him to share with them; and 3) to my wife, Dolores, and daughters—Joyann, Cheriann and Alala—who sacrificed 'vital family time' in allowing me to perform pastoral ministry over the past 30-odd years, when they needed me most.

I am indebted to many benevolent persons, especially of St. Andrew, for volunteering information in interviews, side chats, and discussions that enabled copious notes to be taken in assisting with the compilation of this volume. The invaluable and kind help of the staff of the Archives Department, the National Public Libraries, the Library of Codrington College, and especially, Librarian Karen Bathrobes, the London Metropolitan Archives Library, England, the Most Rev'd. and Right Hon. Dr. Rowan Williams, Archbishop of Canterbury, Bishops—the Right Rev'd. Dr. Wilfred Denniston Wood, KA and The Right Rev'd. Dr. Rufus T. Brome, GCM; Very Rev'd. Dr. Frank Marshall, CBE, Dean of St. Michael's Cathedral, Barbados; Hon. Senator, Dean Emeritus Harold Crichlow, GCM; the Diocesan staff, especially Audine Wilkinson, as well as Canon Lionel Burke, Rev'd. Laurence Small, MBE, and numerous other individuals, is thankfully appreciated. For helping me sort out some of my computer problems I could not forget Tamara Downes, Miles Phillips, Philip Pile, Hadyn Clarke and Curtis Toppin. Those who offered proofreading support include Bob Verdun and Mrs. Muriel Forde, for which I am grateful. But I must single out Mrs. Forde for her ever warm and ready editorial assistance in correcting and helping me make sense out of this volume.

Kind persons, including my sister Haldor Adebowale and Cheryl Hurst, who graciously contributed articles and notes have earned my lasting gratitude.

My daughters Alala and Joyann, and Joyann's husband Curtis, along with Anthony Roett, helped me cut a path through the thick bush and lush undergrowth of the unkempt original graveyard associated with this Church, in order to unearth inscriptions and tombstones; and to them I am obliged.

Table of Contents

Acknowledgement 7
List of Tables 11
List of Figures 13
Introduction 17

CHAPTER ONE
Barbados, St. Andrew and St. Andrew's Parish Church 21

CHAPTER TWO
Early Chronology of St. Andrew's Parish Church (1630s–1850s) 35

CHAPTER THREE
Rebuilding and Consolidating the Church (1840s–1950s) 48

CHAPTER FOUR
Rector Gatherer and St. Andrew's Parish Church (1957–1980s) Phase 1 72

CHAPTER FIVE
Impact of Establishment and Disestablishment on the Church and St. Andrew's 95

CHAPTER SIX
Priest Validates Law and Rewrites Church History (1980s–1990s) 111

CHAPTER SEVEN
The Doors Remain Open (1990s–2011) Phase 2 118

CHAPTER EIGHT
Parishioners of note who attended St. Andrew's Parish Church 139

CHAPTER NINE
Attractions and Places of Significance within 10 minutes drive from St. Andrew's 147

CHAPTER TEN
Graves and Inscriptions connected with St. Andrew's Parish Church 153

CHAPTER ELEVEN
Canon Gatherer and Retirement 158

CHAPTER TWELVE
Edited Excerpts of Tributes to the Rev'd. Canon Edward Gatherer contributed by relatives, members and friends 171

CHAPTER THIRTEEN
"In the Pew"—Any Word to Heed? Any Lessons to Learn? 190

CHAPTER FOURTEEN
And the work goes on (2011 and Beyond) 200

APPENDICES
Appendix 1: Formalising Appointment of Anglican Church Leadership in the 18th century 207
Appendix 2: Hudson's Contribution to and the Impact of Church Music in Barbados 209
Appendix 3: List of Anglican Clergy 1989, According to Date of Ordination 213
Appendix 4: "Only in St. Andrew"—Story of the Green Giant and the Shepherd Boy 215
Appendix 5: Copies of Articles from the Media 219
Appendix 6: Oldest Anglican priest to retire: The Church of England Newspaper, March 18, 2011, p 8 231
Appendix 7: Copies of Correspondence and Notes 233

BIBLIOGRAPHY 237

List of Tables

1. Church Walk Through and Legend 26
2. Glossary 29
3. Government Ten-year Reducing Church Subsidy 102
4. Settlement (*Rev'd. Gatherer* v *Right Rev'd. Drexel Gomez*) 116
5. St. Andrew's Organists and Assistants (1950–2010) 130
6. Clergy and Congregation of St. Andrew's 132
7. Incumbents of St. Andrew's Parish Church 133
8. Inscriptions of St. Andrew's Parish Church 154

List of Figures

1: Parish of St. Andrew, Barbados 22
2: GPS of St. Andrew's Church and Original Burial Ground 24
3: Explore St. Andrew's Parish Church 25
4: Walkers and outline of Turner's Hall, Spring Hall and Rock Hall 32
5: Benn Hill and Babylon Highlands 32
6: Walker's Bay behind vegetated sand dunes 33
7: Vaughan's Tombstone dated 1733 (in Original Graveyard) 38
8: Gaping hole in the roof of a tomb 38
9: Bricks from damaged tomb 39
10: Collection of gravestones 39
11: Dedication Plaque of Cornerstone for rebuilding of the Church 49
12: Plaque in Church foyer 52
13: Rev'd. John Hutson's grave 51
14: Remains of railway terminus platform 52
15: Archbishop Cuthbert Woodroffe, KBE 66
16: Rector Gatherer at work 2010 74
17: Bishop Wilfred Wood, KA 75
18: Chairman Rev'd. E. Gatherer with Erma Rock top right and
    Vestry members 77
19: Pastor Lillian Campbell 86
20: Belleplaine United House of Prayer, St. Andrew 87
21: Cheryl Hurst bidding Farewell 90
22: Open Door 118
23: Buttress of St. Andrew's 120
24: Structural crack above window 122
25: Greenland Landfill under construction 125
26: Augmented Choir at 2009 Christmas Party after cantata 'A Song Unending'.. 129
27: Organist Joyann Catwell 129
28: Church car park 130
29: Cruciform Pavement in grave yard 131
30: 14-foot diameter remains of 100-year old Pride of India 131

31: Barbados' early Vulcan Foundry 2-6-2 Railway Tank Engine 142
32: Fleet of Rocklyn buses 143
33: Picnic at Barclays Park 147
34: Entering the original graveyard 148
35: Wooded graveyard at Top 149
36: Remnant of Farley Hill Plantation House 150
37: St. Nicholas Abbey, St. Peter 150
38: Sand Dunes Bar & Restaurant, East Coast, St. Andrew 151
39: Morgan Lewis Mill, St. Andrew 151
40: Clearing slab of John Foord's grave 156
41: Inscription on grave of John Foord. . . B—1617 156
42: Tombstone of Sir Conrad Hunte 157
43: Slab of grave found near entrance of original graveyard 157
44: Tombstone of Rev'd. John Hutson 157
45: Tombstone of Erma Rock 157
46: Clergy and friends at Retirement Service 165
47: Canon Gatherer's final 'Thank you' at his retirement service 169
48: Fr. Gatherer serving / blessing children 171
49: Sarah E. Hurst 173
50: Alala Moore 173
51: Fr. Gatherer in Bishop's Certificate Awards Ceremony 175
52: Simeon Belgrave 176
53: Rector Gatherer and Cheryl Hurst 177
54: Skit at St. Andrew's Mother's Union Concert, July 2011 202
55: What's a concert without a laugh? 202
56: Congregation at Mother's Union Concert 203
57: Obsolete Rectory, Belleplaine, St. Andrew 203
58: Farewell from the Sunday school 204
59: Farewell from the St. Michael's and St. Andrew's Choirs 204
60: Friends at Fr. Gatherer's 92nd Birthday island tour 205
61: Canon Gatherer—"I fought the fight, ran the race and
    finished my course in St. Andrew's March 2011" 205

Of the eleven parishes in Barbados, St. Andrew, now one of the greatest and most popular, was once the least known in Church history. Dr. Sylvan Catwell by his dedication, devotion and self-imposed duty to the task of producing a most wonderful and much needed publication has filled the void, befitting his skills and learning in the process.

The author richly deserves the honour and attendant rewards which must accrue from his work. The book will enable readers to be fortified and enriched with knowledge of St. Andrew's Parish Church and its impact for the good of the parish in particular, and the country of Barbados as a whole.

Indeed this publication will be of inestimable benefit to generations to come both at home and around the globe.

As one given the honour and privilege to have been in some small way (no pun intended) to be associated with Dr. Catwell's work, I accept it with humble gratitude, and offer him my congratulations with my firm conviction that his endeavours will be a means of equipping readers with further knowledge in the areas of history, education and inspiration. On this publication, to the distinguished author, Dr. Sylvan Catwell, we say, Well Done! Well Timed!

There could be no better time than Now.

To Readers: READ and FEED on knowledge.

Rev'd. Laurence Small

Laurence Small, Priest
The Diocese of Barbados
Church in the Province of the West Indies
Honorary Life Member, Barbados Association of Journalists

I enjoyed this book and learned far more than I had anticipated about both the Church and Father Gatherer. Indeed, I have revised my assessment of the Rector's longevity at the Church and indeed his contribution. Very fascinating!

I really appreciated the legend provided at the outset of the book. It was most informative. Much detail also went into the first 200 years of the Church.

In summary, Dr. Catwell, you have done a marvellous job on a subject which I prejudged to be boring. How wrong I was! The information had to be recorded.

You are doing St. Andrew, the Anglican Church and indeed Barbados a great favour once this is published. Present and future generations will be indebted to you for this outstanding volume.

Harold Hoyte, Editor Emeritus, *The Nation*,
P. O. Box 1203, "Nation House", St. Michael, Barbados

Introduction

During the short period that my daughter, Joyann, was organist of St. Andrew's Parish Church (2007—2010), it became necessary for the choir to acquire new robes, and funds to purchase ancillary items. As very little authoritative material was available on this historic Parish Church, an idea evolved that a booklet could be written for sale, and some of the proceeds used to reduce the cost of robes and meet other minor choir expenses. In 2008, with Father Gatherer's approval and blessing, some interviews were conducted and a few notes compiled for the booklet.

When the booklet was virtually completed and additional notes still remained, the idea dawned that a comprehensive volume on St. Andrew's would be desirable. Fieldwork continued until the present volume was completed.

Research for this project involved reviewing extensive desktop literature. Like looking for a needle in a haystack, one combed the Archives Department and libraries in Barbados and, as much as possible, the Colonial Records in London to unearth information that was not yet in public circulation. The more one searched, the more convinced one became that original information involving letters, notes and manuscripts from clergy and other people who resided in Barbados, were communicated to the Bishops of London for their attention and advice. However, it appeared that much of that information regarding the early history of the churches was lost in Barbados either through destructive hurricanes, or lack of proper storage, and could not be retrieved. Regrettably, much of the information that was sent to England prior to 1700 was also not properly stored, or had not been made available to the public. Additionally, perhaps this information had been appropriated by earlier researchers for personal use and taken out of circulation.

Some brief mentions occurred in references in a few books written on the early history of the churches in Barbados. However, trying to find the original sources in libraries and repositories in the United Kingdom was time-consuming, and yielded little in the way of additional relevant material.

Unfortunately, with no records being retrieved from St. Andrew's over the last 50-odd years, it was necessary to undertake extensive interviews to glean information from senior members of the Church and people of the parish of St. Andrew.

Initially, a thematic chapter approach was deemed impractical as facts appeared difficult to come by. Nevertheless, bits and pieces of data trickled in, which made rewriting and reshaping a continually challenging feature of this compilation. Basically, then, the chapter divisions occurring late in the composition merely attempt to present the book in sections for ease of reference and description, and not principally to delineate a theme, which may ideally be developed in a later work.

The Barbados Diocesan History, dedicated to Bishop Alfred P. Berkeley, D.D., by Rev'ds. J.E. Reece and C.G. Clark-Hunt, is a centenary compilation (1825–1925) on the work of the diocese that celebrated "the hundredth anniversary of the Consecration of the first Bishop of Barbados". It provides information on the Anglican churches of Barbados, including the construction and reconstruction of church buildings that were destroyed by fire, hurricane, or other mishap. The booklet mentions early articles written, for example, by Mr. N. Greenhalgh (Chief School Inspector) and Rev'ds. A.T. Eckel, J.C. Wippell, which apparently contained essential but irretrievable information on the earliest establishment of the churches. Nevertheless, historians advise that this centenary volume should be read with caution as some material regarding the destruction and reestablishment of churches, and relevant dates, has not been validated. It however provided an essential base on which one could begin a serious inquiry, and a list of valuable literary sources to review. It also tendered facts on the rebuilding of St. Andrew's Parish Church and noted that it had escaped destruction in several fierce hurricanes.

Schomburgk's *History of Barbados* "composing a geographical and statistical description of the island; a sketch of the historical events since the settlement; and an account of its geology and natural productions", was one of the most comprehensive and useful sources on St. Andrew. While it did not address the origin and establishment of the Parish Church specifically, in covering a wide sweep of historical events and other general commentary on happenings in Barbados, and notwithstanding the obvious highly subjective packaging of some of the material, this "classic West Indian history", all in all, must be commended for "its wealth of information about the island" of Barbados in early times.

Barbara Hill's interesting *Historic Churches of Barbados* lists and describes many buildings of major importance. It generally looks at the architectural features of buildings and churches from the standpoint of their design and notable structural features, and notes those that escaped hurricanes and disasters. It also included a passing comment, without corroborating evidence, on the likely establishment of St. Andrew's in the 1630s.

While there exists considerable information regarding the settlement of Barbados, not much was captured on the early history and development of the Church in Barbados prior to the tenure of Bishop William Coleridge (1824–1842), the first Bishop of Barbados. In trying to address the paucity of information, P.F. Campbell in *The Church in Barbados in the Seventeenth Century* provided insightful material on the mainline churches. He does not write about the actual church buildings of the time but, like Schomburgk, attempts to provide a rather general eye-opener on the activities of then-existing churches. He adverts to the contemporaneous ministers and

Introduction

their religious and business life in the colonies. Since he apparently had access to early sources of information that were useful, but are not now available, one cannot but wish for more detailed citations involving the works on which he based his research. He provided valuable insight on a few ministers and clergymen, who he reported lived in, owned and sold real estate in St. Andrew, but there was not much recorded specifically on St. Andrew's Parish Church. In fact, Campbell noted that of all of the churches in Barbados, the least information was recorded on St. Andrew's Parish Church and members of the clergy who served in the parish.

Suzanne Ellis' insightful thesis on "Disestablishment and the Challenge of Finance for the Anglican Church in Barbados (1969–1999)" presented the financial position of the Church and how it strove to cope during its first 30 years of disestablishment despite dwindling funds, indebtedness to banks, and the high cost of maintenance of old buildings.

Some helpful papers and theses exploring aspects of disestablishment, and other closely related issues include:

1. Herman Brathwaite. "An Examination of the Way the Anglican Church in Barbados Functions—Its Structure and Actual Operations". Diploma in Theology (External). Final Year Essay, Codrington College, 1983.
2. Ian Norville. "Some Outstanding Events in the Anglican Church of Barbados 1955–1980". Diploma in Theology, Codrington College, 1980. A look at Church Acts, Local Government, the Vestry System, and Disestablishment.
3. Stephen Fields. "A Decade of Disestablishment 1969–1979". B.A. Thesis, Caribbean Studies (UC 300), University of the West Indies, Cave Hill, 1980. Review of the first ten years after disestablishment.
4. Betty Lucas. "The State and the Disestablishment of the Anglican Church in Barbados." B.A. Thesis, University of the West Indies, Cave Hill, 2008. Examination of the government's role in disestablishment.

Audine Wilkinson and Vanessa Knight's unpublished notes, "Selected Writings of the Clergy in the Diocese of Barbados, 1969–2009", and Wilkinson's "Anglicanism in Barbados 1627–2001", both compendia of references on research, biographies, theses, happenings, and misfortunes affecting the churches, as well as other compilations and reading material, provided a ready and helpful resource for the researcher. However, apart from *The Barbados Diocesan History*, these evolving volumes did not list any text on the establishment of St. Andrew's Parish Church, Barbados.

There was abundant information on churches and ministers on the internet resource; although insightful, it lacked specifics on St. Andrew's.

It is hoped that this less-than-perfect volume will excite enthusiasts of St. Andrew's to further compile its history, while filling the gaps in this presentation. In addition, further information and suggestions offered to complement this work will be welcomed and given full consideration. Despite my best effort, I could not meet and interview all of the key persons who, no doubt, had substantial and beneficial information to contribute. And since it is by no means a flawless work, critical evaluation and comments will be appreciated.

Attempts to record the activities and oral history of these earlier institutions are not free from error, even with the employment of the most stringent and careful criteria. Therefore, this book must be seen as a work in progress. The longest journey begins with small steps, of which this is one.

The sad regret the writer personally feels most deeply is that this work was started at least three years too late. Even though the Rector was willing, if not eager to assist, his capacity to recall information was challenged. If he could remember more, he would readily have volunteered needed information.

During my interactions with the Rector, I could not fail to discern his intense love for St. Andrew's Church, the people, and the parish. Although his health was declining, his devotion to his pastoral work and ministry remained strong. No wonder many people readily concurred that, at last, the conferral of a canonry on the Rector on 27 February 2011 was a well-deserved honour, albeit too late. God bless his service!

It is hoped that the passion for which Canon Gatherer lived—the maintenance and preservation of St. Andrew's Parish Church, as well as the primary focus among cares and responsibilities engrossing his attention—will long be honoured by the people of St. Andrew, the people of Barbados, successive incumbents, and all workers and supporters of this Church.

A pledge for the Priest-in-charge, congregation, friends, and well wishers might well be: **"We shall keep the lights of this Church well lit and the plant firmly standing afoot"**.

CHAPTER ONE

Barbados, St. Andrew and St. Andrew's Parish Church

Barbados

Barbados is situated between the Caribbean Sea and Atlantic Ocean, lying just east of the main arc formed by the Windward Islands. It is approximately 108 miles (175 kilometres or km) east of St. Vincent and the Grenadines and 250 miles (402 km) northeast of Trinidad, its Caribbean island neighbours. Roughly triangular in shape, the island is approximately 21 miles (34 km) from north to south and 15 miles (25 km) from east to west at its widest point, comprising 166 square miles (431 square km). Its capital and main seaport is Bridgetown.

From a list of 243 most-densely-populated sovereign states and dependent territories, taken from the United Nations World Prospects Report (2004 revision), Barbados ranked 18th in the highest population densities of the world.[1] The preliminary report of the population of Barbados from the 2011 Census, as reported, 12 October 2011 in *The Nation* newspaper was 277,762, which would equate to a population density of 1,663 per square mile (644 per square km) of land area.

Being the first Caribbean landmass west from Europe and Africa, as well as a main sea and airport destination, has vitally influenced Barbados' history, culture and economic life. Since the seventeenth century, the island has formed a fulcrum connecting Western Europe (especially Britain), the Eastern Caribbean, and the United States mainland.

Interestingly, while Barbados is not part of the archipelago of the Lesser Antilles, it is usually grouped with it. The island is of a characteristically different geological formation; it is less mountainous; has less variety in plant and animal life, and is mainly of limestone, and not of volcanic origin.

Following the British invasion (the so-called exploration of Barbados) in 1625, Barbados remained its colony until 30 November 1966, when it attained independence. While Barbados seeks to foster its own brand of nationalism and nation building, along with a growing attraction to African culture—unlike most other Caribbean islands—it remains essentially very attuned and strongly linked to British culture.

At latitude 13° 11' 23.32" north of the Equator, and longitude 59° 33' 27.26" west of Greenwich Meridian, it sits on the edge of the Atlantic hurricane belt and has been often spared the destruction following several of the region's most ferocious hurricanes. Nevertheless, Barbados has not always escaped, as evidenced by the strong hurricanes it experiences at least every 1:100–120 years, in particular in 1675, 1780, 1831 and 1955.

Over 400 years of intensive sugar-cane production has obliterated much of the original vegetation, and a growing population over the same period, coupled with unbridled conversion of arable land to housing development and golf courses, has eradicated more.

St. Andrew, Barbados

St. Andrew, along with the sloping areas of St. Joseph, St. Thomas, St. James, and St. Peter, falls within the northeast region of Barbados referred to as the Scotland District. Schomburgk[2] opines that the region got its name because it was thought that this rugged part of Barbados resembled Scotland, even though he believed that it more closely resembled North Wales. The Scotland District comprises approximately 150,000 acres or one-seventh of the island's landmass.

Figure 1: Parish of St. Andrew, Barbados

The parish of St. Andrew (see Figure 1),[3] covering 14 square miles (36.3 square km) of land, is one of the less flat parishes of the island delineated by Governor Richard Dutton by 1645. Ranking as one of Barbados' most beautiful areas for its rolling hills, unmatched greenery, and less dense housing development, St. Andrew remains one of the least spoilt parishes of the island.

St. Andrew is the sixth largest parish, with a population of 5,833, according to the 2011 Census. Its density of 417 persons per square mile (161 per square km of land area), ranks it as the least densely populated parish. This is partly due to the steep topography and instability of the land, which render building development unsafe and/or illegal in much of the Scotland District.

Geology of Barbados and St. Andrew

The rocks underlying Barbados consist of sedimentary deposits, including thick shale, clays, sands, and conglomerates laid down approximately 70 million years ago. Above these rocks are chalky deposits, which were capped with coral prior to the island rising to the surface from beneath the ocean. A layer of coral—as much as 300 feet (91.5 metres)—thick covers the land, except in the Scotland District, where geological activity has removed the coral cover.

The government has adopted a proactive conservation plan to control erosion. Having ratified the United Nations Convention to Combat Drought and Desertification on 14 May 1997, Barbados became eligible for funding through the Global Environment Facility (GEF). With GEF, Barbados is better enabled to proactively continue to address the urgent concerns of this erosion-prone area, which could be of intrinsic agricultural benefit to the island.

With assistance from the United Nations Development Programme (UNDP) and GEF, Barbados has broad-based plans for Capacity Building and Mainstreaming of Sustainable Land Management. The proactive National Strategic Plan estimated at approximately $1.2 million includes proposals for the Scotland District and, by extension, St. Andrew. The Plan embraces the layout of a National Park, as well as associated development policies and action plans.[4]

From a geological perspective, Barbados appears of later formation than its Caribbean island neighbours, even though it generally seems similar in geology to Trinidad and Tobago.[5]

The shale and sandstone of the Scotland beds of St. Andrew constitute some of the earliest formations of the island, which may be dated from the Eocene era (54.8 to 33.7 million years ago). If such is the case, the deposits in St. Andrew would indicate that Barbados was situated relatively close to some high land mass or mountainous region with fast flowing rivers which deposited alluvial sediments in geological time. Also to be found are kaolinite, illite, chlorite, and montmorillinite clays (soft clays high in minerals and associated with soil failure) in the Joe's River Formations and Scotland Beds.[6] The presence of peat in the area also indicates a more recent deposit of this organic material, which could have been laid down from river sediments constituted of material brought down from the elevated regions of St. Joseph and St. Andrew.

The oceanic sediments of white siliceous chalk and radiolarian (marine plankton) earth of the Upper Eocene and Oligocene eras overlie the Scotland and Joe's River formations and were laid down in what must have been a period of great subsidence of the ocean bed. J.B. Harrison and C.G. Jukes-Browne suggest that these deposits were formed at a depth of 1,000–2,000 fathoms, basing their theory on fossils that are found only at these depths.[7] In this formation are embedded traces of volcanic ash that fell on the surface of the sea and sank to the ocean bed in layers. This implies that there were active volcanoes within a distance of about 200–300 miles (321.9–482.8 km), possibly arising from the volcanic chain of the Lesser Antilles, consisting of rock formations of the Upper Eocene and Oligocene.[8]

The basal coral, which began its growth in the Pliocene and Pleistocene eras, constituted a shallow water formation. However, findings of coral in some places directly on the Scotland beds suggest that, at some time, a portion of the island appeared above the surface of the sea in the Mount Hillaby and Chimborazo regions of St. Andrew and possibly at Bissex Hill, St. Joseph. There has also been speculation that some of the large limestone rocks/boulders seen in elevated regions, as well as those strewn along some northeast coastal areas, could have been deposited there as the result of tsunami activity of earlier times.

St. Andrew's Parish Church, Walkers, St. Andrew

Figure 2: GPS of St. Andrew's Church and Original Burial Ground

The historic St. Andrew's Parish Church is one of 52 Anglican churches in Barbados. Located on coordinates N 13°15′ 09.2" and W 059°34′ 05.0", it lies on Highway 2 between Belleplaine and Shorey Village, St. Andrew (see Figure 2), near the birthplace of famous cricketer Sir Conrad Hunte. Sitting in the northeast of the island, it is located approximately 50 km from the Grantley Adams International Airport, and 65 km from Bridgetown. Figure 3 following is a descriptive layout of the Church which may be used as a guide, especially for the benefit of visitors and interested persons. Persons not familiar with the Anglican Churches may also find the following Legend and Glossary at Tables 1 and 2 useful.

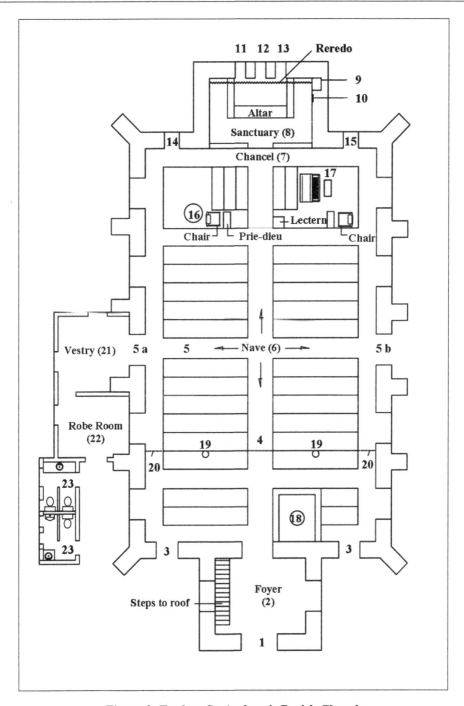

Figure 3: Explore St. Andrew's Parish Church

Table 1: Church Walk Through and Legend

	Legend
1	The **main west entrance** to the Church is located at ground floor of the belfry/bell tower. On entering the entrance, you will see two plaques. On the right door portal, one plaque welcomes you to the present historic Church building of St. Andrew, and the other on the left invites you to spend a brief moment in private worship and thanksgiving in this historic Church.
2	In the entrance **foyer** notice the plaster cast images of the Blessed Virgin Mary with the Infant Babe, as well as Jesus as a boy standing in the Temple. There is an 18-inch wide wooden stair access leading to the summit of the belfry. On ascending the belfry, adventurers get the opportunity to rest on three floors where they will encounter remnants of an old bell, and relics of an earlier organ, including old blowers. Although the wooden stair is somewhat aged, if you dare to take the 99-step trek to the summit of the belfry, and after a few more steps emerge on the roof deck, you will be well rewarded. On stepping out onto the deck of the belfry, you will be overawed by the breathtaking view from one of the most strategic vantage points of Walkers, St. Andrew. You can take a 360° look around the picturesque sloping lands of St. Andrew and St. Joseph. On looking west, you cannot miss the beautiful view of Walker's village and the outline of Turner's Hall, Spring Hall and Rock Hall highlands; and on the south—the rolling hills of Babylon and Benn Hill highlands, St. Andrew, and Bissex and Melvin Hill highlands, St. Joseph, in the foreground; and on the north and east—Walker's Bay behind the vegetated sand dunes (see Figures 4–6).
3	In order to optimise seating, these two **western side entrances** are not regularly used.
4	The **centre aisle** of the Church intersects the north to south aisle.
5	The north to south aisles lead to the vestry via the **north door 5a** used by clergy and workers, and to the graveyard via the **south door 5b.**
6	The 53 ft long by 40 ft wide (16.2 m by 12.2 m) **nave** permits a clear view of the service and associated activities. In 1940–1942, during the tenure of Rector Harvey Reid, the old pews were replaced by a new set with stabilising rails. The pews and rails were built by Kirton Tucker, with assistance from apprentice Newton Bovell. With some chairs added, the Church can seat 500 persons.
7	From the nave, make one step up into the screened (railed off) **chancel**. The 13 ft by 40 ft (3.9 m by 12.2 m) floor was recently covered with green flowered 8-inch square ceramic tiles. Here you will find the choir stalls, organ console, a modern mahogany lectern that is dedicated to the memory ("In Service") of John Hutson (most likely Rector Hutson, who served in the parish 1839–1841), and two old prie-dieus that were used by ministers presiding at service.

	Legend
8	From the chancel (via one step up), you can enter the 11.5 ft by 17 ft (3.5 m by 5.2 m) **sanctuary**. Here the existing altar is approached via two steps. Constructed of beautifully sculptured *Prima Vera* or white mahogany, the altar is one of the main treasures of the Church. It replaced the original altar, a historic masterpiece that was reportedly fabricated by M. Birchet, a famous English artist in London. Two large 4 ft by 5 ft (1.2 m by 1.5 m) inscriptions laid in the floor on the left and right of the altar are dedicated to the memory of Frances Bootman and Janann Thompson—a freed Coloured woman and her three infant children. Also observe the *piscina* and old metal *olea sancta* located on the south of the altar.
9	The ***piscina***, installed in the wall on the south of the altar, dates back to the original establishment of the Church building.
10	The metal ***olea sancta***, lying adjacent to the *piscina*, is a prized relic that was used for the storage of oils for various sacramental rituals.
11	This **stained glass window** depicts St. Andrew the Apostle carrying a cross. *The three stained glass windows located in the sanctuary, and the two in the chancel for bringing light into the Church in the morning, were taken by Rector Gatherer in 1988 to Goddard and Gibbs, Liverpool Street, London, for refurbishing at the cost of £10,700.*
12	This **stained glass window** depicts Jesus the Good Shepherd (in the centre).
13	This **stained glass window** depicts St. Peter the Apostle holding the keys. Each of windows 12, 13 and 14 is separated by a tracery (decorative rib in the church window) and carries a clerestory (the upper section of the window) depicting *Iesus Hominum Salvator (IHS)*—Jesus, the Saviour of Man—α as Alpha (Beginning), and Ω Omega (Ending).
14	This **stained glass window**, located in the chancel, depicts the Prophet Isaiah reading a scroll.
15	This fifth **stained glass window** in the chancel is a portrait of the Prophet John the Baptist holding a shepherd's staff in his left hand, and a picture of a young lamb standing beside him.
16	The 36-inch (3.3 m) diameter **pulpit** comprises an exquisite hexagonal (six-sided) piece of Barbadian mahogany wood-carving. It is mounted on concrete flooring, which sits on a hexagonal concrete base.
17	The rebuilt **Austin organ console** was obtained from the Organ Clearing House, Hampshire, New Hampshire, USA, in the late 1970s.
18	The **baptismal font** located near the main entrance of the Church is elevated on a concrete base. Its 28-inch (0.7 m) wide marble basin sits on a 14-inch (0.35 m) circular rough coralline limestone pedestal protruding from the raised floor base. The ornate, octagonal (eight-sided) cover is crafted from Barbadian mahogany. The shape of the cover, by use of the symbol eight, signifies regeneration through baptism.

	Legend
19	Two modern mahogany wooden **columns** support the mezzanine loft above the western entrance of the Church.
20	This demarcates the edge of the 15 ft deep by 40 ft wide (4.6 m by 12.2 m) **mezzanine floor** which accommodates the organ (pipes) and a few pews for the overflow congregation. The mezzanine is accessed from the outside of the Church, near the sanitary conveniences. The reconstruction of the mezzanine floor was undertaken by Father Gatherer in the early 1970s, after the original floor reportedly buckled under the weight of persons attending a funeral. This renovation replaced the original mezzanine floor that wrapped around the northern and southern sides, stretching not less than three-quarters up the length of the Church. The current loft, which might accommodate only 100 people (when packed), is less than one-third of its original size.
21	The 23.7 ft by 12.6 ft (7.2 m by 3.8 m) **vestry** of stonework, which is located on the north of the Church, was built early in the twentieth century.
22	The **choir robing room** was built and outfitted with cupboards in 1968.
23	The 6.5 ft by 16.9 ft (1.9 m by 5.1 m) **sanitary block**, comprising the males' and females' stone bathrooms, was constructed in 1968. This replaced the dilapidated pit latrines that were located on the western end of the compound.

Table 2: Glossary

Glossary	
Altar	The table in the sanctuary at which the Communion emblems (bread and wine) are consecrated.
Aisles	The passages between rows of seats.
Baptismal Font	A stone receptacle containing Holy water used in infant baptism (paedobaptism, pedobaptism or christening), a ceremony of sprinkling, or pouring water on a person's (baby's) forehead. Baptism symbolises purification or regeneration and is done on admission into the church.
Benefice	This refers to and includes all rectories with cure of souls and vicarages.
Buttress	Part of a wall thickened to provide greater strength. This building-support-structure is used for transmitting the lateral forces pushing a wall outwards (arising from heavy roofs, ceilings, or wind-loading on the roof) across an intervening structure or space and ultimately down to the foundation.
Chancel	The section of the church near the altar that is separated from the nave by a step or rail and in which the choir and officiating clergy sit. It also contains the altar, pulpit, kneelers, and chairs for use of the clergy and other ministers (servers).
Church	In referring to St. Andrew's Parish Church in this text, 'Church' spelt with a capital 'C' is invariably used. When 'church' refers to a general worshipping congregation is used, it is spelt with lower case letters.
Clergy	Clergy or clergyman (incumbent) refers to a Clerk in Holy Orders employed on a full-time basis and paid by the Anglican Church and may include persons under the ministry of Bishops, Priests, and Deacons.
Clerestory	The upper window of the nave or sanctuary, usually positioned above eye level, primarily for bringing in additional light.
Constitution	The Constitution of the Anglican Church in Barbados.
Council	The Synod Council.
Cure	A specified area (Parish) under the care of a clergyman.
Diocese	The ecclesiastical district of Barbados under the jurisdiction of a Bishop.
Disestablishment	This refers to disestablishment of the Anglican Church of Barbados, which occurred on 1 April 1969.
Incumbent	In relation to a benefice, it includes a rector with a Cure of Souls, vicar or curate.
Jamb	The side of a doorway or window.

Glossary	
Laity	Widely used in the Anglican and Catholic circles, it means the members of the church not in Holy Orders.
Lancet	An acute-angled arch; but the term is commonly applied to tall narrow widows, whatever the shape of their arches.
Lectern	This is a stand with a sloping top that is used in reading lessons from the Bible, preaching a sermon, giving an address, a talk, or the announcements.
Nave	The main part of the church where the congregation sits for the service.
Olea Sancta	This now obsolete metal box, located in the wall on the right of the altar in the sanctuary, was formerly used for the storage of oils (Oils of catechumens of the sick and Sacred Chrism) that were used in the sacraments. *Olea Sancta* is inscribed on the metal door.
Piscina	For ceremonial ablution and disposal of wastewater arising from hand-washing during the administration of the Eucharist, a basin with a drain near the altar was installed in the sanctuary. As the water (wastewater) used in ceremonies could not ordinarily be disposed of anywhere, or into the sewer for whatever reason (superstition, e.g. a witch or someone might retrieve it and use it for ritual purposes, including casting of spells), a drainpipe was attached to the bowl for the discharge of all wastewater directly to the ground. The ancient ceremonial washing of hands as a sign of inward purity was associated with reciting Psalm 26:6–12, usually before the service began, after the offering, or before the Eucharistic (Communion) prayer. Nowadays, the clergy normally wash their hands over a bowl carried by a server (generally with no reservations in Barbados about disposal of the wastewater).
Prie-dieu	A portable, shelved wooden desk for use when praying, usually with a low surface for kneeling on and a higher surface for resting the elbows or a book. Along with a chair, it is used by clergy or persons leading devotion and is often seen in the chancel.
Rector	A clergyman licensed and instituted to a Parish and having the Cure of Souls therein.
Reredos	The decorative formwork of marble, metal, stone, but commonly of timber that's positioned behind and above the altar. They often depict religious images.
Rev'd.	Refers to Reverend

Glossary	
Sacrament	An outward, visible sign of an inward and spiritual grace. Seven sacraments practised by the church include the Lord's Supper, Matrimony, Baptism, Confirmation, Penance, Holy Orders, and Extreme Unction.
Sanctuary	Considered the most sacred part of the church, it is the elevated place where the altar is situated apart from the chancel. It is a place where clergy mainly officiates at worship.
Synod	The Barbados Diocesan Synod constituted by the Anglican Church Act 1969.
Tracery	The ornamental stonework dividing windows.
Transept	The arm(s) that may contain room(s) in cruciform (cross-like) shaped churches, and that may be divided, e.g. into north and/or south.
Trustees	The Barbados Diocesan Trustees constituted by the Anglican Church Act 1969.
Vestry	A room attached to, or in, a church where usually the clergy, and other ministers (e.g. servers) change into their vestments, and where the vestments and other liturgical/ sacred items are stored. Depending on its size, it may also include an office, space for preparation for services, and/or a common meeting room. In this account, generally when the word is spelt with a capital "V", it refers to a committee of parishioners who, until March 1959, were elected for administering the temporal affairs of a parish. At that time Barbados changed from the Vestry system to a system of local government that administered government business through parliamentary decision and action.

Figure 4: Walkers and outline of Turner's Hall, Spring Hall and Rock Hall

Figure 5: Benn Hill and Babylon Highlands

Barbados, St. Andrew and St. Andrew's Parish Church

Figure 6: Walker's Bay behind vegetated sand dunes

Notes

1. "List of sovereign states and dependent territories". *Wikipedia, the Free Encyclopaedia.* 2011. http://en.wikipedia.org/wiki/ Viewed on 29 August 2011.
2. Robert H. Schomburgk. *The History of Barbados.* (London: Frank Cass Publishers, 1971), 222–223.
3. Saint Andrew, Barbados - Wikipedia, the free encyclopedia http://en.wikipedia.org/wiki/Saint_Andrew,_Barbados Viewed on 29 August 2011.
4. Government of Barbados, UNDP and GEF "Capacity Building and Mainstreaming of Sustainable Land Management in Barbados". PMS 3408 – Atlas Project ID 00046566. http://asia-pacific.undp.org/practices/energy. Accessed 26 November 2011.
5. J.B. Harrison and A.J. Jukes-Browne: "The Geology of Barbados, 1890", in Alfred Senn "Paleogene of Barbados". *AAPG Bulletin,* Vol. 4, Issue 9, 1940.
6. J.V. DeGraff, *et al.* 1989. Transcribed by Nicholas DeGraff, University of California at Santa Cruz. "Landslides: Their extent and significance in the Caribbean", in E.E. Brabb and B.L. Harrod (eds), *Landslides: Extent and Economic Significance.* (Rotterdam: A.A. Balkema, 1989), 51-80.
Landslides in Barbados - University of the West Indies. www.mona.uwi.edu/uds/Land_Barbados.html Accessed 8 September 2012.
7. Harrison and Jukes-Browne, 1940.
8. *Ibid.*

CHAPTER TWO

Early Chronology of St. Andrew's Parish Church (1630s–1850s)

Original Church

1630s

No records have been unearthed for the origin of St. Andrew's Parish Church. Since early records of the Church were either destroyed or not readily available, no date has been established for its origin. This document will put forward two approximate times for the earliest establishment of the Church or at least a chapel—pending further discovery.

J.E. Reece and C.G. Clark-Hunt noted that Rev'd. Thomas Layne (Lane), the first Rector of St. Michael Cathedral, in reporting to the Archbishop of Canterbury on 'the condition of matters Ecclesiastical in the year 1637', in Barbados, stated that "Our people within these five or six years past have built six Churches beside some Chapels".[1] It is assumed that since St. Lucy's Parish Church was reportedly established around 1629 and there was early connection between St. Lucy's and St. Andrew's[2], at least one of the chapels referred to by Layne existed in St. Andrew. And it is quite possible that a chapel referred to in this context formed the basis for the Church and parish of St. Andrew, as we know it.[3] For this record, a chapel/Church is considered to have existed in St. Andrew by 1631. But this thesis awaits verification.

1636

In defending his thesis that parishes existed long before Bell's parish division in the 1640s, and in also pointing out that the island was divided into at least four precincts, P.F. Campbell reportedly basing his argument on a document—'Memoirs of the First Settlement'—mentioned that a Justice Joseph Gibbs was one of a family of large landowners of St. Andrew and posits that:

> In July 1636 Henry Hawley reduced the number of precincts and instructed that Captain George Bowyer, who was a large landowner in St. Andrew, should 'try all matters in the windward parishes'.[4]

If the thesis is sound, it would indicate that the parish of St. Andrew existed by 1636 and so could have St. Andrew's Church.

1640s

Another notion advanced is one extracted from Oldmixon's *A Short History of Barbados* (1768). This account posits that after Governor William Tufton was executed for mutiny, he was succeeded by Lieutenant Governor Philip Bell on 18 June 1641, who served as Governor of Barbados until 1650. It must however be noted that Tufton died in 1650 (executed) and at least two other Governors (Henry Hawley and Sir Henry Huncks) served before Bell. Oldmixon seems to have got the sequence of events wrong.[5] About Bell, Schomburgk noted:

> Under the mild and beneficent administration of the prudent chief, a new and auspicious era is presented to our view. His enlarged mind embraced a greater variety of interesting objects than had ever engaged the attention of his predecessors; and it was now that the Barbadians began to enjoy the benefits of equal laws and social order.
>
> Sensible of the influence of religion in harmonising the passions and softening the manners of mankind, Mr. Bell's first care was to provide for the uniformity of common prayer, and the establishment of public worship. Assisted by advice of a council consisting of ten persons, whose names are not transmitted to us, he divided the island into eleven parishes, in each of which a church was built and a minister appointed to officiate at the altar.[6]

Since 1629, Barbados had been divided into six parishes—St. Michael, Christ Church, St. James, St. Thomas, St. Peter and St. Lucy—during the administration of Sir William Tufton, Governor of Barbados (21 December 1629—16 July 1630). However, during Governor Bell's rule, the number of parishes was increased to eleven, to include St. Philip, St. John, St. George, St. Andrew, and St. Joseph, and at least one church built in each. By 1651, appropriate salary arrangements were settled, through an Act of Parliament, for the maintenance of ministers of the churches (Anglican).[7] Salary by barter allowed the minister to receive a pound of sugar for every acre of land in his parish[8]. Therefore, at latest, by 1651 St. Andrew's Parish Church existed.[9]

In arguing the case for the existence of a church, or at least a chapel in St. Andrew prior to Bell's final parish division in 1651, P.F. Campbell[10] was at pains to point out that while Bell was credited with increasing the number of parishes in Barbados, there was no mention of when churches were actually built. Campbell also reasoned[11] that St. Andrew, along with other parishes not included among those named by William Tufton in 1629, actually existed prior to Bell's completed list. In support of this thesis, Campbell cited that between 1635 and 1639 rents from St. Andrew were received by Henry Hawley for public charges in the form of tobacco and cotton.[12] Regarding such, he further stated that 2,040 pounds (tobacco or cotton), or 27% of the total quantity collected in Barbados at that time, came from St. Andrew. He suggested that St. Andrew could have existed from as early as 1631, and also indicated that while many deeds bearing the names of respective parishes have not survived, there were references to specific parishes, including St. George, St. John, and St. Thomas in deeds, e.g. in 1640[13], prior to Bell's completed list of parishes. And while we do not know whether the chicken preceded the egg, it is now commonly accepted that the Church preceded the parish or, at least, they co-existed from quite early in their genesis.

It is unfortunate that hard evidence available at present does not allow for the precise determination of the date of the establishment of St. Andrew's Parish Church; nevertheless, in weighing the above information, notwithstanding the paucity of evidence, this writer advances the position that a church or chapel existed in St. Andrew as early as 1631. An earlier date for such establishment, for which no evidence was advanced, is 1630.[14]

St. Andrew was referred to as Overhills (*refer to* "Do you Know?" — Bromley's Message, page 26) as one had to cross the central ridge of the island to reach the parish from Bridgetown. The parish of St. Joseph reportedly formed part of St. Andrew Overhills or Scotland Parish.[15] Although the parish of St. Joseph reportedly existed as early as 1645, its separation from St. Andrew did not take place until twelve years later.

Sir Richard Dutton, Governor of Barbados, was assigned to determine the qualifications and orthodoxy of clergy serving in Barbados in 1681.[16] Dutton reported that a Richard (Matthew) Gray (Grey) was baptising, marrying, and performing other priestly duties without duly holding Anglican authority. In fact Vincent T.H. Harlow reported that Gray had served for 24 years.[17] In support of the notion of paucity of ordained ministers in the colonies, Jeffrey Yeo posits that in the late 1650s, ministers of the Church of England were in short supply, and that by 1653, about half of the parishes were being served by ministers without orders. After Jamaica was captured by Spain in 1655, the parishes in Jamaica were reported to have no serving ordained ministers at all.[18] So Grey reportedly serving as rector of St. Lucy and St. Andrew without being ordained during 1657–1681[19,20] was not anomalous or unheard of. After he was reprimanded, it was reported that with the support of friends and benefactors, he fled the island to England to be ordained; and Dutton reported the incident to Henry Compton, Bishop of London.[21]

In an article "Scotland District — old and new" from *The Barbados Advocate*, the following was noted:

A Parish always had an Anglican parish church. It is interesting to note that St. Andrew's Church was actually located near to but at quite a different location from where it is today. In the time of Mayo's survey it was just to the right of the entrance to the sand pit on the hill which supplies sand for the construction industry. Today this area is known as the graveyard and if you walk through the area you will see a sandstone memorial to Vaughn, dated 1733 along with remnants of other graves. Until early in the 1990s the name Milles could also be found here.[22]

While the writer did not actually verify the aforementioned information and the actual church site near the sand pit as reported, there appears to be merit in the article. And it is concluded that the original chapel/Church in St. Andrew was located near the "Graveyard", St. Andrew. A number of maps[23] indicate the Church was on the opposite side of the road. In addition, the presence of tombstones (see Figure 7), and other remnants of inscriptions (with barely decipherable names) testify of burials in the "Graveyard" (old cemetery), near Benjamin's sand pit, and support the notion of the establishment of an early chapel or Church on the site as noted. The earlier — or what will be referred to as the original chapel or Church — like other early churches, was of timber.

Figure 7: Vaughan's Tombstone dated 1733 (in Original Graveyard)

The original burial ground — Graveyard — west of Walker's beach, located at coordinates N 13°15′ 11.4′″ and W 059°33′ 577.0″ and 903.9 feet (275.5 m) 74.85° ESE of St. Andrew's Church is still evident. The Graveyard, which is situated approximately 400 feet (121.9 m) off Walker's Road, is reported to have been part of the original graveyard of the Church. The plot of 1 acre, 2 rods, 25 perches is now virtually covered by sand and vegetation.

On a recent visit to this site, it was learnt that in mid-January 2012 during the clearing of a track from the sand pit across the old cemetery with a tractor, an eight-foot (2.4 m) square tomb was inadvertently ripped opened. Discussion with Anthony Roett revealed that the tomb was approximately seven feet high and was encased with (10 in x 3 in x 2 in) red clay bricks.[24] Figure 8 displays a gaping hole in the roof of the tomb, now partially filled with sand, and Figure 9 reveals a heap of bricks that were salvaged from part of the arched roof of the desecrated tomb. Figure 10 shows a number of gravestones, including one with undecipherable inscriptions that someone had collected and stored.

Figure 8: Gaping hole in the roof of a tomb

An interviewee from the area said that he physically stood in the tomb, and also reported having met other local people, who reportedly saw entombed leaden coffins.

Could this venue have also been used for the burial of persons who died from cholera during the mid-nineteenth century? Does this site hold the key to an early Arawak, Carib or Amerindian settlement or burial site? Through procrastination, will we lose this heritage site permanently? In any event, here is another urgent plea, reinforcing an earlier one made by the Vestry in June 1911, for the Government to clean up, enclose and preserve this valuable heritage site for posterity. For more information on this old cemetery, the one in current use by the Church, and more on burials and inscriptions, refer to Chapter 10: Graves and Inscriptions connected to St. Andrew's Parish Church.

Figure 9: Bricks from damaged tomb

Figure 10: Collection of gravestones

August 1675 Hurricane

In an article in *The Advocate News*, Maurice Hutt reported that on 31 August 1675, a terrific hurricane struck the island, causing more than 200 deaths and massive destruction of property including "no less than 15 sugar mills each valued at not less than £500 in one parish".[25] In his comment about the devastation caused by this hurricane, Robert Schomburgk remarked that "the country was almost laid waste . . .;" while he indicated that eight sunken ships were driven ashore, the leeward part of the island suffering greater damage to housing, and with most of the churches suffering a similar fate, he never reported any damage to St. Andrew's Parish Church.[26] This hurricane also destroyed the St. James Parish Church, the oldest consecrated church (wooden).[27]

1680

In his article, "The Barbados Census of 1680",[28] Richard Dunn not only noted that Sir Jonathan Atkins, Governor of Barbados, provided a box full of statistical data of prime genealogical, economic, and social value from his early census of the island, but also mentioned that much valuable information was omitted from the published data. In commenting on the census document, John Camden Hotten[29] reported that only a list of householders of St. Andrew was published, and this did not include baptismal and burial registers. Indeed, a comprehensive record of the history of this

Church, as well as missing information on the early development of Barbados, still waits to be unearthed from Colonial records, perhaps lying somewhere, unreported and unpublished.

1700s

In the list of Clergy who came to Barbados after 1710, it was noted that Rev'd. Langton died in St. Andrew and Rev'd. Porter immigrated from St. Andrew.[30] It was not determined where Porter settled, whether the reverend gentlemen served in St. Andrew's, nor was there any information found regarding their interment at St. Andrew's Parish Church or elsewhere, or the circumstance of their death.

1729–30 — People of high standing in St. Andrew

In dispelling the saying that, due to its distance away from Bridgetown, the main centre of activity in Barbados, St. Andrew was 'behind God's back' and was not the place where people of high status usually resided, Governor Worsley of Barbados presented Patrick Rose, his relative from St. Andrew, on 13 July 1721, to Bishop Gibson of London. The Governor also introduced his nephew Charles Rose, who was seeking to become a priest, after teaching Latin in a school in Barbados for three years. Patrick endorsed Charles to be curate, since he himself was getting too old and infirm to perform full-time parochial duty.[31] It was unclear whether Patrick was a priest, but in seeking a curate to replace him implies that he could have been a member of the cloth.

P.F. Campbell recorded the names and pursuits of several ministers, clergymen, and English landowners who resided in or were connected with St. Andrew.[32] Among them were the large Gibbs family, who in 1680 purchased an 80-acre plantation, including part of Walkers Plantation. Zechariah Legard, a member of the clergy and clerk of St. Andrew's parish, was reportedly a landowner and resident. In addition, there were ministers who represented the parish over the years and lived therein. In fact, members of the Colonial Parliament, including James Holigan, Eyre King and Jones Pile, who represented the parish of St. Michael, were also proprietors of large properties in St. Andrew.

"Do you Know" — Bromley's Message?

The distance of St. Andrew from the city and its 'remoteness' from the rest of Barbados, accentuated by the 'long travel time' taken to reach it, is immortalised in a Barbadian folk song.

The term 'Overhills', used in referring to St. Andrew, was not a pejorative reference favoured by the folk of yesteryear. In the small island of Barbados, travelling 13 miles to Belleplaine, St. Andrew, is still viewed by many as quite a distance to cover. Interestingly, apart from the original writer of a Barbadian folk song who sought to conserve his pocket change by not spending on a damsel who wanted to travel 'all the way down' Belleplaine, "Belle Plaine", arranged by Irving Burgie, also reflects Bajans' feelings[33] about 'distant parishes' within the island.

The prolific songwriter Irving Louis "Lord" Burgie[34] of Brooklyn, New York (whose mother was from St. George, Barbados), well known for his songs, "Island in the Sun" and "Jamaica Farewell", memorialised Belleplaine, St. Andrew—and by extension Barbados—by publishing his famous "Belle Plaine" arrangement:

1. You hear what Bromley tell de girl,
    You never go down Belle Plaine out a me.
    You hear what Bromley tell de girl,
    you never go down Belle Plaine out a me.

2. You hear what Bromley tell de girl,
    you never get no car fare out a me.
    You hear what Bromley tell de girl,
    you never get no car fare out a me.

   Refrain

    Out a me, Out a me,
    You never see Belle Plaine, out a me.
    Out a me, Out a me,
    You never see Belle Plaine, out a me.

1731

The information about the 13 August 1731 Hurricane was sketchy. Apart from noting damage to ships in the harbour, no substantial account was recorded, or any damage to churches, including St. Andrew's, reported.

1770s

Thomas Duke, a member of the famous Duke family of Barbados, became Rector of this Church in the early 1770s. His name appears in the List of Parishes and Rectors.[35] The record of his length of service was not found. He, like his family, was a slave owner who belonged to the aristocratic and priestly family residing at Dukes Plantation, St. Thomas.[36]

San Calixto 11, 10 October 1780 Hurricane

In an attempt to emphasise the enormity of the deadliest recorded hurricane in Barbados, it is variously reported, and probably exaggerated, 'that neither dwelling nor trees survived the 1780 hurricane". Some documents from the Society for the Propagation of the Gospel and Rev'd. Hughes, Rector of St. Lucy, supported this position. However, Schomburgk and a newspaper of the time noted that St. Andrew's Parish Church was one of few buildings and churches left standing after *San Calixto 11*, the 10 October 1780 hurricane. This category 5 hurricane, with devastating winds reportedly over 320 km/h (200 mph), destroyed buildings and trees, and left a death toll of over 22,000 in the Caribbean, including over 4,320 in Barbados (other records approximated the number at 4,500), along with untold damage and loss of property. In describing the horrors of this hurricane, Schomburgk reproduced the lament of an eyewitness, taken from Poyer's *History of Barbados,* thus:[37]

> . . .the havoc which met the eye contributed to subdue the firmest mind. The howling of the tempest; the noise of descending torrents from clouds surcharged with rain; the incessant flashings of lightning; the roaring of the thunder; the continual crash of falling houses; the dismal groans of the wounded and the dying; the shriek of depair [sic]; the lamentations of woe; and the screams of women and children calling for help on those whose ears were now closed to the voice of complaint,—formed an accumulation of sorrow and of terror too great for human fortitude, too vast for human conception'.

Schomburgk also noted that only two churches and one chapel—St. Andrew's and St. Peter's Parish Churches and All Saint's Chapel—remained standing.[38] And if we believe Schomburgk's record, it would seem that the St. Andrew's location, nestled between the protective confines of Walker's Highland on the north, and the large sand dune barrier off Walker's beach on the northeast, essentially provided a sound haven from the ferocious winds of *San Calixto 11*.

1785

In the early days, schools were connected to the Church via the school board, whose chairman was the Rector of the Parish Church. The Alleyne School in Belleplaine had its genesis in the following:

> St. Andrew's School, in the parish of the same name, was partly erected and endowed with a permanent salary of £60 currency per annum to the master in the year 1785, by Sir John Gay Alleyne, Bart., then Speaker of the House of Assembly. A bequest of £20 a-year, payable out of Blower's plantation in Barbados, and applied to the above institution, was left by Bryant, Esq., who also left £20 a-year to St. Thomas's parish, and a like sum to the parish of St. James for a similar purpose.[39]

Through the kindness of Sir John Gay Newton Alleyne, the Alleyne School was established in 1785 in Belleplaine, reportedly for poor white boys from the parish.[40]

Sir John (1724–1801), a descendent of one of the first settlers of Barbados, was born in St. James. In 1757, he became the representative member for St. Andrew in Parliament and held the seat for about 40 years, excluding a short break in 1770.

The name of the School was changed many times, from the St. Andrew's School to Endowment School, The Seminary and finally to the Alleyne School on 1 October 1880. In January 1881, it became a Government Grammar (Secondary) School. In 1947, girls were admitted for the first time, thus making it one of the first secondary co-educational schools in Barbados.

It was ultimately the responsibility of the Rector of St. Andrew's to ensure that the construction of the Alleyne School was completed, the Principal properly remunerated as authorised by the Speaker of the House of Assembly, and that grants left in the Bryant's will were properly distributed from Blower's Plantation to the School and the parish churches of St. Thomas and St. James.

1801

Rev'd William Thomas, Rector of St. Andrew's Church, Barbados, died 20 December 1801. Was he, in reality, William Thomas Duke?

1806

Although the total amount of land that the Church owned was not specified, an early map of Barbados (April 1806) indicated that the glebe in St. Andrew comprised not less than 15 acres.

1831

The destructive eight-hour category 4 hurricane, 10 August 1831, destroyed the parsonage that reportedly contained slave registers and other valuable records. With its deadly 17-foot storm surges and over-130-mile-per-hour winds, it levelled the city of Bridgetown, destroyed St. John's Parish Church, and left 1,500 people dead.[41] Schomburgk, in noting Bryan T. Young's account of this hurricane, recorded that it was similar to the 31 August 1675 hurricane in "appearance, duration and fury";[42] and added that "the extent to which human life then suffered was not on record".[43] The *Visitor* newspaper reported that although the Andrew's Church building withstood this assault, by this time it had been so badly ravished by the elements and, no doubt, termite infestation, it had fallen into disrepair, and warranted replacement. A decision was taken to have it replaced.[44]

1834—Grant and sale of property

As early as 4 November 1834, James Maughn, Esq., through a deed of gift, gave 12 perches of land to the Rev'd. Glasgow Lewis for the erection of St. Saviour's Church

School, St. Andrew. Two chapels were affiliated to St. Andrew's—St. Saviour's, which was constructed in February 1836, and St. Simon's, licensed sometime later.

At a Glance

What is historic about St. Andrew's Parish Church?

1. It is the only church reported to have withstood the massive hurricanes of 1731, 1781, and 1831.
2. Unlike many of the other churches in the island, it has never been ravished by fire.
3. Irrespective of its rural setting, the property has been well maintained and its grounds landscaped and regularly manicured; it is one of the finest-kept Anglican churches of the Diocese of Barbados.
4. In spite of the fact that this Church and property has serious structural challenges resulting from construction shortcomings, lack of a solid foundation, too narrow a foundation in relation to the size and density of the building, land slippage problems, etc., it continues to withstand, if not defy, the harsh odds of weather, time and lack of funds, largely due to a prudent preservation programme.
5. Apart from the well kept private cemetery in Christ Church, St. Andrew's has the next-best maintained cemetery in Barbados.
6. Through this Church, the Diocese eventually was able to soundly establish retirement protocols for its clergy and staff and have its Constitution, Canons and Regulations, along with other relevant instruments, duly validated and gazetted (see Chapter six).

Early Chronology of St. Andrew's Parish Church (1630s–1850s)

Notes

1. J.E. Reece and C.G. Clark-Hunt, *Barbados Diocesan History*. In Commemoration of the First Centenary of the Diocese of Barbados, 1825–1925. (London: West India Committee, 1925), 15.
2. *Ibid*, 17. Also refer to Note 19 following, which indicates an early association was established between St. Lucy's Parish Church and whatever church/chapel was initially established in St. Andrew.
3. Barbara Hill, *Historic Churches of Barbados*. (Barbados: Art Heritage Publications, 1984), 44.
4. P. F. Campbell, *The Church in Barbados in the Seventeenth Century*. (Barbados Museum and Historical Society, 1982), 28-32.
5. *List of Governors of Barbados* (1627–1833). From Wikipedia, the free encyclopedia. http://en.wikipedia.org/wiki/List_of_Governors_of_Barbados. Accessed 31 July 2013.
6. Schomburgk, "The History of Barbados: Comprising a Geographical and Statistical Description of the Island", 35. http://books.google.com/books?isbn=1108023312... Accessed 29 August on 2011.
7. Campbell, 28–32.
8. The 1651 law authorising ministers' payment of salary by barter was repealed by 1705 by a law which fixed their salary at £150 per annum; and by 27 June 1815, it rose to £500.
9. Schomburgk, 92–93.
10. Campbell, *28–32*.
11. *Ibid*. While Campbell's reasoning appears plausible, it must be noted that he generally argued his case convincingly outside of hard supporting facts, and he was often careful to point this out.
12. In Campbell, 28–32, reference is made to the rent received in terms of tobacco and cotton collected from St. Andrew as early as 1635–1639.
13. *Ibid*.
14. "Loop Barbados: A North- Eastern Sight to See in Barbados" – St. Andrew's Parish Church/...loopbarbados.com/2011/12/northern-sight-to-see-in-barbados-s. Accessed 8 May 2013.
15. Schomburgk, 222.
16. Reece and Clark-Hunt, 17.
17. Vincent T. H. Harlow, *A History of Barbados 1625–1685*. (Oxford: Clarendon Press, 1926), 249. Harlow reported that Gray had performed priestly duties for 24 years.
18. Jeffrey Yeo. "A Case without Parallel: The Bishops of London and the Anglican Churches Overseas, 1660–1748". *Journal of Ecclesiastical History*, Vol. 44, No. 3, July 1993, 453.
19. Reece and Clark-Hunt, 17, *see* following:

    Governor Dutton in 1681 carried out an investigation of the Clergy to inquire into their orthodoxy and their way of discharging their duties, claiming to act as Ordinary under general instructions issued in this matter by the Bishop of London. He discovered that a man called Grey had been performing Priestly functions without having orders for twenty years. The late Governor Atkins being taxed with having allowed this irregularity, made the cavalierly reply, "If I had known that Grey had not Orders I am sure I could not have ordained him." Grey had been acting as Rector for St. Lucy and St. Andrew, and on his dismissal by Governor Dutton, one of the Parishes he had illegally served called a Vestry, and resolved to smuggle' him out of the Island, contrary to the law for registering intending emigrants, bribing the ship's Captain to take him to England, where they proposed by furnishing him with a credit of £500 to facilitate his Ordination so that he might later return to them.

It is noted that Reece and Clark-Hunt, as well as Harlow, in writing about Richard Gray (Grey) presented similar information for the most part, except for the length of time that Grey reportedly served as rector of St. Andrew and St. Lucy. Harlow stated 24 years. Notwithstanding some ambiguity regarding the length Grey served, taking the sum of evidence presented by these sources, one concludes that someone named Gray (Grey) served in St. Andrew, most likely in association with St. Lucy, as one of the earliest known ministers of that parish.

20. Yeo, 462–463.
21. It was not unusual for an aspirant or other enthusiast to act as priest without formal ordination in the early days. Refer to Appendix 1 for further elucidation.
22. *The Barbados Advocate,* Friday, 25 February 2000.
23. The following maps by Phillip Lea, London 1695; Surveyor William Mayo's Map of 1717–1721 engraved by John Senex, 1722; H. Moll, London, 1739 and Thomas Jeffers, London, 1775 are a few which indicated St. Andrew's Parish Church at an apparently different location from, and south of where it is presently situated.
24. Interview with Anthony Roett, 15 March 2013.
25. Maurice Hutt. "Need for Conservation". *Sunday Advocate News.* 10 August 1980, 8.
26. Schomburgk, 45.
27. "St. James Church, Barbados". *Wikipedia, the free encyclopaedia.* http://en.wikipedia.org/wiki/St._James_Church,_Barbados Accessed 3 September 2010.
28. Richard S. Dunn, 'The Barbados Census of 1680: Profile of the Richest Colony in English America", published in http://www.jstor.org/pss/1922291 Accessed 29 August 2011.
29. *Ibid.*
30. Fulham Papers (official papers of bishops of London), Volume 15, July 16, 1724.
31. Part of the UK archives network. 'Conditions of access: Records after 1910 only to be produced' http://www.nationalarchives.gov.uk ›...› Access to Archives - Cached - Block all www.nationalarchives.gov.uk results. Accessed 29 August 2011.
32. Campbell, 143–161. In the Appendix of his book, Campbell lists several people, Englishmen, landowners, who were ministers, clergymen and residents of St. Andrew.
33. The author of this book understands the sentiments regarding the distance in travelling to Belleplaine, St. Andrew; his wife was from Belleplaine.
34. Irving Louis "Lord" Burgie also penned the lyrics of the National Anthem of Barbados.
35. Fulham Papers, Volume 16, December 1772.
36. Jerome S. Handler, "A Rare Eighteenth-Century Tract in Defence of the Slaves in Barbados: The Thoughts of the Rev. John Duke, Curate of St. Michael". From the *Barbados Gazette,* or *General Intelligencer,* 15–19 March 1788, and recorded in the *Journal of the Barbados Museum and Historical Society,* Vol. LI (2005). http://jeromehandler.org/wp-content/uploads/RareDefense-05.pdf. Accessed 10 August 2011.
37. Schomburgk, 46, quoting from Poyer's *History of Barbados*, 449.
38. *Ibid*, 47.
39. *Ibid*, 105.
40. "Historical Development of Education in Barbados 1686–2000", booklet. Planning Research and Development Unit, Ministry of Education, Youth Affairs and Culture,

November 2000. http://www.mes.gov.bb/UserFiles/File/Historical_Developments.pdf. Accessed 17 February 2013.
41. "1831 Barbados Hurricane". *Wikipedia, the free encyclopaedia*, http://en.wikipedia.org/wiki/1831_Barbados_hurricane. Accessed 17 October 2011.
42. Schomburgk, 56, quoting from Mr. Bryan T. Young's personal report of the 10 August 1831 hurricane.
43. *Ibid*, 56.
44. *The Visitor*, June 15–28, 1987.

CHAPTER THREE

Rebuilding and Consolidating the Church (1840s–1950s)

Old timber building

In the early 1840s, the existing timber (church) building, which reportedly accommodated 300 persons and recorded an average attendance of 150 congregants, fell into disrepair and had to be demolished. Robert Schomburgk reported:

> The former parish-church of St. Andrew was one of the few which escaped the destruction occasioned by the hurricanes in 1780 and 1831. It was situated at the foot of a hill, and was protected on the east by the Dune-like . . . Its age however rendered it necessary to take it down, and a new edifice was rebuilt on nearly the same site.[1]

Loans for the new Church building

This rebuilding would have been effected on the site that the Church currently occupies. Loans from the Government greatly assisted in the initial rebuilding programmes, but were insufficient to complete the work. Additional funds had to be raised through appeals made to the membership and friends, and by way of benevolent donations and gifts.

It was reported on the 9 July 1841 that the Legislature granted £500 for refurbishing and enlargement of the Church.[2] As the building had not been damaged by the hurricane of 1831, it did not receive a Treasury grant of £500 or a loan of £2,000, for which other churches had qualified. However, by an Act of Parliament on 11 May 1844, the House of Assembly passed a Bill granting a loan of £3,000 to the Rector and Vestry of the parish towards the cost of rebuilding the Church.

1841 – Land for St. Saviour's Chapel School and licensing of St. Simon's

It was reported[3] that a deed in the Registry recorded that Jonathan Higginson of Liverpool, England, sold 3 roods, 7 perches of land in St. Andrew's Parish on 5 November

1841, to the Bishop of Barbados for erecting St. Saviour's Chapel School, which was built that year. St. Saviour's Chapel was also licensed for use in 1841.

The Parliamentary Returns of the West Indies and British Guiana, No. 426, June 1845, noted that in 1844, the area of St. Andrew was 13.7 square miles, the population 5,995 persons, and the population density 438 persons per square mile.[4]

1846—Groundbreaking Ceremony and Dedication of Cornerstone

The Barbadian newspaper[5] recorded the laying of the cornerstone for the new Parish Church building, which took place 30 November 1846, by Archdeacon Lawson (Vicar General), along with a number of clergy and distinguished persons. Prominent members of the dedication service included: Speaker of the House of Assembly George Nelson Taylor (1841–1846) who had represented St. Michael in 1834–35 and St James from 1839; he also served as MP from St. Andrew during 1846. Members of the Colonial Parliament representing St. Michael, who were proprietors of large properties in the parish, included Messrs. Jones Pile, Eyre King and James Holigan; James S. Bascom, MP for St. Thomas and Magistrate for St. Andrew, along with Messrs. Charles Packer, Joseph Rock, James King, M. Corbin, Lynch Thomas and J.W. Carrington, MD.

Among the clergy were Rev'd. R.F. King, Rural Dean and Rector of St. Philip; Rector of St. Michael's Cathedral, W.W. Jackson; the Bishop's Chaplain, W.H.B. Bovell; Rector of St. Thomas' Parish Church, H.B. Skeete; H.R. Redway, Vicar of St. Paul's; John Hutson, Rector of the Parish (St. Andrew) with Curates R.J. Rock and M.G. Clinckett. A plaque bearing the date of the dedication of the cornerstone can be seen in the entrance foyer of the Church (Figure 11).

> Welcome to this historic Church dedicated to Saint Andrew. This particular building dates from 1846. The previous building withstood the 1780 and 1831 hurricanes but finally got beyond repair and had to be pulled down.
>
> The present building, as you will see when you look around, is now showing signs of considerable wear. We appeal to you to support our Building Fund by your generous donation so that future generations of parishioners as well as visitors may be able to enjoy this historic place of worship.

Figure 11: Dedication Plaque of Cornerstone for rebuilding of the Church

The procession for the groundbreaking ceremony started from the new primary school in Belleplaine, with children selected from various schools in the parish joining the distinguished guests, visitors, and members of the Vestry and clergy. The stone-laying for the building was performed during the chanting of Psalm 100 at the service where Rev'd. R.F. King and Rev'd. W.W. Jackson served as celebrants and the Vicar-General as preacher. The elevated status of attendees and number of dignitaries attending the dedication of the cornerstone of a church building signalled the high regard that people of the aristocracy held for religion in the early nineteenth century.

The new £5,000 (not less than) incomplete church building of dimension 60 feet by 40 feet (18.3 m by 12.2 m), with gallery (mezzanine accommodation), a tower and recess for a chancel, reportedly housed 1,000 persons.[6] With the mezzanine accommodation, the estimated seating was deemed excessive!⁷ Nevertheless, it was reported that an average of 700 persons attended services in those days. This speaks volumes for the ministry of Rector John Hutson, and Rector John Glasgow, who succeeded him in the 1840s.

Bishop Swaby noted that the altarpiece of St. Andrew's Church was painted by M. Birchet, one of the best among the artists in London; however, nothing further was determined about the altar. This prestigious masterpiece apparently did not withstand the ravages of time, as the current altar lacks any particularly notable features.

The Barbadian of 27 January 1847 reported that the Vicar-General annulled the licence that had been granted for the celebration of the 'Offices of the Church' in the two public rooms of the parsonage of the Parish, and had received licence for the 'Celebration of Divine Services, etc.' in the school building, which had been lately erected near the churchyard of the Parish Church.⁸ The school referred to in the foregoing reference was the St Andrew's Church Combined School.

1850s

> When you come into this church
> remember that our Lord Jesus Christ is here;
> he is present and to be adored
> under the form of his blessed Sacrament
> reserved for Holy Communion.
> Kneel down and worship him.
> Give thanks for your blessings.
> Bring to him your needs.
> Remember all in distress, sorrow and pain.
> Pray that the dead may rest in peace.
> And do not forget those who minister and worship here.

Figure 12: Plaque in Church foyer

By 1850, all funds for continuing the rebuilding of the Parish Church had been exhausted. During May of that year, there was a petition by the Rector and Vestry of the parish seeking a further loan of £500 in addition to the £3,000 already borrowed, in order to complete the construction.⁹ In August 1852, another loan was duly granted to enable them to continue the building work.

The Barbadian of 5 April 1854 reported on a meeting of the House of Assembly that relieved the Church of its outstanding debt of £800 from the earlier £3,000 loan.¹⁰

The belfry of the Church took some time to complete. During the years 1855 through 1857, while mention was made of public worship being conducted, neither was the tower completed nor apparently any consecration of the church performed.¹¹

The editor of *The Barbadian* on 7 November 1857 stated that he had obtained, through a friend, some interesting information regarding the increased accommodation in the newly-built Church in St. Andrew, referred to then as 'Scotland':

> Not long since the parishioners have had the comfort of assembling in the large and commodious Church with which the old parish Church has been replaced. Although not yet consecrated it has for months past been licensed for Divine Worship. . .¹²

The actual date of consecration of the renewed church building was not specified.

One of two plaques (Figure 12) seen in the foyer of the Church, invites visitors and parishioners to spend a few minutes in reverent prayer in the Church.

1876

Of the 24 priests listed in Table 7 who served at St. Andrew's, the grave bearing the name of only one is seen in the graveyard. It is, however, known that at least four leaders have been interred at the Church, three of whom bore the Christian name 'John': John Hutson, John Bradshaw, and John Duke.

The grave of Rev'd. John Hutson is prominently located in St. Andrew's. Apparently, he began his cure in Barbados in 1839. He served as Rector of St. Andrew. While the actual date or length of his ministry in the parish was not confirmed (not less than two years, but more likely not less than eight), he was Rector of St. Andrew's and was present for the dedication marking the start of the rebuilding of the new Church building. This implies that he could have been involved in the Parish Church rebuilding programme and fund-raising drive. During his cure he was assisted by Curates R. J. Rock and M. G. Clinckett. He died in 1865 at age 59, after being a rector for 25 years. He was survived by his wife Susanna, who died at age 84, in May 1891. A three-month-old granddaughter predeceased her in October 1876. Rev'd. Hutson's family was interred at St. Andrew's in his well-maintained grave, located south of and near the small front entrance of the Church (Figure 13).

Figure 13: Rev'd. John Hutson's grave

Although John Bradshaw, MA, BM, TCD apparently was a rector in the parish for about 17 years, no conclusive information was retrieved regarding his place of burial. A cursory search in "The monumental inscriptions in the churches and churchyards of the island of Barbados, British West Indies" by Oliver V. Langford, made reference to the headstones seemingly relating to him and his wife Mary, but the notations were too obscure to be given full weight on the identity of those interred at the specific location cited.[13] However, Reece and Clark-Hunt referred to a Rev'd. John Bradshaw, who served as Rector of St. Peter's Parish Church in 1859. Most likely this incumbent also served at St. Andrew sometime during the mid-nineteenth century, and could have been the person interred at the Church.

Only another obscure inscription is left to the memory of The Rev'd. John Duke, who might have served in St. Andrew's, in which parish cemetery he was interred following his death in June 1803.[14] Like his relative, Rector Thomas Duke, John, too, was a member of the prominent Barbadian Duke family of Duke's Plantation, St. Thomas. He prepared for the priesthood in England and was Rector of St. Michael's Cathedral, 1770–1795 and Christ Church Parish Church, 1796–1803.

Rev'd. Duke was a slave owner and apparently a prolific writer. One of his famous literary pieces included a four-page self-serving tract in defence of slavery in Barbados. In it he argued, contrary to other writings and sentiments at the time, that slaves in the island were being treated well and, according to him, enjoyed considerably greater privileges and freedom than those in England and, in particular, Africa, from which they had originated.[15]

Not much was found on Rev'd. Thomas Duke other than he was still a young priest in 1801, when he died at 46 years of age.[16]

1881 — "Do you know" the connection of Belleplaine with the early train?

The turning of the soil for Barbados' railway network occurred on 23 June 1877. The railway from Bridgetown through St. George to Carrington, St. Philip, was opened on 20 October 1881. By 1883, the line running through St. John, St. Joseph, and terminating in Belleplaine, St. Andrew was completed and ready for public use.[17] Apparently, this replaced the Governor of Barbados, Sir Charles Grey's proposals of 1848, to build a railway from Bridgetown to Speightstown, St. Peter.

In addition to transporting people and goods, the train also transported sugar-cane to the factories (e.g., Bulkeley and Carrington factories). Unfortunately, due to poor maintenance of the carriages, five locomotives, sheds, and especially the tracks, coupled with the genesis and development of the Rocklyn Bus Company, the railway services were terminated in 1937.[18] Was there any truth in the report that the tracks were stripped bare of the rails, and the metal sold to European countries to help provide weapons and other implements of war during the Second World War? Apparently, the dubious history of Barbadian entrepreneurship in 'metal trading' dates back quite a while. The stone remnant of the platform terminus of the train is located off the Ermy Bourne Highway on a grassy landside area, between the watercourse leading to Long Pond and the Belleplaine Housing Area (Figure 14).

Figure 14: Remains of railway terminus platform

1893

In 1893, the government passed an Act to authorise the Vestry of St. Andrew to raise a loan in order to effect repairs to the Church and other buildings in the parish.[19] Other undated Acts included one authorising the Vestry to seek a loan for further repairs of the Parish Church and other places of worship, as well as the Almshouse (charity shelter for the aged) in the parish.

1898 Hurricane

St. Andrew's survived the fury of another devastating hurricane in 1898 that passed south of the island; notwithstanding, the country experienced winds of 135 miles an hour. Following the aftermath, Barbados counted its losses: 83 fatalities, over 9,900 houses destroyed, 4,519 houses damaged, and over 50,000 people homeless.[20]

The St. Andrew's Church Combined School building, located not far from the Parish Church, was a casualty of this hurricane, which forced it to be temporarily closed for reconstruction. During rebuilding on the original site, school was conducted at the old Railway Station at Belleplaine Plantation, St. Andrew.[21]

1900

On 24 August 1900, a plot of land was purchased from Walkers Plantation to provide additional burial ground for the Church; it was consecrated on 18 December 1902.[22]

After reconstruction of the St. Andrew's Church Combined School on the original or current site in 1900, it became a co-educational institution for the next seven years.[23]

1903

A letter of 24 August 1903 from the Vestry authorised the grant of £11.10 to cover the cost of providing running water to the rectory. In its meeting of 31 July, the Vestry approved the sum of £54 for repainting work carried out on the Church.

1904

From the Annual Statement of Accounts noted in the Vestry Minutes of 1904, the stipend of the Organist of the Parish Church was $120, while the Vestry Clerk and organists of the chapels of St. Simons and St. Saviours each received $48.00 per month.

1905

In the Minutes of the Vestry meeting of 16 July 1905, a contractor, Mr. Bayne, was awarded a contract for £835 to repair the rectory, during which time the Rector was to seek alternative accommodation. There was no further word on the outcome of this building project.

1907 — The St. Andrew's Church Combined School

Students of the St. Andrew's Church Combined School regularly attended services (at least one day per week) at St. Andrew's and especially so during the annual Lenten services, and for celebration of important church festivals.

This School, like neighbouring Alleyne School, underwent several incarnations. In 1907, it was divided into the St. Andrew's Boys' and Girls' schools, with this arrangement lasting for 75 years. Following the closure of the Bawden Mixed School in 1982, students were transferred to St. Andrew's Boys' and Girls' schools to form the St. Andrew's Primary and Composite School, a special needs school, which catered to students age three through 16, with learning disabilities. With a transfer of its older students in 1995 to the Alma Parris Secondary School, St. Thomas, the composite School was renamed St. Andrew's Primary School.[24] On 22 June 2011, the St. Andrew's Primary was officially renamed the A. DaCosta Edwards Primary School by Minister of Education and Human Resource Development Ronald Jones.

1909

At the Vestry meeting of 15 September 1909, a report was made that there was a large crack in the Parish Church building. The Vestry asked Chairman and Rector, Inniss Milton Alleyne, to undertake the necessary repairs. No further report of the outcome of this matter could be found.

1911

In May 1911, the old organ from St. Andrew's was given to St. Saviour's along with a grant of £20 from the Vestry for its repair.[25] The Organist and Sexton received stipends of $120 per month.

In June 1911, the Vestry's attention was drawn to the "disgraceful appearance of the original burial ground". In that regard, the Vestry's recommendation was to have the burial ground "enclosed by planting a hedge of silk cotton round it, and affixing a gate to same". Nothing more was said about the motion to secure this heritage site comprising church property. Unfortunately, no work has ever been undertaken to ameliorate the condition, and Government remains oblivious of its existence.

Bees and pecuniary issues in 1912

In 1912, the Sexton was almost dismissed for not disinfesting the Church building of bees—because he asked to be paid for the extra-curricular work involved. One hates to associate St. Andrew's with money irregularities but, apparently, or historically, bees and pecuniary issues have long plagued this Church. It does not escape one's attention that as early as the turn of the twentieth century, fiscal difficulties existed. However, after much rancour, the impasse was eventually resolved. The Sexton was paid the $50.00 charged, and the bees were driven out.[26]

1913

A report submitted by the Sanitary Board indicated that the burial ground of St. Simon's was closed as it had run out of burial space. As a result, all burials were to be accommodated at the Parish Church. On the 1 September 1915, J.H. Taylor offered half-an-acre of land at £160 to St. Simon's Church to provide additional space for burials.

1915—Not Bees, but a hive of activity at the Chapels

When compared with St. Simon's and St. Saviour's churches, the leader of St. Andrew's, and others preceding him, apparently made few requests for refurbishing and upgrading the plant at St. Andrew's. One could not help noting the consistent annual demands, including requests for salary increases for organists and church workers (grave diggers, sextons, and bell ringers), and for washing of the buildings, etc., made to the Vestry on behalf of the chapels. Almost every month a requisition letter from the clergy of either of these chapels was received by the Vestry. Could it be that the Rector, unlike the Vicars—clergy in charge of chapels—being Chairman of the Vestry, had direct communication with the board, and took advantage of the privilege to get things done, without having to make formal requests? In any event, the Vestry's annual statements of accounts did not record regular refurbishment done to the Parish Church, or reflect the urgency and buzz of activity associated with dynamic leadership, as was so evident in the chapels.

Civic and pastoral services of the Rector of St. Andrew's

Notwithstanding the Rectors' apparent reserve in pressing to have the Church's needs met, in the Vestry Minutes of 14 July 1915, the Chairman, Rector Inniss Milton Alleyne, was commended in a motion by fellow Vestry members for patriotically securing a piece of land for Government's use. Accordingly, a motion submitted by The Hon. A.P. Haynes noted that...

> This Vestry wishes to put on record their high appreciation and thanks for the extremely generous and far seeing act of the Rev. I.M. Alleyne, the present Rector of St. Andrew in exchanging the Glebe land in which, the Almshouse is built for another portion of land purchased from Haggatts Plantation by which means the Almshouse now stands on its freehold land which becomes the property of the Vestry of the parish forever.

The glebe land, including ancillary buildings and medical institution, comprised at least 18 acres and 38 perches of land.

The Vestry was the body of members elected by the congregation (Anglican) of a parish to conduct the parish's secular, administrative and ecclesiastical affairs. It also elected the Rector of the church who invariably became its chairman. The chairman and Vestry eventually appointed most civil servants in the parish, e.g. the sanitary officer, the head teacher, district medical officer, sexton and teachers.

Rectors of parish churches were *ex-officio* members and chairpersons of the Vestry, and were responsible for their parish's public services, i.e., telephone, water and light, establishing and maintaining road works and communications, health care (medical, environmental/public health), poor relief ministration, overseeing the ministration of schools, including paying salaries and awarding scholarships, and land tax administration, to name a few. Essentially, they managed the Local Government of the parish, performing service similar to that of Cabinet Ministers in central government, though on a more reduced scale.

Unless one painstakingly notes and carefully recalls the work of St. Andrew's Parish Church—and the Church in general—especially in the early days, there is a tendency today to see the Church only as having defended the cause of the colonists, supported the interest of the plantocracy, and forced the nationals into subjection for the benefit of the colonists. Unfortunately, too often the early and very positive work of the St. Andrew's Parish Church and by extension the Anglican Church, the Moravians, Methodists, Catholics, and many others in managing, refurbishing, and maintaining schools, along with executing all the other pastoral and altruistic ministries—is often ignored or forgotten. And this does not include the cultural, educational, and other social benefits the society received and continues to receive, directly and indirectly, from the Church.

Impact of St. Andrew's on the parish

Over the years, each Church has served the spiritual needs of its parish, and beyond. In addition to having catered to the needs of Barbados in providing sound and solid education through its schools located in every parish, it has attempted to meet the social, physical and emotional needs of its parishioners. St Andrew's Parish Church, like other churches, has provided meals and hampers for the elderly and needy people; it has cared for the homebound, visited the schools within the parish, ministered in correctional institutions, and offered regular teaching in sound Christian and ethical living. Institutions for the sick and incapacitated (hospitals and nursing homes) have welcomed the group ministry of parishioners who offer spiritual enrichment and cheer. Through these various organisations, including the Anglican Young People's Association, Youth Brigades, men's and women's circles, members and adherents were able to not only socialise, but become educated and/or enlightened in many ways, as they participate in the practice of public speaking, crafts, cooking, to mention a few examples.

In reaching beyond the spiritual, the impact of St. Andrew's and the Church embraces the numerous and varied dimensions of life. The need for food and the need to be nurtured spiritually are inseparable. In order to avoid a disservice to the community, the Church has endeavoured not to compartmentalise its ministry, or ignore its members' needs.

And as people benefit from the Church's holistic ministry, they in turn provide reciprocal benefits to the church and other members with whom they fraternise and, by extension, to their parish.

Impact of the parish on St. Andrew's

Pass around St. Andrew's any Saturday morning and you will see members and parishioners voluntarily assisting in cleaning the church, preparing floral arrangements for Sunday worship, and maintaining the grounds and graveyard. From time to time, members and friends of the church give donations to facilitate repairs and maintenance. Members and parishioners have often 'lent a hand' in mixing and applying concrete and mortar, in the course of church maintenance. Members of various church organisations donate gifts, monetary and otherwise, to the needy, as well as offer volitional service in house repair, house cleaning and providing transportation for the sick, thus fulfilling the church's mission by demonstrating the Gospel in action.

Through these deeds and personal sacrifice, church members and parishioners assist the Church and its mission in enabling it to engage in a holistic ministry, as it responds to the world's brokenness by proclaiming and modelling the joy of a right relationship with God, both by works and through 'preaching the Gospel'. Church members, together with the wider community, provide a skills bank which assists the church in effectuating its mission through teaching, organising workshops and concerts, and education-based empowerment of the populace in its environs. Without the members, parishioners and their support, the Church would be unable to reach the community with the whole gospel for the whole person, and there could be no holistic church mission.

And if nothing more were said, let it be known that in its work and mission, St. Andrew's with her sister churches and other 'missions' (other denominations) have unstintingly served the Barbadian community at the civic, pastoral, moral, and every other level imaginable. Indeed the Church's ministry in serving humanity from the cradle to the grave has not been, and never was, merely ecclesiastical. To be so persuaded would be naïve, ignoring the facts regarding how from its earliest years the Church, with its leaders and its outreach, has impacted parishioners, especially the needy, at every level of community life (see Response of parishioners in Chapter 8).

1918 storm

A letter from the Colonial Office to the Vestry of St. Andrew on 29 August 1918 expressed the regret of the Governor of Barbados that "considerable damage was done to the houses of peasants and labourers by the storm which occurred on morning of 22 instant [August 1918]". The letter directed the Vestry to appoint a committee to evaluate the extent of damage and indicate what level of remediation was required.

1919

The Vestry Minutes of 4 September 1918 indicated that £500 were provided to repair 92 severely damaged homes in St. Andrew.

In the Minutes of 14 April 1919, a report of the hurricane committee given to the Vestry noted that a further £152 s2 d9 was required to cover the cost of the repair work done in the parish. The Vestry received a total Grant-in-aid of £1109 s8 d6 to cover the required expenditure incurred by the storm of the preceding year.

The storm moderately affected Barbados and did no damage to St. Andrew's Parish Church or others. It later developed into a category 2 hurricane, with winds of 105 mph (165 km/h), causing damage in Honduras and Belize.

"Only in St. Andrew"—Switch between rectory and District Medical Officer's office

Discussion with senior members of the district indicates some ambivalence regarding exactly where the rectory was originally located. A number of people opined that a Medical Officer, who resided on the compound of the Infirmary, located northeast of the building now comprising the Elaine Scantlebury Home, Belleplaine, effected the exchange of his residence for that of the Rector. They indicated that the Medical Officer disliked being called upon at any time during the night to provide medical assistance and acquired permission to reside in the building (rectory) located nearer to the Church. In other words, the building once occupied by the Rector now became the medical office. This was located approximately 100 metres from the Parish Church, the first building on the right on leaving the Church on the way to Belleplaine. It was allegedly the building set in a slightly wooded area preceding Mrs. Melba Sandiford's residence, adjacent to the bridge and deep watercourse. And so, the Rector removed to the Medical Officer of Health's quarters at the Infirmary site, Belleplaine. There has been no confirmation of this claim of the exchange of the health office and the rectory.

If true, the thesis offers an explanation for the location of the obsolete rectory aback of and northeast of the Elaine Scantlebury Home, Belleplaine. Conversely, Medical Officers of Health of St. Andrew and other familiar district medical practitioners, including doctors L.S. Tappin, Joyce Walton, L. Banister, I. Smyth, B. Brathwiate, S. Renrick, and B. Simon ran clinics in the building located near the Parish Church. The stately, sturdy stone building which served as the District Medical office was refurbished early in 1971 after Dr. Smyth demitted office. The last officiating Medical Officer was Dr. Bromley Simon, who retired in 1979 to continue his practice in Speightstown, St. Peter. Dr. Simon said that the two-foot-coral-stone block building was sound and without a crack.[27] Interviewees said the building withstood many severe hurricanes. Interviewees also remarked that after the St. Andrew's Medical Officer's clinic was vacated for a while, the furniture was stolen, the building was allegedly vandalised, unfortunately to the point that it became obsolete, and was deemed derelict by the Ministry of Health. It was demolished in the mid-1990s.[28]

1920—Rector and Real Estate

On 10 March 1920, an offer was made to Rector A.P. Haynes of St. Andrew's for him to acquire as much land as he wanted for rent at a cost of $15.00 per acre for the cultivation of cotton. This rate compared favourably with the growing cost of cotton per acre at the time. "This offer was unanimously made and accepted by the Rector."[29] Could this offer have eventually led to an increase in the pool of land of the St. Andrew's glebe? Has the Church ever investigated this?

At its meeting of 14 April 1920, the Vestry was asked to provide a curate who would act in the absence of the Rector of St. Andrew's. A similar motion was put forward again later during the year, but apparently no decision was taken.

1926

In January, the organ required repairs costing $100. Only $40 was available to pay technician Hunte, who kindly carried out the repairs on promise to receive the remainder in June that year.

On 23 June 1926, Parliament passed an Act authorising the Vestry to raise a loan, not exceeding £1000, for the repair of churches and the Almshouse in St. Andrew, to be repaid in equal annual instalments over the following 10 years. As a result, £750 was loaned to the Church at 5%, while the other £250 was loaned to the Rector and Church Warden as Trustees for the Alleyne School at 6%.

"Only in St. Andrew"—Two Sisters' Wedding

In adding some romantic flavour to their Centenary volume, Reece and Clark-Hunt included a story of the following dream come true.[30]

Hon. J.G. Alleyne, owner of Bawdens and the River plantations, reportedly decided to cut his losses by selling the family coach and pair of horses. One of his sisters begged him not to sell the coach until she had been to church in it for the last time on the following Sunday.

In one of her dreams on Saturday night, this lady was reported to have gone by coach to church for the last time, where she saw her husband-to-be.

On the 'red letter' Sunday, she and her sister went to church, and waited, and waited. Even up to the time when the clergyman was getting ready to preach, no visitors entered the church. She had no answer for her sister who asked, "Where is your husband?" At last! At last! By the time the priest was ascending the pulpit, in came two gentlemen whom the sexton ushered to a cushioned seat beside the two sisters.

At the end of the service, after breaking the ice and exchanging pleasantries, a relationship struck up between these strangers and the young ladies. Guess what? The dreamer married Admiral Sir Charles Knowles, while her sister, Miss Rebecca, married Viscount Folkestone. Didn't they live happily ever afterwards?

1928

The organist's salary was increased from $120 to $180 per month.

1933

In the Statement of Accounts from Vestry Minutes for the Church ending 24 March 1933: Pew Rent for the year was $70.68, the salary of the organist was $180, that of the sexton was $132 and the grave digger was $92.00. There was a water bill for $6.16. One is not sure what was the purpose of the water bill. It is unlikely that a waterborne system was in place, as earth pits remained in use for many years. Rainwater collection (harvesting) and reuse in some form was not unlikely.

1935

The Clerk of the Vestry noted that all of the Vestry property was presented in a report, except the old graveyard. The Chairman asked to have it included. No record was found regarding the execution of this request. However, the 1935 Registry records reportedly noted that the land comprising the old graveyard was 1 acre, 2 rods, and 25 perches.

"Only in St. Andrew"—Archibald Goodman nowhere to be found

Archibald "Archie" Goodman disappeared from his home one Monday night in 1936, and was never seen or heard from since.

It was reported that Archie was buried in St. Andrew's graveyard. The Rector was asked to test a certain grave in which Archie was alleged to have been buried. On pushing a stick into the grave, the Rector was surprised; it could not pass, never mind however or wherever he angled it; it's path was solidly obstructed.

As the Bishop was ostensibly out of the island, it was said that no exhumation could be undertaken. However, next day, when the Rector reportedly turned up with a police officer to test the grave again, lo and behold, the stick slid smoothly all the way down through the grave. No obstacle!

Tell me, how was this possible? Had Archie been mysteriously removed the night before? He had again eluded them!

Not even a search in Guiana, and afterwards in Canada, found the man!

Like Hall,[31] Archie you can't find at all, at all![32]

1937

An Act was passed authorising the Vestry of the parish of St. Andrew to demolish the buildings comprising the rectory, sell the material obtained therefrom, and raise a loan for the erection of another residence for the Rector.[33] It was not determined exactly which building (rectory) was to be demolished and where it was located; however, it was most likely to have been located on the site near the Infirmary in Belleplaine.

1938

The Parish Church's rectory was in a poor state of repair, and on 10 February 1938, tenders were received for the erection of a rectory at Belleplaine. Plantations Ltd's tender for £1,422 was accepted.[34] By 7 July 1938, an order was passed for the removal of the defective rectory (apparently a chattel structure) at a cost of £110. By 1 September 1938 the new rectory was completed.[35]

In the Statement of Accounts ending 24 March 1938, $7.32 was spent on electric fittings at the rectory. Could this have been used for the maintenance of a generator (dynamo in those days)? Or realising that residents of the parish were expecting electrification in Belleplaine, one may conjecture that the expenditure could have resulted from a wiring installation in preparation for the introduction of electricity from the Barbados Light and Power Company.

Also $15.08 was spent on galvanised-iron plumbing fittings. It is possible that this could have been toward an installation for the collection and reuse of rainwater, as it is unlikely that running water was supplied to the Infirmary (government residential centre for infirm senior people) at that time. The Barbados Water Authority is reported to have provided potable water in the area several years later.

Impact of 1939 War

In spite of the economic hardship prevailing in Barbados (inevitably induced by the Second World War commencing 3 September 1939), a number of projects were carried out at St. Andrew's and other churches. These included major church refurbishing and organ upgrade, as will be addressed later.

Rector Harvey Read and difficult war time

Rector Harvey Read served at St. Andrew's, 1931–1949. His son Anthony ("Tony") Read remembered him as a very strict disciplinarian who was a stickler for time keeping. He believed in starting and finishing services on time. In this way he was a conscientious steward who respected people's time. Although strict, he loved people and got along well with parishioners.

During the hard war times when "little money was available, daddy kept a farm where he grew vegetables and raised rabbits to feed his family."[36]

Rector Read was "a hard worker", who was surrounded by a complement of industrious people, including William Bailey, Kenneth Cadogan and Waple Dash, "school masters" along with MacDonald Smith.[37] These and numerous others served the Church so that under Rev'd. Harvey's leadership, despite the austere war time, he was able to accomplish major refurbishing of the 107-year-old Church. He gutted the woodwork, including the pews, altar rails and wooden ornaments of the sanctuary, and completed major renovation of the building. He installed 'spanking new' pews, altar rails, the current ornamental decoration of the sanctuary, including the reredos, and had the organ rebuilt.

Tony recalls his father, Rev'd. Read, using a Delco plant (generator) for supplying power for lighting during major festivals—at Christmas Mass, early Christmas and Easter morning services, and for Patronal Festivals. He also spoke of the large harvests at which the plantations of the parish liberally donated produce from their land and farms—ground provisions, vegetables, fruits and eggs, along with cash.

1940s

In the Vestry's Statement of Accounts for the Church ending 24 March 1940, the organist's salary was raised to $216, tuning and repair of the organ cost $36.00, the Sexton received $132, the Bell Ringer and Organ Blower (the person who pumped up the leather bellows of the pipe organ), received $90, while the cost of lighting and cleaning was $36.84.

"Only in St. Andrew"—Failure to burn a TB House

In the Sanitary Board meeting of 23 October 1941, chaired by The Hon. J. Haynes, there was an order to destroy a house belonging to a Mr. Small by burning, following the death of a resident from tuberculosis (TB). The owner asked $125 reimbursement for his house which government planned to incinerate (to eliminate contamination); but the cost proved too much for the Vestry to pay at the time.

After the owner refused to accept anything less than his asking price, so that the house could be destroyed to prevent others from entering and promoting the spread of TB, the Vestry, no doubt instructed by the Ministry responsible for Environmental Health, advised the owner of the house: ". . . to open all of the doors and windows in the house and leave it for at least 6 months allowing no one including himself to go near it in the meanwhile."

The Vestry believed that if the advice of the Sanitary Department in the parish were followed, the infective organisms in the house would eventually die and the house could safely have been returned to residential use at the end of the stipulated quarantine period.

1940–1942 Church upgrade

In wartime, during Rector Harvey Reid's incumbency at St. Andrew's, the pews were replaced by a new set and stabilising rails installed. These were built by Kirton Tucker, professional organ builder and woodworker at his home in Hastings, Christ Church, and assembled at the Church, with assistance from apprentice Newton Bovell.[38] There was also a major pipe organ upgrade at the time. In addition to carrying out rebuilding and refurbishing of the organs at St. Lucy, St. Augustine, St. Joseph, and St. Paul churches,[39] Tucker built and installed the reredos in the sanctuary of St. Andrew's. He also rebuilt the chest for the organ pipes, which with the console was located in the western gallery in the belfry.[40] The organ was situated in the centre of the gallery facing the sanctuary, while the choir was positioned south of the organ. In the 1940s, choristers wore their own clothing as the Church had not yet adopted the wearing of robes.[41]

In a 1941 issue of the *Gazette*, there was an account of a loan of $6,048 borrowed under St. Andrew's rectory, of which $772.72 was for repair of the Church.[42] No determination was made on how the Vestry spent the remainder of the loan. A total of $28.32 was obtained from pew rent during 1941.

Early open-air meetings

During the later part of the 1940s, under Rev'd. Harvey Reid open-air meetings were quite a village attraction. Communicant member Emeline Cumberbatch recalls these meetings being regularly conducted in Shorey Village, Belleplaine, Chalky Mount, and Bawden on Sunday evenings and nights with the use of the gas lamps and no loudspeaker! In the absence of television, radio, and internet, 'Open airs' were a popular pastime, especially in a moon-lit village. And in those days, people not only stood by to listen to the Word and ministry, they also enthusiastically participated in the services.

Speakers at open-air meetings included Bros. Kenneth Douglin, Waple Dash, and William Bailey along with Rev'd. Reid.[43] These enthusiasts often walked to open-air sites across the parish. An average of 30 to 40 people attended regularly, and there was usually good cooperation and avid response from villagers to the meetings.[44]

With no electricity during Reid's tenure, Sunday school was held at 3:00 p.m., followed generally by Evensong at 4:00 p.m. on Sundays.[45]

1944—"Do you know"—St. Andrew fanned the flames?

While the Second World War (1 September 1939–15 August 1945) engulfed the European and Asian continents, the smouldering embers of disestablishment of the Anglican Church were being fanned in Barbados. By this time disestablishment had, by indirection, actually materialised in Jamaica since January, 1870, and legally since June, 1870",[46] and was a topic of debate in other Caribbean islands. Persons fanning the embers and flames of disestablishment in this Barbados included Grantley Adams, who introduced a bill for disendowment of the Anglican Church on 30 November 1944, which was seconded by Errol Barrow. Other persons pressing for disendowment included J.C. Tudor, C.E. Talma and Frank Walcott, who also followed Adams in introducing a second Bill for disestablishment and disendowment. On 12 December 1944, J.A. Haynes, MP for St. Andrew, moved a motion for disendowment in a Private Member's Bill, which was also read in the House of Assembly.

The discontent with the status quo emerging in St. Andrew and other parishes led in part to battles engaging the courts in Barbados. The ensuing controversy extended as far as the Privy Council in London. Like the world wars, the St. Andrew's issues—disestablishment, disendowment, and retirement of clergy—would rage internationally across the churches. Chapters Five and Six address the destabilisation of the Church in Barbados and retirement of the Anglican clergy.

1949 Funds for asbestos roof

In 1949, Parliament passed an Act authorising the Vestry to raise loans for repairs of the roof of St. Andrew's.[47] In augmenting the loan, the Church also raised funds through its members, friends, and people of the parish. This was the genesis of the durable, cool asbestos roof that is still in place.

1950s

Interviewees confirmed that the Church was falling into disrepair in 1950. To arrest the situation, the Church began some limited work on the roof, but was hard pressed for funds. In the same year, government came to the rescue and provided over $7,000 in funds to complete the installation of the corrugated asbestos roof of St. Andrew's. It also provided equipment for the new chapel to be reconstructed at Saint Simon's.[48] On completion of the reconstruction work at St. Simon's, the church was rededicated on the Feast of Corpus Christi, 24 May 1951.

In the Statement of Accounts ending 24 March 1950, the Organist received $360, the Sexton $312, and the Bell Ringer and Organ Blower $60. Tuning the organ cost $166 and $67.84 was paid for lighting and cleaning.

In the Statement of Accounts ending 24 March 1954, rectory repairs amounted to $842.62, organ repairs cost $1,376.05, repairs and miscellaneous cost amounted to $1,055.72, while the Bell Ringer and Caretaker were paid $101.64.

The Vestry Minutes recorded under the chairmanship of Rev'd. Woodroffe, chronicled the high standard of debate that Mrs. E.V. Rock and Mrs. E.E. Bourne brought to the Vestry. No doubt, along with the Chairman's guidance, there was an obvious improvement in the conduct of the meetings, as reflected by the perspicacity of the questions, the issues aired and the resolutions passed. Clearly evident were the insightfulness, sharpness of wit, and initiative exercised by the women through the frequency with which they raised and seconded motions, bringing depth, progress, and resolutions to the sessions. During Rev'd. Woodroffe's tenure, typewriting of minutes was introduced.

1954

St. Simon's installed electric lighting in the church and rectory on 5 September 1954, via a 2.75 kilowatt gasoline generator, at a cost of $371.78. Half of the installation cost was donated by the Vestry, as noted in a letter of 13 September 1954, while the church paid the remainder. Did the Parish Church have a similar arrangement for lighting in place at that time? There was no record or indication.

1955

In the Statement of Accounts ending 24 March 1956, the Organist's salary was raised to $680, and the Sexton's was $529.20.

The Vestry granted six months' leave of absence with two weeks' vacation pay to Organist Edward Vaughan. During his absence, his brother Lester acted in his stead and was paid on authorisation of the Vestry at its meeting of 21 July 1955.

Hurricane Janet, 22 September 1955 and Rebuilding

Again, St. Andrew's is one of the Anglican Churches that withstood category 3 Hurricane Janet, which struck Barbados on 22 September 1955. It was a small but powerful system, the centre of which passed not far off the south coast, taking 38 lives. With very minor damage, the St. Andrew's Parish Church provided shelter for members and parishioners while suffering no disruption of services.

On 29 September 1955, the Vestry met to review the hurricane damage. From the assessment made of St. Andrew Parish, the Vestry learned that 330 houses were affected: 45 were demolished, 183 received considerable damage, while 102 received minor damage. The Vestry received a letter from the Government advising that the restoration/

repair was to start first on the least damaged houses. Repairs were performed by a 'gang of carpenters' who started mass renovation of houses at Chalky Mount, St. Andrew.[49]

On agreement of the Vestry, a meeting was called to advise that:

1. Owners of land in the parish were to be summoned to a meeting to discuss making land available for housing purposes.
2. Local materials, including soft stones (limestone blocks) and hollow concrete blocks were to be used where practicable to ensure a more substantial building renewal undertaking.
3. Consequent on the housing repair project, householders should be permitted to own house spots rather than having to lease them for 99 years.

The Janet rebuilding project in St. Andrew was quite proactive. Seeking to allow parishioners not only to have their homes refurbished, but also the opportunity to own both house and land was indeed a visionary and novel endeavour, which several successive governments continue to adopt. The project was a fine example of local entrepreneurship where ordinary people were involved in the supply of land and local materials in executing national housing and rebuilding programmes. Modern governments will do well to exercise such wisdom and realise the benefit in such a system, rather than short-sightedly retaining an oligarchy (investing all power/privileges in a few persons or dominant class or clique) and other building exercises for political ends. Especially at a time like this, in crushing, worldwide recession, sharing the economic and opportunity pie fairly and widely not only avoids partisan conflict and nepotism, but, if prudently administered, alleviates suffering among the masses, while offering more equitable opportunities for a greater number of deserving and qualified people.

Parts for organ

In his letter to the Vestry dated 11 November 1955, organ builder A.D. Hunte of Fairfield Road, St. Michael, relinquished his contract for rebuilding St. Simon's organ for $720.00, after observing its irreparable condition. He also agreed to use the salvageable parts of that organ to repair the organ at the Parish Church at no extra cost, and to keep any remaining parts of value. Alternatively, St. Simon agreed to purchase a small organ for $150.00.[50]

"What's in a name?

"If there is something "Woody" or "Wardy" (Wood, Woodroffe, Edward) about a name with some connection to St. Andrew, take a hint: either expect some invincible position in the service of an incumbent or an individual's meteoric elevation to service.

Rev'd. George Cuthbert Manning Woodroffe

Following Rector William Harvey Reid's incumbency at St. Andrew's (1931–1949), Rector George Cuthbert Manning Woodroffe, a Grenadian, served as Rector of St. Andrew's (1949–1956).[51] Prior to this, he served as Vicar of Simons, St. Andrew, during 1948–1949.

Figure 15: Archbishop Cuthbert Woodroffe, KBE

It is reported that Rev'd. Woodroffe (Figure 15) brought "life and awakening to the parish."[52] The Church was usually packed in the early 1950's as Rector Woodroffe attracted a 'full house'. The enthusiasm was so strong that it was reported that often congregants would begin to assemble as early as 9:00 p.m. for the Christmas midnight Mass.[53] For Good Friday, Easter, and Christmas services, there was hardly standing room as droves of people from Walkers, Chalky Mount, Rock Hall, Shorey, and Belleplaine walked to church to get there early for services.[54] Emeline Cumberbatch said that in order to accommodate participating communicants, often there was need to sing six to eight hymns during the Communion. Emeline nostalgically lamented how worshipping in those days afforded "such a sweet feeling", and with sorry-glad remorse she chuckled that one really wanted to be, and looked forward to being, in church. She said that when Bishop Gay Lisle Griffith Mandeville (1951–1960) asked Rector Woodroffe to assist at St. Joseph's Parish Church, where the attendance was declining, on Woodroffe's first Sunday of ministry, there was no room to accommodate the congregants.

A letter from the Vestry to the Parochial Treasurer's Office communicated Rev'd. Woodroffe's retirement from St. Andrew's Parish Church, slated for 28 December 1956. On 27 December 1956, a letter from the Parochial Treasurer's Office addressed to the St. Andrew's Vestry expressed its regret at his departure. He was moving on, to continue service (1957–1962) in St. Joseph.

Several persons reported that behind the large figure of a handsome rector was a humble person whose message was filled with inspiration, 'solid meat', and charisma. His wife was charming and endearing, as she freely gave of her time and substance in conducting classes for the young women of the parish. The congregation loved this couple and their company and was eager to emulate their example.

After being elevated to Rural Dean (1962–1967) in Barbados and to Sub-Dean in St. Vincent, Rev'd. Woodroffe continued his meteoric rise, becoming the youngest Diocesan Bishop of the Province of the Windward Islands (1969–1986) and Primate of the West Indies (1980–1986).[55]

Of His Grace, the Most Rev'd. Sir Cuthbert Woodroffe KBE, Primate of the West Indies and Bishop of the Diocese of the Windward Islands, who served in St. Andrew, Rev'd. William Dixon reported in his article, "An Outstanding Archbishop", in *The Bajan*:

> ... For me, he is a "Super Priest", a Worthy Bishop and a Historic Archbishop, being the first black man to occupy this high office in the Province of the West Indies. He was, and still is, my idea of a Priest, his high office has not eroded his deep humility. I have treasured his friendship, encouragement and counsel over the years and I wish him a long, healthy, happy and refreshing retirement from his heavy burden as Deacon-Priest-Bishop and Archbishop. His long and successful ministry is an example of what the ministry is all about—servanthood, which is rendered to God and Man, and his example should be emulated by every Caribbean Deacon-Priest-Bishop as well as his successor as the Primate ...[56]

The Vincentian, the National Newspaper of St. Vincent and the Grenadines, reported:

> Woodroffe was noted for his simple and straightforward sermons that went directly at the point targeted. He was a hard worker, a good organiser, an effective manager.
> Above all, he had been the humblest of men, mild-mannered always, that occasionally threw a ball that startled his audience.[57]

He died on 29 November 2012.

Having such a distinguished person as The Right Rev'd. Dr. Cuthbert Woodroffe, KBE, MA, DD connected with St. Andrew (1949–1956) was not a rarity.

Rev. Gatherer's preparation for St. Andrew's

After graduation from Codrington College in 1951, Rev'd. Gatherer served as curate of St. Mary's Church, Bridgetown for 16 months. On 21 December 1952, The Feast of St. Thomas, he was ordained to the priesthood at St. Joseph's Parish Church, where he served until appointed vicar of St. Anne's Church with St. Bernard's Church, St. Joseph, 1 June 1953.

When Rev'd. Edward Gatherer served at St. Anne's with St. Bernard's, it was his first incumbency, but he was no stranger to the parish of St. Joseph, since he had previously served as curate at the Parish Church.

His predecessor as vicar of St. Anne's with St. Bernard's, the Rev'd. J.T. Adams-Cooper was a Glaswegian Scot who had retired to his native Scotland. "Rev. Cooper", as he was known, was a bachelor who was thought to have been somewhat eccentric. He apparently was not particularly concerned about maintaining the property or the grounds of the church, as there was lush vegetation everywhere—bushes all around the vicarage and overgrowing the graveyard. But he was much loved by his parishioners, even though it was alleged that many understood only a small percentage of his heavily-accented Scottish speech. He kept a parrot that he had taught to speak, and it was rumoured that the parrot was equipped with a few naughty words with which to greet unwelcome visitors.[58]

The new, young vicar set about the challenging task that faced him at St. Anne's with determination and vigour. The cluttered sanctuary was cleared and redecorated; celebration of the Eucharist on week-days and Saints' days was introduced; Eucharistic vestments were brought into use; and servers were trained. The priest's vestry was also cleared of an accumulation of outdated papers. The large trees that hid the church were cut down, providing easy access around the church building. The large tree that crowded out the small space outside the west door was removed. The compound was enlarged and covered with gravel so that it could become a car park and the site for the annual church fair.

Rev'd. Gatherer visited in the two primary schools—St. Anne's and St. Bernard's—taking catechism classes, and was an assiduous visitor in the various districts where he took the Blessed Sacrament to the sick and housebound. His tall upright figure in white cassock and knotted black girdle was known everywhere in the parish.[59]

He revived the two Sunday schools, and on 18 July 1954 presented to Bishop Gay Lisle Griffith(s) Mandeville (1951–1960) over 80 candidates (some interviewees insisted over 100), adults and children, for confirmation. He also introduced the first Church Council, and formed the League of Faithful Witness.

His work with young people was quite outstanding. There were two platoons of over 30 boys each in the Church Lads' Brigade, and one platoon of girls in the Church Girls' Brigade (then newly formed). These constituted the basis of the dynamic young people's work and participation in diocesan activities, including the staging of their numerous concerts.

As St. Anne's and St. Bernard's are in the agricultural belt of the island, the harvest gifts were bountiful, including gifts from the local plantations. The harvest services provided a basis for the young people to display their talents in songs and recitations, with much encouragement from the older folk, who turned out in great numbers to support them.[60]

Rev'd. Gatherer's service at St. Anne's and St. Bernard's was illustrious and eventful. There, not less than three promising young men—Wilfred D. Wood, Frank Marshall, and Seibert Small—were profoundly impacted by his ministry, later joined the priesthood and went on to serve at high levels in the Church.

It is not without significance that, although Rev'd. Gatherer was there only just over three years before the Bishop transferred him to be rector of St. Andrew's, two of the young men of the parish later became priests of note, one a bishop (Wilfred Wood) and the other a dean (Frank Marshall).

Notes

1. Robert H. Schomburgk, *The History of Barbados*. (London: Frank Cass Publishers, 1971), 224.
2. J.E. Reece and C.G. Clark-Hunt, *Barbados Diocesan History*. In Commemoration of the First Centenary of the Diocese of Barbados, 1825–1925. (London: West India Committee, 1925), 103.
3. Reece and Clark-Hunt, 103.
4. Schomburgk, 88.
5. *The Barbadian*, 2 December 1846.
6. *The Barbadian*, Volume XXIV, 1846.
7. The figure of 1000 persons seated at St. Andrew's was an exaggeration. A mere 60 ft by 40 ft (2,400 sq. ft.) building accommodating such a number definitely reflects an overcrowding situation, allegedly offering 2.4 sq. ft. per person, and not the optimum 7 sq. ft to 10 sq. ft. per person rule of thumb of recommended space for comfort in churches. When 440 sq. ft. was subtracted for the chancel plus another 550 sq. ft. for existing aisles, this left a mere 1400sq. ft. for seating accommodation. However, if you added another 400 sq. ft., say from the mezzanine accommodation, this allowed less than 500 persons to be 'packed in' (being generous, and allowing, say, 600 during a downpour of rain at a funeral); and this does not include wheelchair accommodation (minimum of 4.6 ft x 2.9 ft per person) for at least 6 persons.

    Ideally, a 1000-member congregation in St. Andrew's would surely be a most desirable feat, and one worthy to attain! *But Shhhh . . . goodness gracious—don't mention 1000 persons being seated (in the hearing of the Environmental Protection Department or Ministry of Health, Barbados)!*
8. Ronald A. Stoute. Undated and unprinted typewritten copy of notes, 2.
9. *Ibid.*
10. *Ibid.*
11. Reece and Clark-Hunt, 103.
12. *The Barbadian*, 7 November 1857.
13. Copious information found on a John Bradshaw, which related to a regicide (person responsible for killing a king) and president, did not fit the description of a rector of St. Andrew's Church, Barbados; nor was such a person buried in this island. This Bradshaw, who was also a lawyer, politician and regicide of England, rose to the distinction of famous judge, and later Lord President of the High Court of Justice, who was set up to preside at the trial of King Charles I.

    In his meteoric rise to power, Bradshaw gained for himself a lucrative, but short-lived career. In what appeared to be a kangaroo trial, at which he presided, Charles I was beheaded in Whitehall on 30 January 1649. Bradshaw died, possibly of malaria, on 31 October and was buried on 22 November 1659.

    When Charles II ascended the throne, through a vote of Parliament on 4 December 1660, he ordered the exhumation of Bradshaw and other regicides who had condemned his predecessor to death, and had them ignominiously hung on the 30 January 1661. Their

heads were displayed on spikes at Westminster Hall, and their bodies were subsequently buried beneath the gallows.
14. Jerome S. Handler, "A Rare Eighteenth-Century Tract in Defence of the Slaves in Barbados: The Thoughts of the Rev'd. John Duke, Curate of St. Michael". From the *Barbados Gazette*, or *General Intelligencer*, 15–19 March 1788, and recorded in the *Journal of the Barbados Museum and Historical Society,* Vol. LI (2005). http://jeromehandler.org/wp-content/uploads/RareDefense-05.pdf. Accessed 10 August 2011.
15. *Ibid.*
16. *Ibid.*
17. "The History of the Barbados Railway". http://www.enuii.org/vulcan_foundryRailway.pdf Viewed on 3 September 2010.
18. Sylvan Catwell. *The Brethren in Barbados: Gospel Hall Assemblies, 1889–1994*. (USA, Michigan: McNaughton & Gunn, 1995), 119.
19. Saint Andrew's Parish (Barbados) Loan Act, 1893.
20. Terry Ally. "Can Barbados be hit?" *Sunday Sun*, 16A. Sunday, 5 September 1999. Accessed 24 August 2011.
21. Joy-Ann Gill. "Renaming Of St. Andrew's Primary School". BGISMedia; published June 15, 2011. http://www.gisbarbados.gov.bb/index.php? Accessed 13 October 2012.
22. Saint Andrew's Parish (Barbados) Loan Act, 1925.
23. Joy-Ann Gill, loc. cit..
24. "St. Andrew's Primary School Renamed". *Nation News,* 22 June 2011. http://www.nationnews.com/articles/view/st-andrew. Accessed 13 October 2012.
25. Vestry Minutes, 10 May 1911.
26. *Ibid*, May 1912.
27. Interview with Dr. Bromley Simon, 17 March 2013.
28. Interview with Melba Sandiford, 24 September 2011.
29. That Rev'd. Haynes was both Rector and farmer was not unusual. Other rectors used the glebe lands to good advantage.

    It was reported that Rector Gatherer reared poultry and sheep; he sold a few eggs. Occasionally he reared a cow or two. When he had a cow butchered, he sold meat (beef) across the parish. Interestingly, interviewee Cheryl Hurst jokingly said that Rector Gatherer "often gave away more milk and eggs than he sold".

    Other incumbents, including one in St. Joseph, are reported to have tended a thriving pig farm.
30. Reece and Clark-Hunt, 73.
31. The pun on Hall draws reference to calypsonian Red Plastic Bag's famous Ragga Soca composition of 20 July 2008—"Can't find me brother". It was a composition on alleged escaped prisoner Winston Hall. The rendition comically portrayed how after a thorough search in Bank Hall, Bush Hall, Eagle Hall, every Kingdom Hall, rather, even in church and every 'Hall' in Barbados, one couldn't find Hall at all. Calypsonian Kid Site also popularised Hall's disappearance by his 1987 Dub-lypso "Babylon Searching And They Can't Find Hall".
32. Interview with Cyrillene Harding, niece of Archibald Goodman, on 29 September 2011.

33. Saint Andrew's Rectory Act, 1937.
34. *Official Gazette*, 19 May 1938.
35. Vestry Minutes, 1 September 1938.
36. Interview with William Anthony "Tony" Read, 20 November 2013.
37. *Ibid.*
38. Interview with Newton Bovell, 19 January 2010.
39. Interview with Michael Tucker, 27 October 2011.
40. Newton Bovell, 19 January 2010.
41. Interview with Emeline Cumberbatch, 12 September 2011.
42. *The Official Gazette,* 26 June 1941
43. Cumberbatch, 29 September 2011.
44. *Ibid.*
45. Interview with Hersie Smith, 31 October 2011.
46. J.B. Ellis. "The Diocese of Jamaica". Project Canterbury: Society for Promoting Christian Knowledge, 1913. anglicanhistory.org/wi/jm/ellis1913/10.html
47. Saint Andrew's Parish (Barbados) Loan Act, 1949.
48. Saint Andrew's Parish (Barbados) Loan Act, 1950.
49. Vestry Minutes, 29 September 1955.
50. Vestry Minutes, 11 November 1955.
51. "UWI honorary degree for Archbishop Woodroffe". *Sunday Sun,* 1 February 1981.
52. Rev'd. Laurence Small, MBE, 4 April 2013.
53. Cumberbatch, 18 February 2010.
54. Interview with McDonald Smith, 8 April 2010.
55. "Cuthbert Woodroffe". en.wikipedia.org/wiki/George_Cuthbert_Manning_Woodroffe Accessed 24 July 2011.
56. *The Bajan*, July–August 1989.
57. "Archbishop Cuthbert Woodroffe Passes". *The Vincentian,* The National Newspaper of St. Vincent and the Grenadines, thevincentian.com/arch-bishop-cuthbert-woodroffe-passes-p1743-10. . . Accessed 19 January 2013.
58. Interview with Dean Frank Marshall, CBE, 3 March 2010.
59. *Ibid.*
60. Interview with Bishop Wilfred Wood, KA, 12 October 2011.

CHAPTER FOUR

Rector Gatherer and St. Andrew's Parish Church (1957–1980s) Phase 1

Edward Godson Gatherer, born 28 January 1922, was the sixth of nine children of Edward and Constance Gatherer of Georgetown, St. Vincent. Through his overarching childhood passion to minister in church, he paid his way from St. Vincent to Barbados to be trained in the priesthood. On completion of his formal training at Codrington College in 1951, he was ordained a deacon in St. Michael and All Angels Cathedral, Barbados, by the Rt. Rev'd. Gay Lisle Griffith Mandeville, Bishop of Barbados (1951–1960) on the Feast of the Transfiguration, 6 August 1951.

Following some short stints of preparatory service at St. Mary's, St. Michael, and then at St. Joseph's, St. Anne's with St. Bernard's located in St. Joseph, Fr. Gatherer was ready to launch out to St. Andrew's Parish Church, St. Andrew, to assume what turned out to have been a lifetime cure, the longest serving period in the diocese.

Gatherer and St. Andrew's

Following Rev'd. Cuthbert Woodroffe's incumbency, "Edward Godson Gatherer became Rector of St. Andrew's Parish Church on 1 May 1957 as a relatively young priest".[1] At 35 years of age, Gatherer was not only young and strong, but was up to the task. He was daring and ready to assume the ministry that he would perform during the following fifty-four years.

It must be noted that Gatherer, on accepting his appointment in 1957, as Rector of the cure of St. Andrew's, no doubt understood that he was serving for life. He joined no less than 13 other clerics, his contemporaries, the majority of whom survived as late as 1989. No doubt, they all had the idea that, in answering their call to serve in the Anglican Church, they would have been doing so until 'death them did part'. At that time there was no question to the contrary as clerics appointed under the Anglican Church Acts 1911, 1928 and 1947 enjoyed certain unambiguous, binding entitlements to housing, glebe privileges, salary, serving for life, to name a few privileges. Without any thought or challenges to entitlements, the young cleric would later need to wade in the uncharted, turbulent civil waters related to breach of contract for service and premature retirement.

In fact there is no recorded information of any discussion then about losing those contractual entitlements. It therefore follows that if there were no conversation[2] about any stipulated retirement, for one to raise the issue later and impose retroactive conditions would in conventional legal terms not only have been a serious breach of contract, but simply unprecedented and acting *ultra vires*. In such an uncharted, turbulent course young cleric Gatherer was destined to enter.

All reports of him regarding his early service indicate that Fr. Gatherer was an industrious, dedicated, devoted worker and fatherly church leader of St. Andrew's. He loved his congregation, was loved by his congregants and parishioners, and shared vicariously in the lives of both young and old, but especially the young.

Accepting his somewhat daunting responsibility, the new Rector understood the refurbishing of the Church as one of his early preoccupations. Joan Smith asserted that "on becoming Rector, Gatherer aggressively repaired the church from day one he took up office."[3] He also assisted at St. Saviour's and St. Simon's when the Vicar of these churches was absent.

Many speak highly of his passion for young people and how he loved, trained and fathered them. Not only did he spend quality time at church and at his home with them, he held camps and took them on educational tours at home and abroad. Often people acclaimed him a Good Samaritan who took the sick and wounded into his care, and as one who would never relinquish caring until he had made a difference in their lives.

One of his great loves and preoccupations was doing his utmost to keep the plant at St. Andrew in remarkable shape. Knowing that the Church was susceptible to gross building stress and structural damage, he never reneged on his life-long dedication to its maintenance and upkeep, despite the cost and sacrifice. Indeed, his penchant for soliciting funds to maintain his church, "St. Andrew's", could have been surpassed only by his love for his God. All knew he dearly loved St. Andrew's, and he worked untiringly to make sure it retained its significance as a well-loved historic church.

How some people felt about Fr. Gatherer

Fr. Gatherer feared God and people highly respected him, while some reportedly grew to fear him, associating him with having supernatural powers. This 'awesome fear' apparently struck terror in some people. And so, numerous stories exist that expressed various myths as people harboured strong and odd ideas about the cleric.

> It so happened that Gatherer appeared at the door of a sugar factory in St. Joseph in order to console and transport one of his church members who was involved in an altercation with another worker. Sometime after, when the worker fell ill, all types of comments were

heard: "Don't mess with Gatherer. He's the biggest Obeah man in Barbados."[4]

Another interesting story:

> A die (tool used for cutting or shaping materials) could not be found at a sugar factory one day never matter whom they asked or wherever they searched. With everyone feverishly looking to recover the die, management was heard to retort, "Bring Fr. Gatherer to help us find the die!"[5]

And were there reprisals for Fr. Gatherer's awesome powers? It was related that when a St. Andrew parishioner was unduly held up at a clinic one day with no respite whatever, one of her friends queried her unfortunate delay, only to be told: "She was one of them who helped Gatherer to show up the Bishop. Don't mind her".[6] For a poor church member, who stood faithful and loyal to her priest, this was a heavy and unfortunate price to pay.

The belief about Fr. Gatherer's supernatural powers took on such currency that when or if an altercation arose, one would often hear: "I'll put Fr. Gatherer on you!"[7] In this regard, some people did not credit the victory in *Gatherer* v *The Bishop* to a judgment for the cause of justice and a vindication of right and what was decent and fair, but rather to, "No, you can't win 'gainst Gatherer!"[8]

About the soft-spoken, dry-humour Cleric the account was retold how at a funeral service one evening, a youngster, sitting in one of the front benches, said that he could not hear what the Rector was saying. On overhearing the comment, Fr. Gatherer replied, "Sunny, if you want to hear what I'm saying don't only come to a funeral; come to church on Sundays.[9]

Figure 16: Rector Gatherer at work 2010

It was rumoured that Fr. Gatherer did not respect the dead as "he never ceased to take up his collection over their dead bodies [at funerals]". In doing this Fr. Gatherer was a trendsetter.[10] It is common practice nowadays to take collection at funerals in order to help defray church expenses and assist in various church projects, involving organ and church building repairs, as well as civic organisations, e.g., the Cancer Society and Heart and Stroke Foundation, to name a few.

Fr. Gatherer (Figure 16) would never want to speak of his personal sacrifice, but many testified of how he unrelentingly and unselfishly gave of his personal substance to ensure that the organ, windows, or whatever at his Church, were kept in good repair. Although St. Andrew's could never be personally owned, it is not difficult to understand that when someone takes such personal interest and expends uncommon effort in unstinting care of property he loves, it would be hard to simply hand over the keys and walk away.

In remaining resolutely attached to this Church, Fr. Gatherer was prepared to fight every battle, brave any storm, and defend any suit in order to stay with his St. Andrew family, while maintaining his legal right to his office and to serve therein.

The *"Wardy"* aspect of St. Andrew's—Edward (Gatherer) touched so many people's lives!

With pleasure and pride, Rector Edward Gatherer often reported that he encouraged young Wilfred Wood to pursue Holy Orders.

Wilfred D. Wood

After completing training at Codrington College, Barbadian Wilfred Wood was ordained Deacon in Barbados and then as priest in St. Paul's Cathedral, England, in 1962. Being affected by the struggles that the black immigrants faced in London, Wood became a champion of the black underprivileged and was lauded for speaking out on racial issues and for social justice. Fr. Gatherer reported that in 1972 he recommended Rev'd. Wood for the bishopric of Barbados, as he was a "beautiful, honest, real highly intellectual and deeply spiritual man."[11] While in England, in 1977, Rev'd. Wood was appointed Rural Dean of East Lewisham and Honorary Canon of Southwark Cathedral. He was Archdeacon of Southwark from 1982 until his consecration as Bishop of Croydon in 1985.

Wood (Figure 17) received myriad accolades and distinctions: as spokesman for racial justice; for launching several initiatives; in 1968, for championing the concept later known as 'the Wood Proposals' that called for some members to be directly elected by minority ethnic associations; in 1992, for co-sponsoring with the Bishop of Liverpool, Bishop David Sheppard, the 'Wood-Sheppard Principles' for ensuring equality practices by employers; for being a Moderator of the Southwark Diocesan Race Relations Commission from its inception; as Moderator of the World Council of Churches Programme to Combat Racism; for protesting the honours bestowed on Enoch Powell upon his death; and questioning the Government and Opposition's attitudes to asylum seekers.

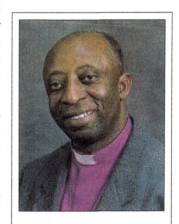

Figure 17: Bishop Wilfred Wood, KA

Wood served on numerous boards and committees, among which were the Mayday Hospital, Royal Philanthropic Society, the UK's Housing Corporation and other housing associations, the Institute of Race Relations, as well as the Royal Commission on Criminal Procedure.

In addition to being an Honorary Freeman of the London Borough of Croydon, he holds honorary doctorates from the Open University, the University of the West Indies, and the General Theological Seminary, New York, at which he was cited as "a wide and trusted defender of the rights of minorities".[12]

From an extract of a speech, 'Inexhaustible faith in the promise of Christ', delivered at the Black and Minority Ethnic Forum farewell to Bishop Wood in May 2002, by the Southwark People, the Ven. Tony Davies, Archdeacon of Croydon, penned:

> I have been privileged to work with Bishop Wilfred for just over eight years and our friendship has developed and deepened through the years...
>
> ...I learnt, by being alongside him, that no one else really knows the daily grind of petty injustices dished out to those whose ethnicity differs from white British. Bishop Wilfred's *crie de coeur* is that minority ethnic people should be able to say for themselves what it feels like, and not be patronised by well-meaning white people who want to tell them what it must feel like!
>
> For Mr Blair, it's 'education, education, education'. You may be tempted sometimes to think that for Bishop Wilfred it is 'cricket, cricket, cricket'. However, those of us who have been privileged to be close to him know that what matters can only be 'Jesus, Jesus, Jesus'![13]

How fitting that, on 30 November 2000, Barbados Independence Day, he received from Her Majesty Queen Elizabeth II, the Knighthood of St. Andrew (Order of Barbados) for his contribution to race relations in the United Kingdom and to the welfare of Barbadians living there!

The Right Rev'd. Dr. Sir Wilfred Denniston Wood, KA, retired as Bishop of Croydon 30 September 2002. In 2004, he was voted by the public as second to Mary Seacole, Jamaican heroine of the Crimean War, on a list of the "100 Great Black Britons."[14]

Bishop Wood in his retirement now resides at home in Barbados.

Frank Marshall

Young Frank, or Dr. Frank Marshall, CBE, Dean of St. Michael's Cathedral, also attended St. Anne's Church, St. Joseph, where Father Gatherer served, at least for a short while. Dean Marshall reported that although he was prepared for confirmation by Rev'd. Lloyd Clarke, shortly after Fr. Gatherer was transferred to St. Andrew, he still vividly remembers Fr. Gatherer's distinguished ministry in the parish. He said that Fr. Gatherer was immensely loved, admired, and respected by young people, his peers, and by himself—who all referred to him as 'Pop Gatherer'.[15] Marshall opined that Fr. Gatherer held such 'presence' and great esteem among the young that in later years many from among them, on returning to the island from overseas, sought him out for re-acquaintance.

Seibert Small

Seibert Small, now Canon Small, reported that in growing up at St. Simon's, he was mentored and prepared for confirmation by Fr. Gatherer in the 1960s. Small fondly recalls how he, with other candidates for confirmation at St. Andrew's Parish Church, was admonished to get to class and church early and once they had been seated, they were to: "... Remember Lot's wife! Never look back, even if the building is [sic] coming down from the back."[16]

1958

As Chairman of the Vestry, Fr. Gatherer received a letter from the Church Warden, dated 27 March 1958, noting a major crack in the wall of the Parish Church.

The Vestry members were instructed to visit the Church and report their findings. While no further report was made on the matter, or any comment recorded in the Minutes of the Vestry, interviewees and church members confirmed that on assuming his cure, Rector Gatherer had passionately taken on the task of refurbishing the Church.

1959

The last meeting of the Vestry in St. Andrew convened by Chairman Gatherer was held on 19th March 1959. Figure 18 shows one of Rector Gatherer's sittings as Chairman of the Vestry.

Electrification in St. Andrew

Many persons spoke quite convincingly of their belief that St. Andrew's Parish Church had electric lighting in the 1950s. They insisted that from a distance they saw lights being turned

Figure 18: Chairman Rev'd. E. Gatherer with Erma Rock top right and Vestry members

on and off and that the Church sometimes kept Evensong at 7:00 p.m. during Rector Woodroffe's incumbency. In the early 1950s, Evensong was usually conducted at 4:00 p.m. on Sundays. However, regarding the "switching on and off" of lights, this was possible when late evening services were occasionally held since, during the early years, gas lamps and, later, a generator producing power for lighting were used in the Church.

Due to the tendency of the land to be easily eroded and dislodged in the Scotland District, electrification of Belleplaine and Walkers posed some problems. Difficulty in installing poles, especially after heavy storms, reportedly delayed lighting in the area. Interviewees reported that residents in the parish had been promised electricity since 1949, and consequently many people had their houses 'wired' in preparation.

At last, electrification came to Belleplaine in 1959. At the grand Christmas lighting ceremony on Monday, 21 December, on the Belleplaine playing field attended by various members of Parliament and Senior Parliamentary Representative of the Parish Mrs. E.E. Bourne (and her husband), The Hon. M.E. Cox, Minister of Trade, Industry, and Labour flicked the switch for the electrification of 12 residences and the Belleplaine Boys' and Girls' schools.[17] MP Bourne expressed the wish to see electricity in every nook and cranny of Barbados.[18]

1960s

In his quest to keep sharp and in step with the demands of the time, Fr. Gatherer spent 1960 through 1961 in study at King's College, London. During that period, Vicar Lionel Burke assumed responsibility for the parish, assisted by Rev'd. Lloyd Clarke, who celebrated monthly mass at Hillaby, Turner's Hall, St. Andrew.

Electrification of the Church

The actual date that the Parish Church received lighting from the Barbados Light and Power Company (BL&P) was not formally recorded. However, the BL&P's records revealed that the Company took lighting to Walkers in 1963; no doubt the Church would have been one of the first places to receive electrification.

1963

St. Andrew's Parish Church branch of the Mothers' Union

Although the St. Andrew Parish Church's Mothers' Union was neither included in the branches of the 48 listed Anglican churches comprising the Mothers Union of Barbados, nor mentioned in the 1998–2000 President's Report of 'The Mothers' Union of Barbados',[19] the movement is alive and well and has continued from its inception early in 1963. It was reported that, in the 1960s, the Union was opened only to married women; this restricted its membership.[20] Sometime later, with the need to be more proactive in ministering to women in general, due to the changes in society, the membership was opened to all mothers—married or unwed—and especially to the young mothers who needed help.[21]

Leaders of the Branch at St. Andrew's included Daphnie Mahon, Melba Sandiford, Nola Wooding and Erma Small.

The first Enrolling Member, Daphnie Mahon, who served three terms (1963–1972) reported that, "Rev'd. Edward Gatherer suggested the need to have such an organisation and the idea was readily embraced".[22]

The branch started with 18 members. Its aims and objectives were to provide support for mothers in the Church in nurturing their children in Christian values. The organisation also sought to enhance the worship experience by providing flowers to beautify the sanctuary, and by cleaning the Church, both inside and outside. Corporate Communion was celebrated on the first Sunday of each month. The branch met once a month to plan and evaluate activities.

Mrs. Mahon also affirmed:

> Social outreach was another part of the Union's ministry. Members visited the sick and shut-ins and provided them with toiletries, words of comfort, and prayers. The making of handicraft items provided vital social intercourse and recreation for members.
>
> The Mothers' Union was actively involved in fund-raising activities including fairs, concerts, and dinners. This ministry proved valuable not only to the mothers, but also to the children and the church in general.[23]

The second Enrolling Member, Melba Sandiford, also served three terms (1972–1981). Mrs. Sandiford reported that she clearly understood her leadership responsibility and undertook her stewardship seriously. In addition to arranging for periodic talks and special services being regularly conducted, the Union branch at St. Andrew's organised large fairs, especially those held on Whit Mondays. Members were happy to participate in providing food, pudding and souse, and snacks for sale on those occasions. Mrs. Sandiford remarked that she was intolerant of anyone meddling with her duties and responsibilities, and particularly 'giving her orders' regarding how to conduct the financial matters of the Union.

It was stated that matters of finance, autocratic leadership, and the Rector allegedly refusing to offer Communion to a young communicant because she was delinquent with respect to her offering dues, led to a discordant and untenable situation,[24] causing members of the Union, including the Sandifords, to leave the Church.

Its third Enrolling Member, Nola Wooding, now deceased, served five terms (1981–1996). Apart from the usual visitation of the sick, and members faithfully attending the Union's functions at other churches throughout the island, interviewees reported that there was no particularly outstanding mission during this phase of the Union. Some spoke of the interpersonal conflicts arising from the alleged dictatorial style of leadership of the priest, simmering squabbles over money and who held the reins of responsibility. This was also the tumultuous period during which the case involving the Bishop and Rev'd. Gatherer occurred. It must have been very unsettling for the Church and its organisations. The observation was made that the membership ceased to grow during this period.

Mrs. Erma Small, its fourth and current Enrolling Member, led the branch for five terms, commencing in 1996. In 2007, when the Provincial Council finally agreed to bring the Mothers' Union Organisation of Barbados in line with those of the other dioceses in the region, Enrolling Members were renamed 'Branch Leaders'.[25] In 2007, Erma Small became one of the first Branch Leaders of Barbados.

Although the 1990s was a very difficult litigious time when the Church fell into its stormy civil battle, Small's leadership reportedly saw nine members added to the branch, bringing the drooping membership back to twenty during 2003. Small noted that in spite of the difficulties, the few members maintained a vibrant group that held regular concerts and fish fries, and participated in exchange visits with other branches.

One reason advanced for the lack of development of this organisation was the reportedly over-protective, domineering disposition of the Rector, who allegedly maintained that only he should be ultimately responsible for all church funds.

Yes, some interviewees said, they understood the Rector's proclivity for collecting funds that he spent maintaining the church plant that was so riddled with structural problems. Many praised him for keeping the Church in good repair (refer to "Money and dissension" later in this Chapter), but others opined that the Rector often insisted on having things done his way, to the exclusion of members' perspectives and efforts.[26] This approach frustrated those members who felt that their interest was not appreciated; the resulting friction did not augur well for dedicated persons continuing their service and membership.[27]

The Union members of St. Andrew's, even though small in number, continue to hold their own within the 3,000-odd Mothers' Union family of Barbados, and are usually well and regularly represented as they participate in and support the Union's corporate activities across the island.[28]

"Only in St. Andrew"—Coin minting?

An interviewee related how, as a student of St. Andrew's Girls' School in the 1960s, she attended service at St. Andrew's with her school every Monday morning. It was something she looked forward to, as she enjoyed Fr. Gatherer's teaching, and the interesting and effective way he was able to interact, entertain and minister to school children. 'He just had a way with them', she said.

She also fondly dramatised how, when it came to offering time, he never settled for less than the amount he planned to obtain. He would urge and coerce the school children to give more and more. If they gave $5.00 he would implore them to raise it to $5.50. When he got $5.50, he would then urge them to increase it to $6.00. And on and on! And so, she humorously recalled how a little girl wrapped foil over a lesser coin in order to simulate a silver coin and then placed it in the collection to help to supplement the amount Fr. Gatherer sought.[29]

Fr. Gatherer was renowned for leaving no stone unturned in acquiring his offering target, regardless of whether he exacted collection from prince or pauper, from the palace or pew, from young or old!

Legend of St. Andrew

Saint Andrew, the brother of Peter, while still a fisherman became one of the first disciples called by Jesus Christ. This Christian Apostle's extensive ministry included Asia, and he became patron saint of Romania and Russia. He is also the patron saint of Scotland and of women.

Tradition holds that he asked to be crucified in Patros, Greece, on an X-shaped cross, as he thought he was not worthy to be crucified on the same type of cross as his Lord. After allegedly being whipped severely by seven soldiers, they tied his body to the cross with cords, to prolong his agony. His followers witnessed that, on being led toward his cross, Andrew saluted it with these words: 'I have long desired and expected this happy hour.' Affirming that the Cross has been consecrated by the body of Christ having hung on one, he continued to preach to his tormentors for two days until he expired.

St. Andrew's Church's favourite hymn

Although there is no prescription in Scripture for celebrating St. Andrew's Day, in venerating the celebrated Apostle Andrew, the church does well to remember a dedicated, devoted disciple of Christ. Andrew may be most honoured for bringing his brother, Peter, into Christian service. How we need to become fishers of men like those early apostles, and especially so in first ministering to our own family!

In celebrating St. Andrew's Day in Andrew's honour, one of the hymns regularly sung is:

1
Jesus calls; us o'er the tumult
Of our life's wild, restless, sea;
Day by day His sweet voice soundeth,
Saying, "Christian, follow Me!"

2
As of old the apostles heard it
By the Galilean lake,
Turn'd from home, and toil, and kindred,
Leaving all for Jesus' sake.

3
Jesus calls us from the worship
Of the vain world's golden store,
From each idol that would keep us,
Saying, "Christian, love Me more!"

4
In our joys and in our sorrows,
Days of toil and hours of ease,
Still He calls, in cares and pleasures,
"Christian, love Me more than these!"

5
Jesus calls us! By Thy mercies,
Saviour, may we hear Thy call,
Give our hearts to Thine obedience,
Serve and love Thee best of all.

In her hymn, "Jesus calls us," Mrs. Cecil Frances Humphreys Alexander (1818-1895), well-known, prolific hymn writer invites her readers to follow and serve Jesus. She wrote this hymn for her husband, who was preparing to preach at a St. Andrew's Day celebration. It was popularly sung to the tune "Galilee" or "Jude", which was composed in 1887 by William Herbert Jude, organist of the Blue Coat Hospital in Liverpool.[30] This hymn is loved by St. Andrew's Parish Church and particularly Fr. Gatherer, who prefers the St. Andrew's tune composed by E.H. Thorne in 1875.[31]

Mrs. Alexander radically calls us to follow Jesus—leaving work and family for Jesus' sake. She challenges us to decide whether we love Jesus more than competing idols. In a world steeped in materialism, her hymn is a timely reminder that the people of God must not fail to submit to Christ unreservedly, whether "in our joys . . . sorrows . . . toil, and hours of ease".

In concluding her hymn, she passionately pleads that her readers might voluntarily submit to the prayer: "Saviour, may we hear Thy call; Give our hearts to Thine obedience, Serve and love Thee best of all."

St. Andrew and Barbados' Independence

The official date of Barbados' Independence is 30 November 1966, the Feast of Saint Andrew, the first recorded Apostle, who readily responded to the call of Jesus. Because of the chosen date, Andrew has been commemorated as the Patron Saint of Barbados.

The date was announced by Premier Errol Barrow at the conclusion of the Independence conference in Marlborough House, London. It was reported that toward the end of one of the official talks, Mr. Barrow broke for a brief private consultation with the Deputy Leader of the Barbados delegation, J. Cameron Tudor, who was also a leading churchman in Barbados.[32] Fr. Laurence Small, MBE, said that Mr. Barrow told Mr. Tudor, "We have achieved Independence but really, I haven't thought of a date". To this Mr. Tudor is reported to have promptly responded, "30 November—St. Andrew's Day".[33] The conference resumed and Premier Barrow made the official declaration.

The father of Barbados' first Prime Minister, Rev'd. Reginald Barrow, was a curate of St. Andrew's Parish Church and Principal of the Alleyne School, St. Andrew. Could this be another reason why Barbados National Hero Errol Barrow so readily acquiesced to such a date for the country's formal achievement of independence?

It is reported that on learning of the date for Barbados' independence, Rev'd. Gatherer approached members of the government to state that since Barbados' independence was to be formalised on St. Andrew's Day, something depicting St. Andrew should be adopted. Consequently, the Cross in the Emblem was allegedly used.[34]

The Independence Service held at West Minister Abby, London, to mark the official date on which the Barbados Flag was dedicated, was attended by The Right Excellent Errol Walton Barrow PC, QC. The Right Rev'd. Dr. Sir Wilfred Denniston Wood, KA, preached the sermon.[35]

Simeon Belgrave said that as a part of the Independence celebration, St. Andrew's Parish Church hosted a flag-raising ceremony, which was held at The Pavilion, St. Andrew Community Centre, Belleplaine. The celebration involved a gala performance by a number of community church choirs at a large gathering. It culminated at midnight with the raising of the Barbados Flag by a boy scout.[36]

St. Andrew's Parish Church was the first church to publicly recognise and celebrate this ecclesiastical patronage, as it coincided with its Patron Festival. At early morning Mass just a few hours after the official historic midnight celebration, 29 November 1966, at the Garrison Savannah, Bridgetown, Fr. Gatherer invited Rev'd. Laurence Small, then a well-known radio commentator, to address the congregation on the national proceedings.[37]

Saint Andrew is honoured by the name of Barbados' highest national award, The Order of Saint Andrew. Additionally, the symbolic X-formation of two sugar cane stalks to comprise a cross on the national Coat of Arms of Barbados reflect the shape of the one on which St. Andrew died.[38] The Order of St. Andrew and the Coat of Arms were adopted at Independence in 1966 by the decree of Queen Elizabeth II.

The original "Order of Saint Andrew", or the "Most Ancient Order of the Thistle", is an order of Knighthood that was reserved for the King or Queen of England and sixteen others. It was established by James II of England and Ireland (who was concurrently James VII of Scotland) in 1687.

As was the case in Scotland, the highest national honour in Barbados is also the Order of the Knight or Dame of St. Andrew (KA or DA). It is bestowed on a Barbadian citizen in recognition of extraordinary or outstanding contribution to the nation or humanity. This meritorious award, along with others,[39] was instituted in November 1980.

1968

Church's vestry room and communal sanitary block

The 23.7 ft by 12.6 ft (7.16 m by 3.81 m) concrete vestry room situated on the north of the Church was an early twentieth-century addition; it was subdivided in 1968 to accommodate a choir robe room, outfitted with cupboards. At that time, also, a 6.5 ft by 16.9 ft (1.98 m by 5.11 m) communal sanitary convenience was added in stone. This improvement, which lacked a covered walkway from the Church for shelter, especially in inclement weather, replaced the tattered choir robe room located on the northeastern section of the mezzanine gallery, and the old earth pit toilets that were situated on the western end of the compound.

Church Army 1969

A not-to-be-forgotten Church Army branch evolved under Rev'd. Gatherer. The 30 founding members were enrolled on St. Andrew's Day, 30 November 1969.

These members stood solid in their support of the Church and regularly met in the St. Andrew's Primary School.[40]

Army members zealously carried out several programmes of benefit to church members and parishioners. They conducted visitation among members who were sick, aged and infirm, which was well received. In addition to holding members together, the organisation effectively reduced sagging membership as persons kept in touch with the Church through the visitation and relational ministry.

In sharing practical fellowship, the Church Army members collected monetary donations, and received gifts that they gave to deserving persons during visitation. It was reported that the issue of dealing with various funds caused considerable upheaval in the Church.

1970s — Disagreement

Open disagreement surfaced between the Rector and the Church Army around 1970, shortly after the return of Fr. Gatherer from six months' overseas leave. It was reported that Rev'd. Dr. Frederick Walcott, who had been left in charge of St. Andrew's, advised Fr. Gatherer on his return from overseas, without success, 'to leave the Church Army and matters related to its funds alone'.[41]

Money and dissension

Interviewees said that the Rector ordered that all monies collected should be given to him, so that he might manage its distribution. This caused sore disaffection, as Church Army members felt that they were sufficiently organised and capable of managing the funds for which they were entirely responsible. They did not mind reporting on the programmes they planned and the offerings they held, but had difficulty with the *carte blanche* delivery to the Rector of funds they had personally raised.

However, Fr. Gatherer maintained that all funds ultimately belonged to the Church and should be given to him. This became a tumultuous bone of contention, which was never solved. Interestingly, interviewees never disputed Fr. Gatherer's use of funds or ever associated him with abuse of money. Several people were high in praise of his prodigious and efficient maintenance of the church property; but his penchant for soliciting, if not exacting funds, and then wanting to be exclusively responsible for the administration of all financial matters caused much 'dis-ease' and dissension.

In respect of Fr. Gatherer and his dealings with church finance, note that there are always, at least, two perspectives for consideration. While there were critical reports regarding Fr. Gatherer's eccentricities relative to his strict control of money, there were others who commended him for his actions.

There were apparently occasions of serious haemorrhaging of funds from fairs and from organisations of the Church. One report stated that when a careful calculation of $7,000 net profit was estimated from a certain activity, which was considered the most successful of the time, unfortunately only $4,000 was realised prior to meeting expenses. Some interviewees mentioned that pages from an account ledger went missing in regard to questions about certain funds. Others also passionately pointed out that "Fr. Gatherer never called the police or made an unruly song and dance" about infelicities connected with people and church money. There were instances of considerable delay being encountered in some workers producing the takings from fairs and other church activities. Interviewees said that Fr. Gatherer often had to wait until persons received their pay packets in order for them to settle their outstanding church arrears. And so there were those who showered praise on Fr. Gatherer for acting with abundant empathy and fatherly grace.

Consequently, with respect to the aforementioned, some interviewees held the strong position that Fr. Gatherer acted prudently and correctly in requiring strict accountability and taking full responsibility for church funds arising from every organisation and activity at the Church he was empowered to nurture and shepherd.

It should be noted that the 1911 Church Act was established to increase Rectors' power. It gave the Rector virtually exclusive power in his parish, so much so that it was he who invited the Bishop to officiate at services, not the other way round. While the Bishop, for example, conducted the rite of confirmation and might address the confirmands after he had finished, any other participation was at the behest of the Rector.[42] This is to underscore that the pervasive powers of the Rector, which by no means excluded matters of finance in his church, squarely qualified him to be totally in charge, despite how members or organisers of the Church felt or acted.

In the early 1970s, apparently a bone of contention arose respecting a sum of money (about $29), a subscription which the Church Army membership had established to assist members who were ill. The subscription had been made during the period that Fr. Gatherer sojourned overseas. On his return, the Rector reportedly maintained that it was money collected under the banner of the Church and should be handed over to him. On the other hand, the Church Army leadership decided that it was money they had collected for a specific purpose, and had no intention of giving in to Fr. Gatherer's directive.

The unresolved incident grew into a major squabble as neither side was prepared to compromise. A number of unsavoury remarks were being bantered around. Moreover, what apparently made matters worse was an allegation by some members of the Church Army that the Rector was directing scathing remarks towards them when they attended Church.[43] It is reported that members resented these potshots being scattered during the service.[44]

During that period, a disaffected group visited other churches, including St. Saviour's, St. Alban's, St. Peter, and St. Thomas. On the 1971 Christmas midnight service, a busload of members from St. Andrew attended St. Peter's Parish Church, where Rev'd. Rufus Brome was Rector. In welcoming the group, Rector Brome remarked that he was not going to send them away, and that he would hold them for the Church [Anglican Communion].[45] Some of them remained with St. Peter, while others resettled at other churches where they felt more comfortable.

Wandering Sheep debacle

Dissatisfaction continued to seethe without respite. Another incident that exacerbated the conflict occurred in mid-August 1972. At the funeral service of Clarissa Small, a member who had left the Church Army, it was reported that Fr. Gatherer announced the Ancient and Modern hymn 258:

> I was a wandering sheep, I did not love the fold;
> I did not love my Shepherd's voice, I would not be controlled.
> I was a wayward child, I did not love my home;
> I did not love my Father's voice, I loved afar to roam.

The Church Army, apparently convinced that the hymn was grossly inappropriate for the occasion, and a slap in the face that was patently condemnatory of one of its beloved past members, openly protested during the singing of the hymn.

Apparently the problem was reported to the Bishop and the parties were summoned to the Bishop's headquarters. But whatever was discussed obviously did not make much of a difference because the impasse continued.

In 1972 unease at St. Andrew revolving around the monetary and other burning issues became too intense and unmanageable. Approximately 35–40 of the disaffected Church Army members, led by then Church Army Leader Lillian Campbell (Figure 19), felt the need to leave the Church. The action was fuelled by the allegedly 'disquieting attitude' of the Rector, his reported carping "wuhna stop coming down here humbugging me", and other allegedly personal remarks uttered during the services.[46]

Figure 19: Pastor Lillian Campbell

This group too visited other churches, including St. Saviour's, St. Thomas, All Saints, St. Peter, St. James, and St. Alban's. They eventually decided to meet on their own in the Belleplaine Primary School. During one of the meetings at the school, it was alleged that the Rector intervened and turned on the Rediffusion (radio of the day) broadcast.

After Mr. T. Campbell (Lillian's husband) acquired and renovated a residence at the corner of Worrell Road and Belleplaine Main Road, St. Andrew, the group convened there, finally seceding from the Parish Church, and establishing the Belleplaine United House of Prayer (BUHP),[47] referred to as Campbell's Church, in 1973.

It was reported that the unbridled personal attacks and criticism of members by the leader of St. Andrew's during services led to severe discomfort of those who felt targeted and to their continued exodus from the Church. Interviewees—who insisted on anonymity—reported that as long as the disturbing attitude of the leader continued unabated, it was unrealistic to expect the haemorrhaging of members to cease.

With the loss of members from the Church Army continuing during the 1970s and onwards, as would be the case with a military force, substantial defence and support of the Church was lost.[48] Several church members of significant standing in the parish retracted from fellowship, leaving the Church denuded of an influential core body capable of making a difference in the life of the congregation. When ordinary people—teachers, civil servants, people of substantial standing in the community—simply walk away heartbroken from the place of choice where they had worshipped over decades, without recourse or address, it leaves much to be regretted![49] Such a situation the Church can ill afford, and must definitely avoid.

As in normal life, haemorrhaging continues until the root cause is excised or addressed; similarly, cancerous relational problems cannot be left to chance without inevitable imperilment and death of the organisation/institution. And the situation at the Church led not only to secession, with an alternate church being established, but to a weakened body as several other members fled from the membership, while others simply stayed on with no recourse or respite.

New leadership of the Belleplaine United House of Prayer

Andrew Campbell took over the care and management of the Belleplaine United House of Prayer (BUHP) after his mother fell ill in 2007. On the death of Lillian Campbell in January 2010, Andrew assumed pastoral leadership of the church.

Due to morbidity and mortality of the elderly members, the BUHP membership had waned somewhat. On assuming leadership, Pastor Andrew embarked on refurbishing of the former 20 ft by 40 ft (6.09 m by 12.91 m) chattel building (residence). This involved replacing much of the timber with stonework, basically on the same footprint (Figure 20). An aisle at the western front section of the church, near the altar, was enclosed to provide access to the covered accommodation in the rear building. There are plans to convert this covered space into office and utility accommodation. The pastor also sees the potential for using a covered shed at the north of the building for accommodation of the Sunday School and other children's activities.[50]

Like its parent Church, which celebrates its Feast Day on the 30th November, the BUHP has chosen to memorialise this date also. On 30th

Figure 20: Belleplaine United House of Prayer, St. Andrew

of November 2010, the BUHP celebrated its 37th Anniversary, not the 43rd as many members were reporting in error.

The refurbished plant, costing approximately $50,000 was the scene of a Gala Thanksgiving Service on 2 October 2011 in celebration of its 38th Anniversary.

With a renewed plant and vibrant community outreach, the church boasts a membership of approximately 50 and growing, and a Sunday school of 25 students. With divine enabling and strategic planning, this young church seems poised to 'take off'.

So what is the lesson here? Out of death still comes—life, and from adversity and challenges—great possibilities! St. Andrew's Parish Church now has a thriving adult daughter church in the same parish.

Kudos to Church Army Leader, Pioneer, Mother, Pastor Lillian Campbell, and a few faithful members who, undeterred by circumstance, left no stone unturned in planting the Belleplaine United House of Prayer to the glory of God!

1974—Renovations continuing

During the rainy season, water entered the St. Andrew's Parish Church. Fr. Gatherer replaced guttering on the north and south sides of the Church in 1974. He also replaced the roofing and floor, and the 4 inch by 8 inch (0.10 m by 0.20 m) wood beams and 3 inch by 8inch (0.08 m by 0.20 m) floor supports of the bell tower.

1975

As early as 1975, redevelopment of the graveyard had started.[51] It involved levelling steep hillsides and inaccessible sections, the removal of dead trees and stumps and doing general landscaping that transformed it from partially overgrown woodland to the second-best-maintained cemetery in the island.[52] Unfortunately, during the landscaping of the graveyard, many headstones and other grave markers were permanently lost.

The gallery of the Church, which fell into to disrepair in the late 1960s, was completely replaced by Rev'd. Gatherer by 1975. Renovation work involved the reduction of the gallery to its present structure, providing protection rails and replacing the circular 8-inch (0.08 m) supporting wooden columns on the ground floor.[53]

Father Gatherer and children

Rev'd. Hugh Sandiford

Rev'd. Hugh Sandiford said that Fr. Gatherer was responsible for his early spiritual nurturing. He recalled with pleasure how, in addition to serving at St. Andrew's as Altar Boy and Server, he was mentored by Fr. Gatherer at summer camps; and not only he, but at least 25 other children at the time—Anglicans as well as young people from other faiths, including Pentecostals and Adventists of the parish.[54] He reminisced how Fr. Gatherer used his car and hired other transportation to take the young campers to view "The Sound of Music" at the Vista cinema, Worthing, Christ Church.

Fr. Gatherer, he said, was interested in more than just the spiritual segment of life; he embraced every opportunity to equip the wards under his care in the most balanced way practicable. He personally took the campers on hikes through the village at least three times weekly. Rev'd. Sandiford lauded him for personally helping in his spiritual, social, and emotional development, as well as in many other children's early progress.

Here again Fr. Gatherer also helped in grooming another Anglican priest. It is only left to Rev'd. Hugh to pursue the high calling to which "Edward's" ministry leads: to the Deanery or the bishop's palace.

"Only in St. Andrew"—Blows at class

Rev'd. Gatherer was not only a priest or Chairman of the Vestry who exercised sweeping powers in his parish; he also served as Schoolmaster—and from all reports, a very strict one!

Stories abound of how Fr. Gatherer never spared the rod lest the lack of its tempered use spoilt the student. In conducting confirmation class he demanded that you be attentive, sharp, and do well in the examinations that followed. Those who scored poorly were literally flogged.

It was reported that adults too actually fell under the snap of Gatherer's belt for alleged misdemeanours at church.

Do you recall the bacchanal with E. from the parish and Fr. Gatherer? E. allegedly didn't score high in E's confirmation class examination. Without his glasses on, the joke went, Fr. Gatherer didn't see well. So who told him to lock horns with E? As Fr. Gatherer proceeded to administer the belt, off went his glasses (taken by E), and there was no telling who really received blows that day. "No, neither the joke nor victory was Fr. Gatherer's!"[55]

Gatherer the lifesaver

In addition to being a priest, Fr. Gatherer was a life saver. He prepared lunch/meals for many young and old needy people, repaired houses of the indigent,[56] and took children overseas on camp.

Fr. Gatherer was a man of deep spiritual understanding, one who was intensely interested in people—both young and old. He demonstrated this by a devotion whose source was a deep well of sympathy and willing sacrifice. Committed to ministering to his ordained brethren, he displayed a true pastoral heart for fellow clergy whom he visited in illness, counselled in crisis, held their hand when they were in distress, and spoke for them when they lost their voice. They could depend on him when they were going through 'hard times'.[57]

1979

Children's camp in St. Vincent

By the time hurricane David was approaching the Caribbean, Fr. Gatherer and his St. Andrew's group were already packed for a trip to St. Vincent. Trusting God for protection and security, they proceeded on their mission and took a number of children to that island for an uneventful, and reportedly very exciting, educational visit of a lifetime.

1980s

Transport Board Choir in concert

In September 1983, the Transport Board Choir rendered a Sunday evening concert at St. Andrew's. Owing to Fr. Gatherer's openness and willingness to have guest participation, it was easy for the choir to arrange the programme to minister through their music. The performances of the young choir, under the direction of Richard Clarke and organist Sylvan Catwell, were as welcome as the proceeds raised!

Maintenance and preservation work in 1985

As part of the ongoing maintenance and preservation of the church plant, slipper drains were installed and other upgrades undertaken to channel storm water away from the building as quickly as possible. Work also involved the construction of reinforced concrete retaining walls around the borders of the elevated land and graveyard on the northwest of the Church to restrict their perennial movement, and the refurbishing and provision of double metal gates at the south entrance of the graveyard.

Ms. Cheryl Hurst

No history of St. Andrew's Parish Church would be complete without due recognition paid to worker and leader Ms. Cheryl Hurst. On returning from her one-year training in Mission and Evangelisation in Austria in 1985, and a subsequent three-year stint of training in Human Relations in Britain, Cheryl (Figure 21) commenced an illustrious period of service at St. Andrew's, while assisting Fr. Gatherer. She not only drove him around, assisting him in the

Figure 21: Cheryl Hurst bidding Farewell

performance of his numerous parochial duties,[58] but also truly served as nurse, doctor, cook, chaperone, advisor and server "in the forefront of everything" related to the Church. She took oversight in transacting the financial matters, organised fetes and programmes, and along with the Priest, brought church plans to fruition. Whether it was calling a meeting after church without prior announcement, organising the annual luncheon, or making announcements, she executed the job on her terms.

For seemingly acting like her Rector in being resolutely committed to ensuring the job was done, her service and personal style were not always appreciated or accepted by some people; nevertheless, she plodded on in completing the tasks at hand. Many people opined that without her help and support, the Rector could not have rallied on so long at the Church. She is to be highly commended for her yeoman support at St. Andrew's. During her 26 years' service at the Church, she faithfully stood solidly behind the Rector all through his difficult days to the end of his ministry.

Her graciously accompanying the Rector on his overseas trips for medical attention is to be highly applauded. Many interviewees expressed great delight and pleasure that someone so kind was available to administer such vital and essential help and sympathetic care to the Rector in times of critical need.

In so many ways, Cheryl must be seen as the answer to prayer and the medium that God used in fulfilling His Word, in not allowing his servant to be forsaken, or to beg for survival. Cheryl served God in providing the hands and feet that ministered to God's servant. In Fr. Gatherer's retirement, we have no doubt that God has elected her to assist him as old age advances, and care becomes crucial. God bless her work and grant her the courage, grace, and strength to press on in her noble endeavour to care for someone who spent his entire life in caring for so many!

1986

Church Driveway

Fr. Gatherer completed paving the entrance driveway to the Church around February 1986.[59] This work involved excavating approximately 18 inches (0.5 m) of topsoil from the existing driveway, importing marl fill, levelling and casting approximately 4 inches (0.1 m) by 130 ft by 11 ft (39.6 m by 3.4 m) of concrete from the roadway to the entrance of the Church, at an approximate cost of $15,900.[60] Prior to this work, there was only partial vehicular access to the Church. Vehicles, including the Rector's, had to be parked along the roadway. The former entrance to the Church was a poorly contrived path, comprising 'step ups' that were inaccessible to vehicular traffic. At last, the concreted driveway facilitated access right up to the door of the Church for funerals and weddings, and particularly so during inclement weather.[61] Following the completion of the driveway, the southeastern pillars and the wrought iron double gates were also refurbished.

Refurbishing of stained glass windows in 1988

The relatively modern double-height windows with gothic arches and large openings for optimising ventilation are made of diamond-shaped clear glass and timber mullions.

Like other seventeenth century churches, St. Andrew's also boasts five stained-glass windows on the eastern walls of the sanctuary and chancel. To arrest their deterioration, Fr. Gatherer took them to Goddard and Gibbs, Liverpool Street, London, in 1988, for refurbishing at a cost of £10,700. Three of the windows positioned on the eastern wall of the sanctuary above the altar (from north to south) depict: 1) St. Andrew with his cross, 2) Jesus the Good Shepherd (in the centre), and 3) St. Peter holding the keys. The top section of these windows also depict *Iesus Hominum Salvator (HIS)*—Jesus, Saviour of man) as—α (Alpha) and Ω (Omega).[62] Regarding the other two stained glass windows installed in the eastern wall of the chancery, the one on the north depicts the Prophet Isaiah reading a scroll, while the other on the south is a portrait of the Prophet John the Baptist holding a shepherd's staff in his left hand, and a picture of a young lamb standing beside him.

In earlier times, in addition to vividly telling Bible stories in colour to persons who could not read, stained glass windows brought in light, and also served to conceal the contents of the church. The latter was apparently not the case in a modest country church like St. Andrew's, where the windows are aesthetic show-pieces located at a high level, and thus not really essentially designed for concealment of the church interior.

To summarise, Fr. Gatherer's work in this Church will remain uniquely significant not only in terms of his physical sacrifice related to the plant and general pastoral work, but also for the deep impact that his mission has had on the diocese and the Church international.

Rector Gatherer and St. Andrew's Parish Church (1957–1980s) Phase 1

Notes

1. Interview with Canon Lionel Burke, 11 October 2011.
2. Interview with Rev'd. Dr. Michael Clarke, 21 January 2013.
3. Interview with Joan Smith, 12 December 2009.
4. Extracted from a speech given by Simeon Belgrave at Canon Gatherer's 91st birthday party, January 2013.
5. *Ibid.*
6. Extracted from a speech given by Bishop Wilfred Wood, KA, given at Canon Gatherer's 91st birthday party, January 2013.
7. Simeon Belgrave's speech.
8. Bishop Wood's speech.
9. Extracted from jokes shared by Neville Kirton during Fr. Gatherer's 92nd birthday bus tour, 28 January 2014.
10. Simeon Belgrave's speech.
11. Notes extracted from Fr. Gatherer's personal diary, 24 December 2009.
12. Wilfred Wood (bishop) - *Wikipedia, the free encyclopaedia.* en.wikipedia.org/wiki/Wilfred_Wood_(bishop), Accessed 28 December 2009.
13. Tony Davies, Ven. Archdeacon of Croydon. "...Inexhaustible faith in the promise of Christ". *The Bridge*, Vol. 7 No 7—September 2002. Southwark People: The Diocese pays tribute to Bishop Wood. www.southwark.anglican.org/thebridge/0209/page11.htm Accessed 20 December 2009.
14. Wilfred Wood (bishop)—*Wikipedia*, Accessed 12 May 2013.
15. Interview with Dean Frank Marshall, CBE, 3 March 2010.
16. Canon Seibert Small. "A Tribute To Father Gatherer" in the booklet, *The Holy Eucharist and Commemoration of the Ministry of The Reverend Edward Godson Gatherer.* Sunday 27 March 2011.
17. *The Barbados Advocate,* Wednesday, 23 December 1959, p. 7.
18. *Ibid.*
19. "The Mothers' Union of Barbados, 1998–2000". http://www.cariblife.com/pub/mothersunion/default. Accessed 27 September 2011.
20. Interview with Erma Small, 23 July 2011
21. *Ibid.*
22. Interview with Daphnie Mahon, 26 July 2011.
23. Daphnie Mahon. Information was extracted from her unpublished, undated notes, 21 August 2011.
24. Interview with Melba Sandiford, 7 September 2012. Mrs. Sandiford demitted leadership of the Mother's Union in 1983 and with her family transferred their membership to St. Peter's Parish Church.
25. Interview with Mrs. Jennifer Maynard, 8 November 2012.
26. As a case in point, an interviewee said that if a member, in enthusiastically decorating the Church placed a table mat right side up for a particular function, invariably the Rector would call someone else to remonstrate that 'the mat looked hideous', and would have it turned other side up. This behaviour reportedly led to frustration, hurt and disagreement and members walking away from their church.
27. Interview with Cyrillene Harding, 29 September 2011.
28. Erma Small, 2 August 2011.
29. Interview with Dolores Catwell, 18 February 2010.
30. "Jesus Calls Us". http://homeschoolblogger.com/hymnstudies/564962/ Accessed 5 November 2011.
31. "ST. ANDREW (Thorne)"—http://www.hymnary.org/tune/st_andrew_thorne. Accessed 5 November 2011.
32. Interview with Rev'd. Laurence Small, MBE, 13 March 2013. Rev. Small was Rediffusion's Radio commentator covering the Barbados' Independence celebration.
33. Extracted from Rev'd. Small's unpublished, undated notes, 13 March 2013.

34. Interview with David Goring, 19 February 2013.
35. Interview with Bishop Wilfred Wood, KA, 28 November 2013.
36. Interview with Simeon Belgrave, 17 March 2013. Belgrave said that due to the challenges in obtaining transportation from Belleplaine to the Garrison Savannah for the national Independence Celebration, the Church hosted its own Independence celebration in conjunction with other churches in the parish.
37. Rev'd. Laurence Small, MBE, 13 March 2013.
38. "Andrew the Apostle"—*Wikipedia, the free encyclopaedia*. en.wikipedia.org/wiki/Saint_Andrew, Barbados. Accessed 30 August 2011.
39. Other national awards include:

    The Companion of Honour of Barbados (CHB) is presented for distinguished national achievement and merit.

    The Crown of Merit—either in gold (GCM) or silver (SCM)—is given for highly meritorious service or achievement in science, the arts, literature, sport, civic duties, or any other endeavour worthy of national recognition. Persons who are not Barbadian citizens may be presented with honorary awards.

    The Barbados Service Award—either the Barbados Service Star (BSS) or Barbados Service Medal (BSM)—is presented for meritorious work in civil, fire, military, police, prison or other protective services or in any other field of endeavour.

    For acts of bravery in hazardous circumstances, the Barbados Bravery Medal is awarded.
40. Interview with George Beckles, 26 July 2011. Beckles volunteered information from his unedited and published notes.
41. *Ibid.*
42. Rev'd. Laurence Small, MBE, 8 March 2013.
43. *Ibid.*
44. Interview with Emeline Cumberbatch, 18 February 2010.
45. Interview with Bishop Rufus Brome, GCM, 12 October 2011.
46. Cumberbatch, 18 February 2010.
47. Cumberbatch and Beckles, 26 July 2011.
48. Interview with Everton Bovell, 26 July 2011.
49. *Ibid.*
50. Interview with Pastor Andrew Campbell, Belleplaine United House of Prayer, 30 October 2011.
51. Interview with Perometta Watkins, 27 July 2011.
52. Interview with Patrick Clarke, 18 July 2011.
53. Interview with organist Hutson Drakes and organ builder David Burke, 21 January 2013.
54. Interview with Rev'd. Hugh Sandiford, 1 October 2011.
55. Interview with Nigel Williams, 1 October 2011.
56. Cyrillene Harding, 16 March 2010.
57. *Ibid.*
58. Everton Bovell, 2 August 2011.
59. Interview with Erma Small, 24 September 2011.
60. Interview with Oliver Solomon, 26 September 2011.
61. Cyrillene Harding, 26 September 2011.
62. Interview with Dean Emeritus Harold Crichlow, GCM, 20 December 2009.

CHAPTER FIVE

Impact of Establishment and Disestablishment on the Church and St. Andrew's

The Anglican Church of Barbados

The Anglican Church has been established for over 380 years and is one of the oldest institutions in Barbados. Originally referred to as the Church of England, it was brought to the West by the English settlers in the early part of the seventeenth century. "It was the Church of the Englishmen who resided in the colony, the clergy for the most part being persons who came largely on their own to minister to the settlers."[1,2]

The Bishop of London also held responsibility for the churches in the British colonies in the early seventeenth century and eventually for the British West Indian Islands from 1776. In 1675, as a result of a recommendation made by the Bishop of London through the Board for Trade and Plantations, the churches that were formerly controlled by the plantations or local governors, were brought under the management of the Bishop of London, and concomitantly under the vestries and government in 1681.[3]

In assuming responsibility for the Church of England, the government essentially supported the Church. "Nevertheless to the State, thus in its constitution effectively secular, the Establishment secures complete legislative and judicial control of the Church;" and in turn,

> . . .The Enabling Act (1919) did indeed confer on the Church Assembly the power of drafting measures to which Parliament might, if so pleased, give statutory force, but the unlimited legislative power of Parliament was expressly preserved.[4]

The Bishop represented the Church on the Legislative Council; while salaries of the bishops and clergy were paid by government, the Vestry paid that of the church officers. Officers of the church enjoyed the same privileges as civil servants. In this way, the church held the status of being established; accordingly, Bishop E. Lewis Evans of Barbados (1960–1971) noted that

> ... an alliance exists between the church so established and the state, in which the state has accepted the church and the religious body in its opinion truly teaching the Christian faith, and has given to it a certain legal position and to its decrees, if rendered under certain legal conditions, certain civil sanctions.[5]

In vividly portraying his understanding of 'establishment' as it related to the Church of England, the late Sir William Anson provided a farsighted and rather timeless explanation in positing that society, including the church, was

> . . .in necessary subordination to Parliament, because Parliament may make the profession of its opinions unlawful, may subject the performance of its acts of worship to a penalty, may impose tests which disqualify its members for the office of franchise.[6]

He also mentioned that any transaction of property or business required approval of the state. In fact, in his work, *The Law and Custom of the Constitution*,[7] he offered a long and provocative analysis of the deeper implications of the "established church":

> ... the Established Church has a closer connexion with the State than this necessary subordination to Parliament and liability to have its doctrine discussed and interpreted in the courts of law. The King is Head of the Church, not for the purpose of discharging any spiritual function, but because the Church is the national Church, and as such is built into the fabric of the state. The Crown itself is held on condition that the holder should be in communion with the Church of England as by law established...[8]

The Law and Custom also held that Church Convocations were summoned, prorogued, and dissolved by the Crown, which appointed the church's administrative officers and judges of ecclesiastical law, constituting the Lords Spiritual in the House of Lords. It also made clear that the church's canons and liturgical articles of religion, though not formulated by Parliament, invariably required parliamentary sanction, thus favouring the synthesis of state and church. And this position with the Church of England and the state would hardly be grossly unlike what obtained in the Anglican Church in Barbados, since this country fell under British rule. As part of a constitutional monarchy, Barbados closely followed England in the letter and spirit of the law, until it developed its own legal system after independence.

With establishment, the church also enjoyed the status of being endowed as the state provided funding, grants, contributions, and other largesse for its maintenance and support of its staff and mission. Indeed, establishment and endowment constituted a marriage that bequeathed significant benefits to the church and its appointed leaders and staff. Subsequently in this chapter, establishment will generally be used to imply endowment and, invariably, all it involves. Similarly, later disestablishment will also be used to generally imply disendowment—being deprived of government finance and other privileges.

Since the Bishops of London were regarded as having responsibility for the churches in the colonies in the early seventeenth century,[9] the same status and privileges the English Church enjoyed from government were conferred on the churches in the British West Indies colonies. Therefore, as established, the Anglican Church in Barbados received numerous benefits, its leaders endowed with larger government grants for their church than were other organisations, in addition to being funded from London. Its Bishop and clergy were treated and paid like civil servants, having security of tenure and a pension. In time, Barbadian legislation incorporated these rights and privileges and bestowed them on the local church.

The Anglican Church 1911 Act gave rectors the right to, and control of, the glebe and the rectory, along with a monthly government salary. Through the Parish Vestries, the rectors, as chairmen, hired and fired government workers—teachers, school principals, health personnel, including medical officers, chief sanitary officers and their staff, to name a few. With the Barbados' Widows and Orphans Pensions Act of 1928 and the Pensions Act of 1947, officers of the church were entitled to the same rights and benefits as civil servants; they received leave passage, long leave, and even franking privileges (having free stamps and postage paid for by government).

Rectors received benefits from glebe lands, and bearing in mind that some glebes were large, it afforded an opportunity through which the more industrious and entrepreneurially adept clergy could generate sizeable extra incomes. Indeed, many of the early clergy (sometimes referred to as ministers) were noted, as revealed from their real estate transactions, to have carried out extensive trading in large plantations—selling, buying, and reselling 19, 80, 100 acres of land and more. This merchandising was conducted with land quite apart from the large parcels of glebe lands that rectors would have inherited on assuming their cure (refer to "People of high standing in St. Andrew", Chapter 2).

Similar to what occurred in the English church, the Anglican Church in Barbados, through the Vestry system, funded and supervised churches and burial grounds, parish cottages and workhouses with common lands and endowed charities, oversaw the repression of vagrancy and relief of destitution, the mending of roads, suppression of nuisances, eradication of insects and vermin, furnishing of soldiers and sailors and, substantially, the enforcement of religious and moral discipline. Essentially, government fully empowered the church. Underwritten by the central authority, the Vestry expended vast sums of money on the upkeep of the parish. These were among the multitudinous duties executed by the Parish Vestry, its officers, and the church by the law of the land.[10]

Notwithstanding the existence of Moravians, Methodists, and others sects such as the Brethren (Gospel Hall Assemblies) that gave solid voluntary assistance, buttressed by Government endowment, the Anglican Church held an enviable position in being able to assist the community and poor of Barbados. Consequently, the Anglican Church, albeit with other churches, made a stellar contribution to education in Barbados and in the administration of schools. Anglican rectors, as *ex-officio* officers of the parish vestries, were responsible for the administration of the parish schools. In their role, they administered not only the ecclesiastical but also social and financial affairs of the parish on behalf of government. Thus, the Anglican institution played a significant role in establishing the General Hospital, with the then Bishop and the Archdeacon serving on its Board at the time. The Bishop and Archdeacon were also instrumental in establishing the Barbados Mutual Assurance Society.

In addition, the Anglican Church's contribution in music is unforgettable. Undeniably, the development of music can easily be traced to the mid-nineteenth century when numerous young organists and choirs sprung up across the island. During the 1960s to 1980s, traditions of music evolved around distinguished persons who gave long service as organists, e.g. Gerald Hudson,[11] organist and choir director of St. Michael's Cathedral (1921–1974), Appendix 2.

Truly, the church both received and earned its benefits, admirably and honourably husbanding the fund derived from government. These benefits lasted until disestablishment and disendowment, a movement impelled by a rapidly changing Barbadian society and laws aiming to reflect the radical socio-political climate of the 1930s and onwards. Around that time, the winds of independence, political, social, and ecclesiastical self-determination began to blow.

Much is written on the growing self-awakening and nationalism of young Barbadians who were beginning to leave no stone unturned in signalling the need for greater democratic consciousness and for nationals and Caribbean peoples to determine their own destiny and leadership, rather than accepting oligarchic and colonial forms of leadership. In her reference to F.A. Hoyos'[12] description of the social revolution occurring in Barbados around the 1930s and 1940s, Suzanne Ellis remarked that[13]

> This mood, marked by an upsurge of democratic consciousness which swept across the Caribbean calling for change and recognition, saw the development of the trade union movements, the formation of political parties and the rise of prominent leaders who had been trained primarily in the mother country, England, championing the cause of the masses.

Increasing self-awakening was not restricted to the society at large; it was being experienced in the church as well.

Reservations about Establishment (and Endowment)

While some people extolled the benefits that the church received from government, a number of others felt that the church, in being the beneficiary of government's largesse, was unable to be truly objective and had to be subservient to its power. Others complained that the church was biased in favour of the ruling class, ". . . the symbol of stability, respectability, and legitimacy".[14] This matter became an issue of concern, if not disquiet, for church leaders and politicians in a nation that was going through the pre-independent throes of national actualisation; and in this regard F.A. Hoyos referred to the period as a social revolution.[15]

People were developing a strong voice to speak out on matters that affected them. The idea that the church had been supported by government and was subject to its direction, i.e. having to accept instruction mandated by the existing legislation, was becoming a contentious issue.

On 12 December 1944, interestingly enough, J.A. Haynes, MP for St. Andrew, raised the motion for disendowment of the Anglican Church of Barbados in a Private Member's Bill, which received its first reading in the House of Assembly. Moreover, Bishop James Hughes (1945–1951), was an outspoken critic against establishment and the entrenched government system that constituted the basis for his appointment. He was quite dissatisfied that the church was not free to manage its own affairs, staff, lay representatives, clergy and other church dignitaries (e.g. bishops) apart from government's advice or involvement. In his very first charge to Synod 1945, he remonstrated that "The Church is not a Social Club or Ethical Society which needs the support of the state in order to do its work. . ."[16] and called for the severing of church and state relations.

The Bishop felt unable to serve in a church which was subservient to a government given to actions

> . . . he believes inimical to the best interests of the Church, and [the] rejection of his nominee by the Appointments Board for the Parish of St. John has convinced him that he must resign.[17]

Ultimately, for Hughes, the issue of the church not being free to select its own bishop 'broke the camel's back'—he resigned.

In Parliament, other avid advocates of disestablishment and disendowment led by Grantley Adams, who at the time had not long returned from England, included J.C Tudor, Errol Barrow, C.E. Talma, and Frank Walcott. Their pleadings and protests led to the government informing Bishop Gay Mandeville (1951–1960) on 25 September 1954 of its intention to disendow the church. This signalled the beginning of the end of government's facilitation of funds and benefits to the church. It was to be followed on 28 June 1955 by The Anglican Church (Partial Suspension) Act 1955, which hastened the end of the church-state relationship, abolished the Vestry system (1959), and repealed the Anglican Church Act of 1911 that had brought the church under the direction of the state. And finally, after a long battle, on 1 April 1969 the church was formally disestablished.

Now the church that had served the state of Barbados so faithfully in educating its masses, coordinating much of its civil and administrative policy via the Vestries, at last had its essential financial support curtailed. No more could it depend on financial backing for maintaining the fabric of its parish churches and cathedrals, which picturesquely adorned the country by their presence and pageantry as national showpieces of historic heritage. The government would continue to use the cathedrals for state funerals and religious observances. As government subventions receded, church properties would eventually deteriorate through lack of funds for renovation. Nevertheless, the church was finally free to initiate and direct its own policy regarding discipline, rules, and regulations. With the state shackles broken, it could breathe a sigh of relief at the prospect of living its long-sought dream of spiritual independence and self-respect.

Dean Emeritus Harold Crichlow said that many young clerics at that time supported disestablishment, which he opined "turned out to be much better for the church". The Dean also said that "generally Anglicans felt a greater sense of ownership of the church after disestablishment and many of them increased their monthly contributions".[18]

The 1955 Act affirmed that all clergy appointed prior to its proclamation would continue to receive their benefits and pensions from government, while clergy appointed after its enactment would receive only stipends, but not fringe benefits and pensions. It also temporarily disallowed additions to the stipends of the clergy to match salary revisions for government employees in 1956 and 1961, as well as any increase in the clergy's pensionable emoluments.

Four years after the 1955 Act, the Vestry system was replaced by a system of Local Government. The Local Government too was phased out during 1967–1969 in Barbados, and replaced by the Parliamentary Representative System, or National Government, which carried out the provision of services across the eleven parishes of the island.

With the Partial Suspension Act 1955, the financing of the church and its personnel and all ancillary activities were to be transferred to the Local Government via the Local Government Act 1959. Both these Acts were preparatory to divorcing the church from the state (as would be occasioned by disestablishment).

In preparation for disestablishment, the church began to develop means for its funding and support. Bishop Mandeville had proactively introduced a means of "Sustentation" in 1954 by which he encouraged members to support their church by proportionate giving.

Post-independence church giving

Giving generally, and by way of Proportionate Sustentation, was not one of the more welcome acts in the post-independent period. Bishop Evans tried to address this challenge by pleading with members to increase their giving. Dean Crichlow reported that in an effort to encourage members to give, Bishop Evans suggested that, bearing in mind the large membership of the Anglican Church at the time, if each member had donated at least 36 cents per month, the financial needs of the church would have been met. Following the Bishop's appeal, one of the wealthiest men in Barbados presented his "Sustentation" of 36 cents to the Dean of the cathedral claiming that the Bishop had said that each member should give that amount.[19] Proportionate and sacrificial church donation still remains a practical way forward, especially during such times as the crippling worldwide recession 2007–2013 which is likely to last for at least another decade!

The Anglican Church Act 1969 (Cap. 375)

With the proclamation of the Anglican Church Act 1969,[20] Section 3 (a) and (b), disestablishment finally occurred on 1 April 1969, approximately 24 years after it was formally proposed. *The Advocate News* noted the famous proclamation Bill accordingly:

> The Anglican Church Act of 1911 which brought the church completely under the direction of the state was repealed by the House of Assembly on Tuesday night bringing the Church-State relations to an end.
>
> This Bill, one of the most important pieces of legislation in Barbados, was passed with little comment and ado. The bill also repealed the Anglican Church (Partial Suspension) Act of 1955.[21]

Some salient issues of the Anglican Church Bill Settlement

1. The Anglican Church Act 1911 was repealed.
2. The Anglican Synod was to receive the stipulated grants (Table 3) during the 10-year period commencing 1 April 1967.
3. After the tenth year, the Government would pay to the Anglican Synod a subsidy that would be in line with the amount paid to other denominations, proportionate to the total membership of the Anglican Church and those denominations, in an amount of not less than $10,000 per annum.

Table 3: Government Ten-year Reducing Church Subsidy

Period	Grants
1967–68	248,000
1968–69	213,000
1969–70	213,000
1970–71	213,000
1971–72	213,000
1972–73	177,000
1973–74	142,000
1974–75	106,500
1975–76	71,000
1976–77	35,000

4. Government Pension Liabilities would be honoured for persons to whom the Anglican Church (Partial Suspension) Act 1955 did not apply.
5. Clergymen still serving under the Anglican Church (Partial Suspension) Act 1955, at the date of the repeal of that Act would receive one month's salary for every completed year of service, with the proviso that service of six months or more, which was completed before 1 April 1967, was to be regarded as the equivalent of one year's completed service.
6. Pensions, along with compensation for abolition of office, would be payable immediately upon disestablishment.
7. Contribution of the clergy to the Widows and Children's Pension Scheme would be treated in the same way as the contributions of civil servants who leave the Service.
8. Service in church and state should not be deemed equivalent.
9. Payment of leave passages earned or payment of long leave was discontinued for the clergy unless such leave had begun prior to the repeal of the Anglican Church Act 1969.
10. Franking privileges enjoyed by the church would cease.
11. Bishop's Court (former official residence of the Bishop of Barbados) and its maintenance would be the responsibility of the Anglican Church.
12. The existing arrangement between the Anglican Church and the state regarding school buildings would continue.
13. The Anglican Church would cease to be the "Established" Church in Barbados, and its clergy and church officers would be removed from the Establishment, subject to the existing interest of the present holders of an ecclesiastical office.

Protracted settlement

As outlined at item 2 of issues covered by the settlement, in order to help the church absorb the crushing financial shock resulting from loss of state revenue following disestablishment, government agreed on a financial settlement to make a ten-year payment to the church from 1 April 1967 by contributions over each of the first five years of amounts that would or should have been paid prior to 1969, less the cost of pensions, gratuities, and certain other specified allowances, but not less than $213,000. However, from 1 April 1972, the amount would have been progressively reduced until 31 March 1977, after which the Anglican Church would receive a subsidy based on proportionate membership as explained at item 3.

Government pension would be paid to all retiring, eligible clergy.

The relationship between church and state regarding church schools that existed prior to disestablishment would be continued, except that upon revision of the existing appointment system, the role of clergy in appointments would also be changed as determined by relevant legislation.

Self governance of the Church and vesting of church property

Under the Anglican Church Act 1969, Cap. 375, Section 3 (b), the Anglican Church would have full control over its affairs under the Barbados Diocesan Synod (Sections 23, 24 and 30), while church property and funds would be vested in the Barbadian Diocesan Trustees (Sections 6, 7, 8, 25, 26 and 30).

Impact of disestablishment on the Church

With the proclamation of the Anglican Church Act 1969, Section 3 (a) and (b), the Anglican Church was disestablished, and became responsible for managing its own affairs, paying its clergy, and maintaining its buildings. The age of accountability had arrived when the church would be master of its destiny in directing its own spiritual policy. It was expected to be able to exclusively determine its rules of discipline and enforce them, and be free from the disadvantage of state connection, which tended to compromise church action and practice. But disestablishment would inflict on the church the strain and sacrifice of being self-sufficient, such discomfort, however, being mitigated by concomitant restoration of its desired self-respect, autonomy, and the exercise of an unfettered voice. With no longer any support from government through the Vestry, the church needed to be wholly self-supporting in order to address or cope with the following (list is not exhaustive):

1. payment of church personnel emoluments,
2. the ability to increase personnel's wages when civil servants' salary was being revised upward,
3. maintenance of church buildings, properties, graveyards, and clergy's residential accommodation,

4. members having no avowed commitment to give an offering, or volunteer time, or labour on the church's behalf,
5. pensions for clergy and other staff,
6. payment of National Insurance, sick benefits, accident entitlements and, not least of all,
7. (incidental but vital) car loans, house loans—simply loans.

The time had come when effective and strong governance of the church requiring greater hierarchical control was necessary. Having its property (glebe lands, buildings, and the rent therefrom, etc.) under central management and better supervision for the benefit of the diocese seemed to be the viable option. What therefore was the best way forward?

Under The 1969 Anglican Church Act, three corporate bodies were established for the autonomous (no longer having government's permission, acquiescence, or intervention) governing of the church: the Diocesan Synod, the Barbados Diocesan Trustees, and the Dean and Chapter of St. Michael's Cathedral. This move provided the church with some capacity to develop its mission in an independent country.

With regard to the Diocesan Synod and the Barbados Diocesan Trustees, Bishop Drexel Gomez posited in his April 1990 Bishop's monthly radio broadcast that:

> These bodies which represent the Anglican Clergy and laity in Barbados are composed of clergy and laymen who have been elected or appointed because of the high regard in which they are held for their knowledge, integrity, and reasonableness.[22]

The Diocesan Synod

The Diocesan Synod consisting of the Diocesan Bishop, Bishops and Clergy, and Lay Representatives essentially constitutes the administrative and consultative arm of the Anglican Church and is invested with full powers to administer the affairs of the diocese and be responsible for its action and decision-making under the Anglican Church Act.

The functions and powers of Synod include, but are not limited to:

- assumption of responsibility for making, administering, and revising the constitution of the Church,
- receiving rules, ordinances, canons, and regulations made by the Provincial Synod of the Province of the West Indies,
- making rules, ordinances, canons, and regulations for general church management, discipline, and governance,
- developing and regulating general church rules and day-to-day matters,
- assisting and administering pastoral and personnel matters related to clergy appointments and resignation, and devising regulations for same, and

- setting up tribunals; appointing councils, committees and officers to carry out church business.

The Barbados Diocesan Trustees

The Anglican Church Act also provided for the establishment of the Barbados Diocesan Trustees, which comprises the Bishop, Archdeacon, one member of the House of Clergy, and five church members elected by the Diocesan Synod. Through this corporate body, all church property was vested in the Trustees to be managed by the Synod and held in trust for support of the parishes, the payment of stipends of the holders of ecclesiastical office for the benefit of the church, and the furtherance of public worship.

The Trustees' functions basically involve:

- collecting and administering matters regarding rents and glebes,
- disbursement of loans and general administering of funds—the Consolidated Trust Fund and Diocesan Pension Fund,
- holding of all church property,
- transacting matters relating to loans, rents, and repairs or restoration of buildings, and the
- development of church lands and property.

While the Trust serves the useful purpose of legally administering property left in trust, it does not seem disposed to address the situations of donations made directly to named persons, or a particular church, as opposed to those made to the larger diocesan organisation. Provision should be made for a named recipient or organisation to benefit from a gift or property donated/prescribed as the giver specifically wishes or bequeaths.[23]

Dean and Chapter of St. Michael's Cathedral

The 1969 Church Act, Section 31, mandated that there should be a Dean and Chapter for the Cathedral of St. Michael and basically outlines, along with the Constitutions, Canons and Regulations:[24]

- its composition—the Rector of St. Michael shall be the *ex officio* Dean of the Cathedral and the Canons of the said Chapter shall be the Archdeacon of Barbados for the time being, and not more than eight nor less than three other priests,
- broad duties and functions of the Dean,
- who acts in the absence of the Dean, and
- the appointment, designation and duties of Canons.

The road after disestablishment

Individual Anglicans, as well as a plethora of literature, note that the road after disestablishment was rough and hard. It required the church to climb the steep curve of self-management without subsidy or any dependable source of income. The bishops, with the support of Synod, the Diocesan Trustees, clergy and laity, strove hard to make ends meet. No block grant was given by the state for repairs to the churches, some of which were 100 years and older.

Matters presenting some difficulties and struggles to the church:

1. No substantial funds granted or made available at disestablishment,
2. Diminishing grants from government,
3. Low cash flow and salaries and benefits of clergy,
4. High and rising cost of salaries and allowances,
5. Struggle of the clergy to honour the wish of Synod to promote better management (parochial) with little funds,
6. High maintenance/rehabilitation costs arising from numerous aged and 'sick' buildings—churches, rectories, schools, and clergy's residences—continually falling into disrepair or obsolescence,
7. Destruction of property (churches) by fire—St. Philip Parish Church on Ash Wednesday, 23 February 1977, St. Peter's on 21 April 1980, and St. Leonard's on 8 July 1981—and the high cost of having to rebuild/restore these,
8. Difficulty in receiving funds in respect of work done on behalf of the church,
9. Government's tardy remuneration attempts to settle arrears for the use of church property—schools and graveyards—and also its failure to readily return such property in a satisfactory, reasonable state of repair or on terms as were agreed,
10. Inability to access loans, and
11. High litigation costs involving the *Diocese* v *The Barbados Water Authority and Sintra*, the *Bishop* v *Gatherer*, and the dismissal case involving the Rector of St. John the Baptist.

Attempts at redressing difficulties

Notwithstanding the foregoing, with astute management and determined sacrifice, the church struggled on to redress some of its difficulties and garner financial support for its mission and sustenance through, for instance:

1. Assessments levied on parishes for meeting the pastoral responsibilities and the general administration of the diocese,
2. Government subventions (which assisted with personnel emoluments),
3. Management and development of church property and investing of assets for the benefit and upkeep of the church,

4. Rental of some church buildings for cultural events,
5. Launching of the Bishop's Restoration Fund for liquidating outstanding church debts,
6. Financial payment from government in lieu of the proper repair on return of the church's property,
7. Formation of an Advisory Property Development Committee,
8. Legacies bequeathed to the church,
9. Sale of land, including 44,000 square meters from The Glebe, St. George, and 1,115 square meters sold to Brydens (a large commercial enterprise),
10. Sale of properties, e.g. in St. Michael—St. Ambrose's rectory, Ellesmere, The Nook, Vermont, and Cherhill, and in St. Joseph—Hillside (this list is not exhaustive),
11. Income from the rental of lands used in residential housing, and
12. The sale of glebe land to tenants at ten cents per square foot, on which very expensive residences are built.

The church owns considerable real estate that needs to be suitably developed and converted into income-producing assets by effective use; but, of course, this requires essential capital that is not readily available. There is also the possibility of the church allowing approved investors (foreign) to develop its land. What about using one of the increasingly popular project financing ventures: Build-operate-lease-transfer (BOLT), or Build-operate-transfer BOT, or Build-own-operate-transfer (BOOT)? These types of ventures would require more than a grasp of theology or politics, or indulgence in wishful thinking. They do call for an entrepreneurial approach, business acumen, a realistic property development project proposal, and the will and wisdom to act.

Of all the inherent and prevailing problems caused by disestablishment, cash flow remains one of the continuing demons.

Disestablishment: A way forward

Bishop Gomez saw the need to centralise management of church property, bringing it under diocesan control. Subsequently, Bishop Rufus Brome in commending the wisdom of such a proposal in his 1996 charge to Synod said:

> The centralisation of all church property for the benefit of the whole church was done to remove the disparity between parishes, and to emphasise the spirit of community which characterises the life of the early church.[25]

Bringing church property, e.g. glebe lands, buildings, and the rent therefrom, under the hierarchical control and better supervision of the diocese would be a desirable option, but a formidable ordeal!

For the Bishop to have direct authority over the churches and parishes rather than the rectors was a strategic option. This, however, implied that a considerable sweep of power and freedom would have had to be wrested from them. Transferring a rector from his parish and rectory would analogously be seen as uprooting a lord from his castle and divesting him of his inherent rights. Rectors could not be moved without their consent. Priests-in-charge can be moved.[26] Asking a rector to resign from his cure and 'supposed lifetime endowment' would be an anathema. Notwithstanding, there was need for tactical leadership and a more pragmatic approach to make the desired changes.

With disendowment and disestablishment having been realised, how in one fell swoop was the church going to adequately procure funds to control its property and effectively address conditions of service of its personnel of so varied a tenure and status?

Herein lay a portentous dilemma for the leader of the Anglican Church—indeed a tall order, an exceedingly gruelling if not insurmountable task! How was the Bishop going to curtail or withdraw privileges and lifetime rights of his personnel, retire them in quest of achieving equanimity, unanimity, strategically reallocate personnel in the best interest of all concerned and optimise effective leadership in his diocese? The Constitutions, Canons and Regulations of the Diocese of Barbados did not allow the indiscriminate movement of rectors. The institution of a priest to a parish (cure of souls) meant that a rector had a permanent appointment. A priest-in-charge, unlike a rector, could have been moved. His licence states that he served at the bishop's pleasure, which was not the case with a rector.[27] How could opening the legal cans of worms and swallowing the bitter administrative pill be best undertaken by the Bishop amidst an ominous impending war?

Implications of disestablishment for Rev. Gatherer

As alluded to earlier in this chapter, it was necessary for the Bishop to assume greater autonomy over church property and management of the church. He had authority to delegate power to his clergy, within limits. Indeed transferring long-entrenched staff (those appointed prior to the Anglican Church Act 1955) would be problematic, and altering or removing their rights to glebe and rectory privileges would have been grave. To replace Rev'd. Gatherer by a younger or more charismatic person, to ask him to retire, give up his residence and glebe benefits, to end his life's mission as he saw it, and take away 'his church, his life' was a tall order. And to attempt such tasks without being fully seized of the law, the ramifications, and collision with the laity's sheer, "good old Bajan common-sense" would inevitably cause trouble. Challenge reticent, weak people, or people who are unaware of their rights, or those who are simply unwilling to defend their rights, and you may succeed; facing down a tenacious, determined rector and his adherents can be a daunting exercise.

A look at the 'List of Clergy According to Date of Ordination' in the 1989 Diocesan Synod Report (Appendix 3) revealed at least ten other clergymen, along with Rector Gatherer, who qualified for exemption from the restriction of the 1969 Act because of their prior appointment, and who were being asked to resign on reaching age 65. Some of these honourable, reverend gentlemen—B. Ullyett, G. Hazlewood, A. Simons,

C. Curry, W. Brathwaite, E. Payne, M. Maxwell, G. Hatch, L. Burke, and L. Clarke, caught in a predicament similar to that of Rev'd. Gatherer passed on, retired humbly, or waited upon the outcome of the retirement saga. Reverends S. Walcott, I. Jones and H. Tudor similarly held prior appointment, but had not been appointed to cures. But this was not to be the case with the no-nonsense, astute St. Andrew cleric. He would not let sleeping dogs lie!

The time had come for the post-independent church to get it right, to amend, improve, and validate its archaic Acts, Constitution, Canons and Regulations of the Diocese and let justice prevail, rather than relying on sentiment or grandpa's good old 'turn-the-cheek' faith.

In England, prior to 1985, the Church of England had no retirement age. Priests who were appointed before 1985 were allowed to remain in office until they were certified by two physicians to be incapable of serving the church, or until they died. There was no undue haste to depose of senior clerics; the church would remain for centuries to come![28]

At what age should clergy and diocesan staff in Barbados retire? What proper industrial relations and civil routine would have been required in dealing with staff whose appointment predated the 1955 Church Act, and who accordingly did not expect to be ousted by any subsequent legislation? Was the church required to conform to civil legal practices in issues not relating to its doctrine? Therefore, could the law exercise jurisdiction over the church regarding ecclesiastical matters?

In a post-modern Barbados where people's rights and independence were coming under increasing social pressure to be respected and preserved; when freedom of expression and information more than ever dictated that justice should be done and not merely given lip service; when the pound of flesh is being required without a drop of blood being shed; indeed, in our growing, litigious society, all sectors, the church not excepted, need to be prepared to yield on some matters to advance the common good.

Therefore, to settle the industrial questions which were arising; to legally address the matter about when to retire, who to retire, and by whose dictate; to resolve the related uncertainty and legal implications about retirement; and to chart a clear and proper way forward—all these perplexities led to the *Bishop* v *Gatherer* case being seen as a way to address some of the burning issues at the time, and to bring resolution to the brewing industrial relations and civil issues within the church setting.

Notes

1. "History of the Anglican Diocese of Barbados". http://www.anglican.bb/hist. Accessed 20 November 2012.
2. Suzanne L. Ellis, "Disestablishment And The Challenge Of Finance For The Anglican Church In Barbados (1969–1999)", M.A. thesis, University of the West Indies, Cave Hill, 2008.
3. "History of the Anglican Church in Barbados". http://www.anglican.bb/hist. Accessed 22 November 2012.
4. Herbert H. Henson. *The Church of England*. (Cambridge University Press, 1939), 44.
5. Bishop E.L. Evans quoting from R.J. Phillimore, in an article addressed to the Church in the *Barbados Diocesan Magazine*, May 1967, 8.
6. William R. Anson. "Church And State", in Henson, *op. cit*, 47.
7. Sir William R. Anson, *The Law and Custom of the Constitution*, 3rd edition (1908), Vol. 2, Part 2, 218.
8. Anson, in Henson, *op. cit*.
9. "History of the Anglican Church in Barbados". *Email Webmaster*. Last Modified: 13 August 2007. http//www.anglican.bb/hist Accessed 17 March 2013.
10. "Vestry". *Wikipedia, the free encyclopedia* http://en.wikipedia.org/wiki/Vestry. Accessed 2 December 2012.
11. Interviews conducted with Neville King, Hariet Lowe, Canon Lionel Burke and Fr. Laurence Small, MBE, on 20 November 2012 revealed that organist, music director and composer, Gerald Hudson, who taught Music Appreciation and Singing at Harrison College, Combermere, and others secondary schools, was not only an outstanding organist and musician, the "only one in his class qualified to teach music" King opined, but someone who unselfishly taught many budding organists in Barbados, thus enriching their musicianship. These 'Hudsonites' continued to enhance the standard of music across Barbados by their improved pipe organ playing, and in teaching their respective church choirs. Like Hudson, they also taught others to play the pipe organ. Unfortunately, the rich patriotic tradition of 'teaching organ and enhancing musicianship' apparently died with Hudson.

    In terms of someone being a music lover, and someone who has prodigious memory of Hudson and his contribution to music, the assistance from Fr. Laurence Small, MBE, must be gratefully noted. It was through his wealth of information that this expanded note was made possible. Also refer to Appendix 2, to which Fr. Small primarily contributed.
12. Ellis quoting from F.A. Hoyos' *Grantley Adams and the Social Revolution*, (London: Macmillan, 1974).
13. Ellis, Thesis, *op. cit.*, 12.
14. John Holder. "Religious Trends in Barbados during the last Sixty Years". *The Journal of the Barbados Museum and Historical Society*, XLII, 1994:59. 58–59.
15. F.A. Hoyos, *op. cit*.
16. *The Barbados Advocate*, Saturday, 14 March 1946, 12.
17. *Ibid.*, Friday, 25 August 1950, 1.
18. Interview with Dean Emeritus Harold Crichlow, GCM, 15 March 2013.
19. *Ibid*.
20. The Anglican Church Act 1969, Chapter 375 was proclaimed on 1 April 1969.
21. "Disestablishment. The Anglican Church Bill 1969 Explained". *The Barbados Advocate*, 3 March 1969, 4.
22. Extract from Bishop Drexel Gomez's April 1990 radio broadcast, 5.
23. Crichlow, 15 March 2013.
24. Constitution, Canons and Regulations of the Diocese of Barbados, S.I. 1992, No. 77, Regulation C3, 20.
25. Bishop Rufus Brome, GCM. Charge given to the 1996 Annual Session of Synod, *Synod Journal 1996*, Diocese of Barbados.
26. Crichlow, 15 March 2013.
27. *Ibid*.
28. *Ibid*.

CHAPTER SIX

Priest Validates Law and Rewrites Church History (1980s–1990s)

In alluding to the possible impact that disestablishment could have had on the Gatherer saga, The Right Rev'd. Drexel Gomez (Bishop or Bishop Gomez) in his 1990 radio monthly broadcast noted:

> It is perhaps not surprising that in the first decades after Disestablishment and Disendowment, we should have found it difficult to extricate ourselves from the ties of Establishment without resorting to the law.[1]

The Bishop's reference to the law has to do with his eventually prosecuting a case he brought against Rev'd. Gatherer for rejecting his order to resign as Rector of St. Andrew on reaching age 65. About the case, the Bishop went on to state:

> ...the core issue is one which is to be determined, not by narrowly religious considerations, but by the law. The core question is—At what age, in law, shall priests of the Anglican Church retire?[2]

This chapter briefly summarises events leading to a determination of this historic question—what is the age of retirement for clergy? In confirming age 65 as the legally-adopted age of retirement, eventually the church had to engage in a fierce lawsuit reaching as far as the Privy Council in England, after the church and brilliant law luminaries failed to solve the problem. One significant outcome was that the church had to amend and legally validate its Constitution, Canons and Regulations, and duly put instruments in place to regulate the age and other relevant matters pertaining to the retirement of its personnel.

Rev'd. Gatherer was ordained Deacon in the Anglican Church on 6 August 1951. He went on to serve as Deacon at St. Mary's, and Vicar of St. Anne's Church. He was ordained priest on 21 December 1952 and served at St. Joseph's until he became Rector of St. Andrew's Church from 1 May 1957. With his ordination as a cleric (Appendix 3) and appointments to serve (Chapters 3 and 4) in the church prior to the Anglican Church (Partial Suspension) Act 1955, he and other clerics appointed with him understood that they qualified for all of the benefits arising from establishment and endowment—having no retirement date along with acquiring possession and responsibility for the vicarage and glebe lands for life

Prior to 1985, clergy who were appointed to parishes could remain in them for life. In the UK, occasionally persons kept their parishes much beyond their ability to function. Unless these priests were forced to retire on grounds of being medically unfit,[3] they died in office, some of them with impaired capability, to the dismay of onlookers.

On 15 January 1987, a week before Father Gatherer's 65th birthday, the Bishop of Barbados notified him to vacate his office of Rector by 31 January 1987. In writing to Fr. Gatherer, the Bishop used the Anglican Church Act 1969, stating:

> A Clergyman shall vacate his office on the last day of the month in which he attains the age of sixty-five, but shall be eligible for appointment of Priest-in-charge or assistant curate.

The Bishop invited him to continue serving as Priest-in-charge.

Fr. Gatherer reportedly made it known that he would not accept the Bishop's terms, and continued to occupy the rectory, conducting services as usual as Rector and not as Priest-in-charge as was instructed by the Bishop.

Interviewees maintained that strong representation to the Bishop, especially from mature clergymen, not to proceed with forcing Rev'd. Gatherer to retire as Rector and leave the rectory, as there was really no solid ground or sound reasons for so doing, was not heeded. There was a strong opinion, held then and even now by a number of mature clergy and church legal advisers, that since Rev'd. Gatherer was appointed prior to the 1955 Act, and was then an elderly person, he should not have been asked or coerced to retire, since doing so would have been acting *ultra vires*. Moreover, it was also reported that contrary to the common opinion of the church, the Bishop obtained 'advice from a legal luminary who wielded influence rather than practised law', and, as Bishop, proceeded with termination and eviction orders. Interviewees alleged that it was held that the action was to 'teach Gatherer a lesson and make him an example'.

On 31 January 1989, the Bishop terminated Rev'd. Gatherer's appointment as Rector of St. Andrew's Parish Church, requiring him to vacate the rectory and cease holding services in the Church, with effect from the same date. In a writ to the Bishop, Rev'd. Gatherer remonstrated that he was entitled to serve as Rector and receive all the benefits of the office. He also had an order served requesting the Bishop not to disturb him in performing his office as Rector.

An article in the *Daily Nation* summarised Rev'd. Gatherer's case:

The plaintiff priest had asked the court to declare that he was still the substantive Rector of St. Andrew, a post he held since 1957 when he went through the process of institution and induction.[4]

On 20 December 1989, the High Court of Barbados (Davis, J.), ruled that the Constitutions, Canons and Regulations established by the Synod on 10 December 1979 for the Diocese, having not been published in the *Official Gazette,* had not taken effect or come into operations, and so were not valid, and decided in favour of Rev'd. Gatherer. The Court held that Fr. Gatherer was entitled to occupy the rectory, and ordered that he should continue in his office as Rector of St. Andrew's Church, while receiving all the emoluments and benefits of that office. Consequently, Father Gatherer was allowed to continue to receive all the emoluments of his office together with the rights, rents, and profits of the glebe attached thereto and to occupy the rectory of St. Andrew. No damage was awarded, only costs for Rev'd. Gatherer's counsel.

The Bishop appealed on 5 April 1990. The Court of Appeal in Barbados set aside the Judgment of the High Court, ordering that Rev'd. Gatherer should give up possession of the rectory and glebe to the Bishop, with which decision Rev'd. Gatherer complied. The Rector was also ordered to pay $200 per month from 1 February 1989 to the date on which he delivered up possession of the rectory.

Pursuant to the decision of the Appeal Court, the Bishop obtained an interim injunction which restrained Fr. Gatherer from functioning as Rector of St. Andrew's without written permission from the Bishop.

Things turned ugly at St. Andrew's. Pictures appeared in the media showing the doors of the Church barricaded and/or "locked or bolted from inside" (Sunday Sun, 15 April 1990, Appendix 5). With the doors barricaded, members could not enter. To accommodate churchgoers dressed in their "Sunday best" a senior priest of the area, with a few church 'faithfuls' armed with hammer and other tools, removed a window pane, gained entry, restoring a degree of sanity, allowing services to be conducted.

The Rector, not one to "curl up his feet" and lie down, appealed to the Privy Council in England, the final court of appeal for Barbados, in the famous case *Gomez v Gatherer*. He was granted leave to appeal on terms including that the Judgment of the Appeal Court be executed and that the Bishop enter into a Bond of $40,000. The case, *Gatherer v Gomez*, [Privy Council. Appeal No. 29 of 1990] was heard before Lord Griffiths, Lord Jauncey of Tullichettle, Lord Lowry, Lord Mustill and Lord Slynn of Hadley. English barrister Sheila Cameron, QC and Chezley Boyce of the Barbados Bar (instructed by Winckworth & Pemberton) appeared for the plaintiff, while Allen Dyer (instructed by Radcliffes & Co) appeared for the defendant.

The Privy Council in its deliberations on 18 June 1992 set aside the Judgment of the Appeal Court in Barbados and ordered that:

1. The Judgment and Order of the High Court of 20 December 1989 be restored and that Rev. Gatherer's claim for damages was to be referred back to the High Court, and
2. Rev. Gatherer was to be paid his costs of Appeal.

With reference to old ecclesiastical English laws that governed the Anglican churches in England and Barbados prior to the Anglican Church (Barbados) Act 1891, the Anglican Church Act 1911, and the Anglican Church (Amendment) Act 1949, there was no provision of a specified retirement age for Anglican clergymen. In Barbados, as in England, clergymen were treated as civil servants and received government salaries and pensions on retirement.

Fr. Gatherer had been serving in the diocese prior to 1955. In fact, he had been appointed since 1952 (refer to Appendix 3). Moreover, his appointment to St. Andrew's in 1957 fell within the net of enforcement of the Anglican Church (Partial Suspension) Act 1955, which stated that no new appointments to any vacancy in the offices of Rector, Vicar, or Curate were to be made under Section 9 of the Anglican Church Act 1911, so long as the Suspension Act remained in force. However, the Anglican Church Act carried an exception, where the office of a Rector, Vicar, or Curate, who was in office at the time the Suspension Act came into force, was to be filled. The exception clause allowed for Fr. Gatherer's appointment, so that he therefore filled the vacancy as a rector appointed under the 1911 Church Act.

Father Gatherer maintained that the provision quoted in the Bishop's letter of termination to him was null and void and of no effect because the procedure for its proper implementation was not followed. Consequently, he technically maintained that he was entitled to remain in office until death or when he chose to retire or resign, or unless he was legally removed for misdemeanour.

Notwithstanding, in the historic Privy Council appeal, Lord Slynn ruled that the 1947 Pensions Act applied to Rev'd. Gatherer, legally requiring him to retire at 60. The Judgment also concluded that from the date of disestablishment, service in an ecclesiastical office ceased to be regarded as public service, so that from 1 April 1969, the Pensions Act also ceased to apply to an incumbent in the position of Rev'd. Gatherer. Therefore, technically, Rev'd. Gatherer had not acquired life tenure because a compulsory retirement age had been in force.

Moreover, the Privy Council also ruled that based on Section 9 of the Anglican Church Act 1969 no retirement or pension date was fixed for clergy as that responsibility had been left to Synod. It also noted in Section 16(1) that every enactment should be published in the *Official Gazette* unless the enactment otherwise provided; and that Regulation C10 paragraph 11 (which requires a clergyman to vacate his office at 65) could only have been binding based on the date of its publication in the *Official Gazette*. Consequently, since the enactment was not duly published as mandated, it never took effect or came into force, and no retiring age was properly prescribed as required by the Anglican Church Act 1969.

The Privy Council (the Committee) also found:

> . . . the appellant was right in his contention that he could not be required to retire at the end of the month in which he attained his sixty-fifth birthday and that the order of the Court of Appeal was in error in so far as it required the appellant to deliver up possession of the rectory and glebe land to the respondent.

Accordingly, following the ruling of the Privy Council, it was necessary for the church to sort out its Constitution, Canons and Regulations, along with other relevant instruments, and have them duly validated and gazetted.

It was said that Godson (God's son) Gatherer won the case not because God was on his side. It was because Fr. Gatherer was on God's side. "He was a person who stood for right, justice, and what was principled",[5] a stand reflective of one of Fr. Gatherer's favourite hymns:[6]

> For right is right, as God is God, And right the day must win;
> To doubt would be disloyalty, To falter were to sin.

It is interesting that the ruling of the Privy Council basically accorded with that given in the High Court of Barbados, where Justice Woodbine Davis determined that the Constitution, Canon and Regulations should have been published in the *Official Gazette* for them to have effect of law. Following the ruling Father Gatherer was allowed to continue in his office with all of the rights and privileges attached thereto,[7] while the Bishop graciously resigned from his bishopric without any solicitation from the clergy or Church in Barbados.

Unfortunately, too little credit has been given to Justice Davis for his wise, incisive, and timely judgment, confirming that 'local isn't less'.[8] From discussions with interviewees, it was determined that there was an abundance of wisdom and sound advice prevailing among older members of the clergy and other persons of calm manners, who cautioned that Rev'd. Gatherer should not have been forced to resign, and that a legal case or an appeal against him was not necessary. Interviewees opined that the Bishop, having taken the case to court, should have been made to be personally responsible for the cost, and not the church, which covered the expenses. Of course, they were also interviewees who felt that Fr. Gatherer had already given of his best in the parish and should then have made way for some other person, for the greater good of the church and all concerned. On hindsight, one cannot but concede that the letter of the law may require a penalty, but it is the spirit of the law that brings satisfaction!

Having won the case, Fr. Gatherer claimed not less than $11 million for suffering and other costs. Some people opined that unfortunately, with this judgment determined locally (not overseas), he ended up being awarded only approximately $200,000.

The resultant lawsuit amounting to $286,623.88 in costs and fees (see Table 4) proved to have been exceedingly costly for a diocese that continues to struggle financially to make ends meet after disestablishment.

Table 4: Settlement (*Rev'd. Gatherer* v *Right Rev'd. Drexel Gomez*)

Description	Cost $
Total Housing Allowance	86,400.00
Stipend	61,166.67
Utilities	5,200.00
Seniority Allowance	4,100.00
Travel Allowance	1,800.00
Glebe 1	400.00
Glebe 2	180.00
Subtotal	**159,246.67**
Total Interest	46,152.21
Subtotal	**205,398.88**
Attorneys Fees	
Messrs. Carrington & Sealy	14,375.00
Mr. Leroy Inniss Q.C.	21,850.00
Mr. Chezley Boyce	45,000.00
TOTAL	**286,623.88**

Information extracted from: Synod Report (1998) II

In addition to striking a blow to the church's reputation, the debilitating spiritual and mental trauma inflicted on the Anglican congregation and enthusiasts as a result of the case was overwhelming.

Unfortunately, at least 13 other clergymen were caught in the anomaly of undetermined resignation date, some of whom surrendered in death and others quietly or unwittingly giving up their service. The final determination was that the church is required to conform to civil legal practices in issues not relating to its doctrine. Therefore, the church was not free to act outside the boundaries of civil law.

In reference to the impact of Fr. Gatherer's court case on the diocese, Rev'd. Laurence Small commented: "Wherever there is church in Barbados, the name of Rev'd. Gatherer will be written".[9] Indeed, Rev'd. Gatherer will long be remembered nationally and further afield as the one through whom the Anglican Constitution, Canons and Regulations of the Diocese of Barbados were rewritten and made valid. The case set a precedent for retirement not only in Barbados, but throughout the region.

With judgment determined in the Rector's favour, and the fact that he was legally still Rector, the time came for him to resume his cure and get back to work. At last he would enter the doors of his beloved St. Andrew's again, for another two decades.

Notes

1. Bishop Drexel Gomez's April 1990 radio broadcast.
2. *Ibid.*
3. In England, if and when it was determined that elderly or infirm clergy were unable to perform reasonable functions, on the advice of at least two medical practitioners, the church could have them extricated. This would occur in extreme cases with persons who were determined to be too ill to continue to perform normal duties.
4. "Priest remains at St. Andrew". *Daily Nation*, 21 December 1998.
5. Simeon Belgrave. Speech given at Canon Gatherer's 91st Birthday party, January 2013.
6. *Hymns Ancient and Modern*, (Norwich, UK: Canterbury Press, 1988). Hymn 739.
7. *Daily Nation*, 21 December 1998.
8. Interview with Rev'd. Laurence Small, MBE, 4 December 2012.
9. Rev'd. Laurence Small, MBE, on his 90th birthday 2013.

CHAPTER SEVEN

The Doors Remain Open (1990s–2011) Phase 2

. . . I know your works. Behold, I have set before you an open door, which no one is able to shut . . . Revelation 3:8 ESV[1]

And to the angel of the church in Philadelphia write: The words of the holy one, the true one, who has the key of David, who opens and no one will shut, who shuts and no one opens. Revelation 3:7 ESV[2]

Figure 22: Open Door

St. Andrew's Parish Church, like an ancient steel bulwark, is enduring. The doors of this Church have always remained open, as if in fulfilment of the quoted passages of Scripture; neither hurricane, fire, diminishing congregation, nor civil suits could close them (Figure 22).

Description of the Church

This modest rectangular 60 ft by 40 ft (18.29 m by 12.19 m) building was fabricated from one-foot-thick coral limestone blocks.[3] Its massive coral stone buttresses on the exterior, interspersed with large double-height, pointed-arch windows, lend support to the structure. Built in typical east to west church orientation, the building was constructed to optimise ventilation as there was no electricity, mechanical ventilation, or air-conditioning in those days.

The symmetry of the building is interesting and attractive with similar rectangular size and shape of the narthex (entrance porch comprising the base of the bell tower) on the west and the sanctuary on the east. Symmetry and spirituality promoting balance and equality were significant tenets of classical European churches. At St. Andrew's, symmetry—signifying balance—is interrupted only at the communion rails from where the sanctuary, standing apart, leads to God, signifying hierarchy.[4]

The 23.7 ft by 12.6 ft (7.16 m by 3.81 m) vestry on the north of the Church, was an early twentieth century addition, with some later extension in 1968 to provide the sanitary block.

Architectural Features

Equally-spaced windows between the vertical load-bearing buttresses provide not only an aura of grandeur, but also of order, precision, and rhythm.

The double-seamed parapet around the roof and supporting walls recalls the look of Georgian architecture, while adding structural strength to and protection of the building (roof) from strong winds.

Interior

The pews, rails, reredos, tiles and altar comprise modern restoration work that was completed during the Second World War.

Walls of the Church ascending up to the 21 foot (6.4 m) high arched ceiling (also a modern feature), are thicker at their base for support of the roof and gallery (mezzanine floor), which sat on the north, west, and south sides of the Church. Apart from the 15 ft x 39 ft (4.6 m by 11.9 m) repaired upper floor, which overhangs the western main entrance, all other mezzanine features were removed in the 1970s due to disrepair. With their removal, the clear view of the altar was accentuated by the elimination of several timber columns from the nave.

Roof

The steep slope of the roof was exaggerated to give the illusion of soaring height, while allowing water to drain quickly. Its durable asbestos roof covering, dating back to 1949, remains in good repair and keeps the building cool.

Belfry

From the roof of the bell tower, one of the highest points in Belleplaine, a spectator can enjoy the enchanting, picturesque rugged slopes of St. Andrew and beyond: the green rolling hills of Walkers highlands (north), Bawden, Turner's Hall (northwest), Ben Hill and Chalky Mount (south to southeast). With its pointed-arch windows and elaborate buttresses, the imposing 64 ft (19.5 m) high square belfry also mimics quaint medieval design. In medieval British architecture, church buildings incorporated some of the finest expressions of Gothic designs.[5]

From base to apex, the buttresses (Figure 23) of the bell tower are increasingly reduced in size every 1/5 of the height of the tower. Without the modern extensive reinforcing of walls employed today, buttresses provided the support that the walls and structures needed, as well as essential stability for counteracting the side thrust of the Church's heavy roof. Note too, that with the gradual reduction in size of the buttresses, depending on how one looks at the Church, one is apt to get an idea that its tower is leaning to the east. The "leaning tower effect" not only gives St. Andrew's a lofty soaring perspective, but richly adds to its Gothic grandeur.

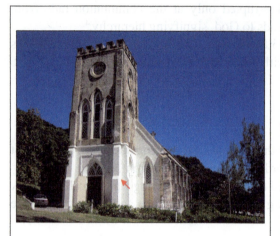

Figure 23: Buttress of St. Andrew's

Geology of the parish

St. Andrew is part of the Scotland District (or 1/7 of Barbados) which is without a limestone cap. The limestone cap has been eroded, exposing approximately 500 feet (152.4 m) of deep soils comprising clays, shale, sandstone, to name a few. The area is also devoid of basal coral limestone, which is otherwise prevalent over the remainder of the island. With no coral cap *in situ*, vast erosion has taken place, resulting in the characteristic steep slopes of the Scotland District region.

Perennial structural stress in the church building

St. Andrew's Parish Church was erected on Scotland and other montmorillinite clays (clays rich in minerals).[6] The high proportions of clay minerals in some of these soils can expand and increase in volume as water enters the crystal structures of the clay.[7] Infiltration of water from rainfall or underground streams adds to the weight, force, and stress of the soil slopes, which eventually lead to slope instability and failure. Failures occur when the clay-rich soil experiences a decrease in strength, resulting from increased pore-water pressure. Eventually, when the clay dries out, the loss of water results in a decrease in volume, and resultant shrinkage of the clay. The same phenomenon occurs with peaty soils. This combined expansion and subsequent shrinkage of the soil constitute common occurrences in St. Andrew, which adversely impact the Church building.

Another problem may occur where pore-water pressure builds up on perched water tables within the bedding of older clay-sealed slip surfaces.[8] Along the edges of these slip surfaces, especially in elevated areas, may be seen seepage of subsurface water or streams in the Scotland District, especially during or after the rainy season. However, sometimes when enough soil-water collects in the interface of sub-soil clay, slippage is facilitated, which occasionally causes the movement of vast tracts of land, taking along trees, buildings and other objects in its path.[9] This familiar phenomenon of the Scotland area resulting in significant slope movements was experienced in the "Terrible Landslip in Boscobel" in 1901 when between 40 and 80 houses, along with estate buildings, mills, and cottages, were levelled and/or submerged.[10] This landslide followed four days in which between 9.5 and 20 inches of rainfall was recorded in St. Andrew, the higher figure representing the downpour in Boscobel.[11]

As noted earlier, other potential problems arise from subsurface water—from rain, storm water, obsolete or defective water mains and wastewater—collecting on the clay beds, causing clay-type soils to expand and contract, especially during the wet and dry months of the year. This subsoil activity—expansion and contraction—exerts severe differential pressure and movement that affect the stability of buildings (especially large ones), which can result in their fracture or collapse. The heavy stone structure of St. Andrew's Parish Church has suffered continual structural stress, differential settlement and factures over the years. Other factors threatening this church building and that have remained perpetual and devastating menaces include:[12]

- its softstone block foundation with less than acceptable bearing footings in the clay subsoil,
- lack of conventional steel reinforcement,
- inadequate site stabilisation,
- distress in the building substructure,
- storm water (including rainwater and roof drainage), water from defective water mains, and wastewater entering the subsoil of the Church,
- less than satisfactory drainage of the site, and
- lack of funds to appropriately address the plaguing subsurface water problems in a timely manner.

Whether or not Rev'd. Gatherer understood these dynamic hydrogeological and geomorphologic factors at work, he nevertheless was indefatigable in his gallant attempts to mitigate the perennial problems of the building, and its surrounding lands. He continually ensured that the Church plant was kept in reasonable repair,[13] unlike what is seen in many other churches outside of the Scotland District, many of which merely require only the usual regular painting and building maintenance. His tireless efforts and goodwill yielded rich dividends in preventing the structure from crumbling, and the adjacent sloping lands from sliding and engulfing the building.

In reporting on the endeavours to maintain and refurbish the Church in 1987, *The Visitor* (Barbadian newspaper) noted:

> Damage to the main structure caused by huge settlement cracks, heads a list of problems, which includes heavy termite infestation, rust, and damage to both stained glass and the church organ.
>
> According to Reverend Gatherer, vicar of the parish for the past 30 years, repairs to the main structure alone are expected to cost in

the region of $50,000 despite work already completed through the generosity of parishioners and other private individuals.[14]

The Visitor also reported that settlement problems were evident from the main entrance to the churchyard, and that renewing the termite-ridden bell tower alone was estimated at $6,000. Extensive cracks in the walls, bell tower, floor and foundation have had to be continually repaired over time, and urgent work had to be undertaken in the 1980s. At that time, wide fissures had developed in the southeastern (Figure 24) and northwestern walls, in the bell tower, and the floor. It was also reported that vibrations of the building were felt as heavy vehicles traversed the adjacent highway.[15]

Figure 24: Structural crack above window

Brian H. Claxton Associates Ltd. carried out extensive engineering works to address many of the problems. In brief, some of the major remediation exercises involved underpinning the Church's substructure, replacing defective gutters and roof parapets, and redirecting water away from the building.[16]

Thanks is due to the foresight, vigilance, and dedication of Rev'd. Gatherer, along with the cooperation of the local Church Council, the wisdom of the Diocesan Secretary, the Barbados Diocesan Trustees, and not least, the skill and kindness of engineer Brian Claxton of the then Brian H. Claxton Associates Ltd, and cooperation from his counterparts, including Richard Edghill. Concerned companies such as the Barbados Light and Power Company Ltd., C.O. Williams Construction Ltd., and other anonymous benefactors and generous firms, through whom major problems have been arrested/remedied, deserve recognition and praise.

Sustainable programme

All efforts to alleviate structural problems to the building have had to be rigorously pursued including:

- maintaining the building in good repair,
- timely remedying of defective guttering and walls,
- eliminating leaks,
- preventing water from entering the building and its subsurface,
- disallowing indiscriminate building development around the Church plant, most certainly not on or near the higher elevation adjacent to the Church, and
- aggressively soliciting money for general plant upkeep.

Like Fr. Gatherer, the incumbents of this church and the congregation have to be serious about, profoundly committed to, and united on plant sustainability, in order to prevent the building from crumbling to the ground in a few years.

Regarding the matter of prudent preventative upkeep, there must be continual vigilance and astute plant management, with no lapse in the maintenance regimen. Unlike other churches, every rainy season followed by drying out of the soil, constitutes potential problems and challenges for this building. That the Church has survived myriad challenges caused by nature and humans over the years, and has been kept in the current and reasonable state of repair, speaks eloquently to the ingenuity, dedication, and tenacity of purpose of its leaders generally, and particularly that of its longest serving incumbent (over 54 years service), who unswervingly persevered in the preservation of the plant. For his sacrifice, untiring and skilful efforts in maintaining this problem-ridden church building and making the entire plant (especially the burial ground, which is one of the best maintained in the island) a truly national attraction, by day and night, the Reverend Canon Edward Godson Gatherer deserves national honour/ recognition. The bestowal of a canonry is not enough.

1989

As noted in Chapter 6, the period 1989 through 1992 was a stormy litigious one for Rev'd. Gatherer who, on reaching age 65, was expected to retire. During this time, much work had not been done on the church building, following the Rector's court eviction from the church, rectory and parish. Rev'd. Gatherer eventually won the court battle and was allowed to continue serving in the Church, thus setting a precedent in the annals of Anglican Church history.

1990

Finally, with knowledge of the court eviction notice of 5 April 1990 on the way, Rev'd. Gatherer vacated the rectory in St. Andrew and resided in Rockley, Christ Church. He remained there until he won the case before the Privy Council in London on 18 June 1992, when he moved to St. Joseph. From St. Joseph, being nearer to his cure, he resumed service at St. Andrew's.

With no one occupying the rectory, unfortunately it was vandalised (allegedly in 1994), the windows removed or stolen, and the building partially burnt. It was finally destroyed by fire in the summer of 1999.[17]

1991

The Diocesan Trustees sought the assistance of the priest and Church Council of St. Andrew's in compiling statistics relative to the use of glebe land in the parish, as the potential for development of over 18 acres of land seemed a viable option. This was followed by a proposal that was agreed to and a lease signed on behalf of the Diocesan Synod for the rental of 602.5 square metres of land adjacent to the disused rectory to the Ministry of Health at $100 per annum.[18] The land was to provide recreational accommodation for children in the parish and the residents of the adjacent Children's Home, now called the Elaine Scantlebury Home. In addition, the Synod

Report of April 1990–March 1991 noted that an estimate of $76,549 was determined for renovation of the disused rectory. The Diocesan Trustees planned to undertake the renovations with the funds realised from rental of developed glebe land in the parish. With 18 acres of glebe land in St. Andrew alone, there was potential for profitable diocesan investment to enhance the Church's small revenue; and this potential exists not only in St. Andrew, but in respect of the vast land bank owned by the Anglican churches all across Barbados. Accordingly, a sum of $7,800 was spent on Phase 1 of the project.[19]

However, with a change in circumstances wherein Rev. Dr. Eustace McCollin, the interim Priest-in-Charge of St. Andrew's, and his family were given rental accommodation in Mullins Terrace, St. Peter, and a raging civil suit between the substantive Rector of St. Andrew's and the Bishop, the project was shelved.

1992

Following the Judgment given in favour of Rev'd. Gatherer, he resumed work and repairs at St. Andrew's. It was doubtlessly a very traumatic episode for him. One will never know the ultimate effect this case had on him and on his ability to effectively resume and carry on his ministry. Although he returned to a few members who stood solidly beside him all the way throughout his litigation in Barbados and England, he also had to face those who were less enamoured with him, and who did not welcome his return to the Church. In fact, some persons left the Church when he returned.

It was reported that Fr. Gatherer resumed his work at St. Andrew's with much pain and hurt, but he proceeded in his calm and resolute manner "working with zeal, thankfulness and determination to right things".

Again he commenced the repair of the Church and beautification of the grounds, spending many hours "toiling and making sure that all went well as the work was being carried out". Some faithful members who insisted on anonymity reported how he did all in his power to ensure that the Church was upgraded even to the extent of spending his own funds in doing so.

Greenland Landfill

The early British settlers thought that the northeastern parishes of Barbados resembled the hills and fields of Scotland. This led to the hilly area, including St. Andrew, being called the "Scotland District". To preserve the beauty of this parish, protect its fragile environment, and control its soil from erosion, it was proposed that the rugged coastal region of St. Andrew and the neighbouring hilly parishes should be preserved and developed as a national park. Despite the tentative proposals for the national park, in 1997 the Government of Barbados constructed a so-called state-of-the-art landfill on pristine St. Andrew land, at an approximate cost of $40 million. Many people contended the expenditure was not less than $100 million. This caused a considerable furore among residents of the area and lovers of the environment, regarding what they considered to have been a thoughtless decision in placing the facility in Greenland (approximately 1.5K northwest of the Church). With various problems and issues reportedly arising with the landfill, caused by heavy rains, settlement, slippage of land, and an earthquake, 15 years after its completion the facility remains idle, with little or no attempt by the government to utilise it for the purpose for which it was planned (Figure 25).

Figure 25: Greenland Landfill under construction

1999

St. Andrew's Parish Church Men's Fellowship

Behold, how good and how pleasant it is for brethren to dwell together in unity Psalm. 133:1

Men's ministry is an integral part of any church congregation. How the nation yearns to have more men with passion on fire for God, men who will faithfully lead their families and country and support the churches!

The St. Andrew's Parish Church Men's Fellowship (Fellowship) was started in June 1999, by Everton Bovell and a few men (church members).[20] Bovell said:

> We tried to focus on activities that would support the ministries of the Church—uplifting members and stimulating the membership—while spreading the gospel.

During the 8:00 a.m. Sunday Worship Service, 28 November 1999, Rector Gatherer enrolled Everton Bovell as the First President of the Men's Fellowship of the Church, Trevor Best as Deputy President, Ghandi Morris as Treasurer, and Adrian Belgrave as Secretary, along with 14 other members.

Objectives of the Fellowship

1. To reach and encourage men of integrity who love God,
2. To help men to be godly examples and true role models in their family, church, and community (Mark 12:30),
3. To help men grow in Christ and in fellowship among Christian men through worship, prayer, service, and
4. To train and help men to be leaders in their home, family, church, and community (Ephesians 4:12–13).

Some functions involved

1. Encouraging and strengthening one another,
2. Praying together,
3. Upholding the church's principles,
4. Fostering closer relationship with Jesus Christ,
5. Promoting evangelism,
6. Helping to build solid homes, and
7. Forging links and fellowship with other men and men's organisations of St. Andrew's and other churches.

The Fellowship sought to accomplish its mission as it met monthly for worship, fellowship, discussion, and ministry of the Word and prayer. On the third Sunday of every month, members met for corporate worship, when they sat together, participated in reading the Scripture lesson for the day, and assisted in ushering. They also took part in the cleaning and maintenance routines of the Church.

One of the highlights of the Fellowship was the 2005 musical concert, which had a grand turnout. The Barbados Defence Force Band, the Evangelical Singers, and the Church choir performed to swelling applause.

Due to the demise of many of the older men and lack of new members joining the Fellowship, there has been marginal growth over the years. The membership, which needs revival, stood at approximately eight persons early in 2011. The president hopes that, with new church leadership coupled with training of members in personal evangelism and outreach mission in the parish, the group will be revived, and more people will join.

Enhancement Projects

The Government undertook an $11 million Greenland to Walkers road enhancement, which was scheduled to be completed by December 1998.[21] The project, executed by C.O. Williams Limited, included realignment of the river course, the laying of footpaths, provision of a roundabout by the Parish Church, and widening of the roadway.

Construction work on the road adjacent to the Church and the roundabout commenced late in 1999, and was assiduously completed early in 2000 at a cost of approximately $400,000. The project partially constructed a 4-foot (1.2 m) wall on the south of the graveyard, next to the roadway. This left to the Church the necessity to complete the enclosure which involved extending the columns and enclosure walls, finishing the ornamental columns (including the circular plinths), installing the beautiful decorative lighting along the enclosure, and providing the wrought-iron entrance gates leading to the graveyard.[22]

The overall construction work enhanced the Church. Due to the realignment of the road, a 611-foot (186.3 m) lighted lay-by, north of the road and adjacent to the graveyard, was created. This comprised a concrete parking-bay 390 feet long by 25 feet wide (119 m by 7.62 m) with a 4-foot (1.22 m) concrete curb. There is also a 122-foot long by 18-foot wide (37.2 m by 5.5 m) grassy area which is bordered by a 4-foot (1.22 m) concrete curb.

On completion of the enhancement work, St. Andrew's Parish Church was awash with beautiful lighting—thanks to Rector Gatherer. When viewed at night from the cul-de-sac on the elevated section of Franklin-Doughlin Road, Belleplaine, the Church appears as a brightly lit beacon, not only at Christmas time, but as a year-round beautiful spectacle.

While noting the breathtaking beauty that Fr. Gatherer sought to generate in the parish, an excerpt of Dean Emeritus Crichlow's sermon delivered on the 35th anniversary of Father Edward Gatherer's ministry as Rector of St. Andrew's Church amply captured his sacrifice:[23]

> ... Driving from the Park [referring to Farley Hill National Park] into St. Andrew, you never expect to come across such a very beautiful church as the historic Parish Church with its lovely atmosphere of beauty and tranquillity. Its surroundings are a credit to this island and diocese. I have often said that ordinands in training at Codrington College should be sent here to learn about the care of churches, which will be a life-long job for them. I know the time, effort and expense that go into making a church—both inside and outside—look like this. I know, too, the example shown by the Rector in this area of church life. I commend all of those parishioners who have assisted in the beautification of the grounds and the cleaning of the church all year round...
>
> Recently I was so struck by all of this beauty that I asked the Rector if I could spend my off-days taking some photographs. I see they are posted on the notice board and I hope they have helped you the members... A visitor stopping in here could have his or her life transformed by the visit. God does not only use sermons and sacraments. The old saying: "Cleanliness is next to godliness" is very meaningful in terms of St. Andrew's Parish Church... It is really refreshing to see these grounds around this Church..."

For all of his work and the untiring sacrifice in making St. Andrew's Parish Church a national showpiece, Fr. Gatherer surely deserves more than a posthumous honour.

Organ(s)

Apart from the sparse mention gleaned from Vestry documents, only meagre documentation was available on early organs of the Church. Very little information was available on the early nineteenth century organ that was located in the southern end of the chancel, where the present console stands. That organ was repositioned by Kirton Tucker in the gallery in the early 1940s. It was manually supplied with air until the 1960s, when major refurbishment was undertaken, and an electric blower designed and installed by the late Samuel D. Burke, father of the present Curator of St. Michael's Church.[24] Over the years the organ fell into disrepair, and a small keyboard was loaned by McDonald Smith. Later, a small electric Yamaha organ was used, and this was replaced by an electric organ borrowed from St. Barnabas' Church in the 1960s.

"Only in St. St. Andrew"—speaker set returned

A speaker set was given to the Church by MacDonald Smith. It so happened that one day in a service when MacDonald reminded the priest that he had given the Church the set, it was reported that the priest immediately fetched the set and rejoined: 'Mr. Smith, here is your set."

Organ Replacement[25]

On recommendation from David Burke, who was residing in England, Fr. Gatherer travelled to the UK in 1974 to acquire a pipe organ, which was obtained through the Church Commissioners.[26] With Burke's help, in 1976, for only £50, he purchased a disused English organ built by Vincent Organ Works of Durham, from a redundant church in Durham in northeast England. Fr. Gatherer contracted David Burke and his assistants to travel from London to Durham to dismantle the organ, and transport it at a cost of £300 to Burke's workshop in London, where a £1000-refurbishing-job to tropicalise the woodwork and general repairs were undertaken prior to its complimentary shipment to Barbados.[27]

On arrival of the organ at St. Andrew's in July 1976, rebuilding and upgrading works were carried out by David Burke, Burke Pipe Organ Service, of Oxnards, St. James. It was necessary to reduce its height by six feet (1.8 m) in order for it to be accommodated in the loft. Following damage to the imported English console during shipment (Gatherer's car, also in shipment, allegedly rolled on it), a rebuilt Austin console had to be obtained from the Organ Clearing House, Harrisville, New Hampshire, United States.[28] The old tubular pneumatic action was replaced by modern electro-pneumatic actions, built in Barbados. The drawstop actions are electric.

After several suspensions over the years due to insufficient funds, work on the organ was finally completed in 2004 by David Burke and Eugene Jordan through Burke Pipe Organ Service. Mrs. Jordan is a local resident who has been with Burke Pipe Organ firm since 1996. The value of the completed organ was approximately £30,000.

The organ was dedicated by the Bishop of Barbados, The Most Reverend Doctor, the Honourable John W.D. Holder, 30 November 2004, at a recital by Philip Forde, FRCO.

When in good repair, the present organ is one of the most splendid pipe organs in Barbados. In size and sophistication, it falls third in its category after the organs of St. Michael's Cathedral and St. James Parish Church. It is a straight 3-manual organ with 25 speaking stops, over 23 ranks of pipes, and a total of 1,299 pipes. A clarion stop is currently being fabricated for installation on the Swell organ (upper manual on most two-and three-manual organs; it is so called because the sound of its pipes can be made to swell and diminish).

One cannot help but appreciate the happy marriage between an impressive historic building and the rich acoustical sound of the St. Andrew's Church organ. The resonance and acoustics are so unique that the impression is produced that the organ and building were custom-designed for complementarity. Superb synergy of sound and enchanting organ music make this historic Church not only renowned for meditation and worship, but ideal for weddings, recitals, and recordings.

Figure 26: Augmented Choir at 2009 Christmas Party after cantata 'A Song Unending'

One of its notable recitals, which attracted rave reviews and drew an audience from over the island, was its 2009 Christmas cantata, *A Song Unending*, composed by John W. Peterson. Figure 26 shows part of the augmented choir that assisted in the recital, while Figure 27 shows the organist and choir director, and part of the audience.

Figure 27: Organist Joyann Catwell

Organists and Assistants (1950–2010)

Over the years St. Andrew's has attracted a number of distinguished organists. The information provided in Table 5 was obtained from senior choir members at the 2009 Christmas Party. With no documentation available, the veracity and completeness of the information could not be verified.

Table 5: St. Andrew's Organists and Assistants (1950–2010)

Organists	Approximate Dates of Service
W. William Worrell	1950s
Charles Vaughan	Charles served in the 1950s until 1959 when the organ used a bellows and was located on the mezzanine floor. Young church members lined up for their turn to pump the organ.[29, 30]
Lester Vaughn	July—December 1955
Louis Marshall	1959–1967
Arlington Brathwaite	1969–1970
Hutson Drakes	1976–1977
Geoffrey Yarde	Few months
Ovid Horton	Few months
Vernon Leacock	Few months in 1979
Cyrillene Harding	1974–1987
Wilbert Cox	2 years in 1980s
Charles Vaughan	1 year in 1980s
Colbert Belgrave	1987-1999
Seymore Allman	3 years
Goldbert Maynard	2001–2005
Livingstone Bowen	2005–2007
Emerson Scantlebury	Few months
Arlington Brathwaite	Few months
Joyann Catwell	2007–2010
Roger Worrell	Few months in 2010
Livingstone Bowen	2010–present

2005—Car Park

Figure 28: Church car park

In his quest to have his Church the best it could be, Rector Gatherer provided a public car park (Figure 28) east of the graveyard for use by persons attending church functions. The 540 square metre car park project, for which arrangements were concluded in June 2005 by Pavements and Foundations (Caribbean) Limited, Black Bess House, Black Bess, St. Peter,[31] was a major undertaking involving:

1. excavating the site to a depth of 18" (0.5 m) approximately, and disposing of the rubble from the site,
2. importing, compacting and levelling the marl-fill,

3. placing approximately two to four inches of crusher-run (2-down) to the existing marl base, grading, compacting and levelling, and
4. applying four inches of concrete (of 3,750 PSI strength) to the compacted area, overlain by A-98 BRC reinforced mesh; broom finishing the surface, and then cutting the edges to prevent cracking.

Indeed, since anything worthwhile exacts a cost, the expenditure estimated at $116,500 for providing a firm foundation for parking to serve this historic Church, which has ably stood the test of time, was justified. Many admirers and users of the car park unceasingly commend the Rector for his foresight in providing such enrichment to the plant. Where else in Barbados do we have such vision in the management of church property, was a question that was proffered but for which no answer was provided!

Figure 29: Cruciform Pavement in grave yard

As an extension to the car park, there was also the installation of a 3.35 metre-wide cruciform-like pavement in the graveyard (see Figure 29). This walkway, costing some $14,950, attractively enhanced access to the plots in the graveyard, especially for use during wet conditions.

In summary, there was a new car park and a levelled, well manicured graveyard with hard-surface cruciform pavements, which traversed its length and breadth. Indeed, Government's enhancement work adjacent to the Church, coupled with Gatherer's unflagging upgrade of the plant, constituted a stellar addition to community beautification that greatly benefited St. Andrew's and the parish as a whole.

2008
Fallen Pride of India

Figure 30: 14-foot diameter remains of 100-year old Pride of India

The ant-ridden Pride of India *(Koelreuteria)* deciduous tree (Figure 30), which flowered beautifully in summer, was the largest tree on the compound, located off the west entrance of the Church. It fell in March 2008 during a morning communion service. To the blessing of the congregation, no injury occurred. For enhancing the landscape of the church grounds, and in the interest of public safety, the tree stump and remains were removed.

2009

In his zeal for continually improving the plant, Rector Gatherer replaced the asbestos roofing and leaking copper guttering of the sanctuary with permaclad sheeting and copper guttering in 2009.

Relationship and membership

Over the years, as the congregation of St. Andrew's grew, additional clergy was provided to serve. For example, in the 1830s and '40s, when the numbers swelled from 300 to 700, at least two priests were delegated to serve. While the incumbents serving in 1834 were not identified, it would appear that they and present-day Rectors like Rev'd. G.C.M. Woodroffe, were able to command crowds and a large congregation. Since growing congregations are associated with leaders' charisma and interest in people, it would seem reasonable to surmise that those early priests, who had remarkable followings, were also charismatic and possessed excellent people-oriented skills (Table 6). This thesis must seriously challenge a church hierarchy that is responsible for selecting and training personnel for leadership today. If the church wants to attract and increase its numbers, and keep congregants, a specific type of aspirant for church leadership must be encouraged. And most significantly, the selection of persons capable of empathetic relations with both the congregation and the parish at large must be made a priority.

Table 6: Clergy and Congregation of St. Andrew's

Year	Clergy	Average Attendance/Congregation
1825	1	100
1834	2	300
1846	2	700[a]
1950s	1	400 odd
2007	2[b]	250
2010	2[c]	200

a. The Church was reported to be able to accommodate 750 persons.
b. Bishop Casper Springer, Rector Gatherer's friend, faithfully assisted him during 2007–2008, especially when Fr. Gatherer was receiving treatment for his eyes and failing health.
c. Dean Emeritus Harold Crichlow, GCM, assisted at St. Andrew's, 2008–March 2011.

Incumbents of St. Andrew

Over the years, the names of at least 24 Rectors, who served the parish for at least one year, have surfaced. This list does not include the unknown number of ministers who would have served in this Church, especially during its early establishment, and the time when incumbents went on leave, on holidays, and for other reasons. Rev'd. G. Cuthbert Woodroffe, who served 1949–1957, also served as Bishop of the Windward Islands and Primate of the West Indies. Succeeding him was Rector Edward Gatherer.

During 1989–1992, while Rector Gatherer was evicted from the Church, other priests lent assistance at St. Andrew's. Rev'd. Laurence Small acted as priest-in-charge for four months. Following Rev'd. Small's stint of service, Rev'd. Dr. Eustace St. Orban McCollin-Moore, who returned to the island from Canada, acted in the cure, just short of two years, from September 1990 until the Privy Council's ruling on 18 June 1992. However, based on the Judgment of the Privy Council in *Gatherer* v *Gomez*, holding that Fr. Gatherer had been wrongfully evicted from his cure, for the record in this book, Rector Gatherer is considered as not having left the parish.

During 1961 and 1962, Rector Gatherer spent a year in training at St. Paul's, London. In his absence, Rev'd. Lionel Burke, who was Priest-in-charge of St. Simon's and St. Saviour's, served at St. Andrew's. Albeit, in this record Rev'd. Gatherer's incumbency as Rector is deemed to have existed from 1 May 1957 to 31 March 2011.

Of the 24 listed incumbents of St. Andrew's (Table 7) Rector Gatherer recorded 54 years of service, followed by Rev'd. Richard Hotchiss and Rev'd. Inniss Milton Alleyne, who served 28 and 27 years, respectively. Comprehensive records for the incumbents were not found; however, in leafing through some Vestry Minutes, one could not help but commend the work for and attention to the churches under their care, and note that many of these incumbents were chairpersons of the Vestry.

Table 7: Incumbents of St. Andrew's Parish Church[32]

Nos.	Incumbents	Time Served	No. of Years
	?	?	?
1	Matthew *William (Richard)* Gray (Grey)	1657–1681	24 odd
2	Thomas Gibbs	1682–1694	12
3	Richard Hotchiss	1694	28
4	Adam Justice	1741	
5	Thomas Duke	1772	
6	William Thomas (died 1801 at 46)	?	
7	John Duke John Bradshaw	?	17
8	William Maynard Payne	1838–1839	1
9	John Hutson John Glasgow Lewis	1839–1847? 1840s–	? ?
10	William Henry Moore	1865–1876	11
11	Henry Hutson	1876–1884	8
12	Edward Lisle Smith	1884–1891	7
13	Philip Lovell Phillips	1892–1897	5
14	Harold Grenville Emtage	1897–1898	1
15	Inniss Milton Alleyne	1898–1925	27
16	Walter Eric Dash	1925–1931	6
17	William Harvey Read	1931–1949	18
18	George Cuthbert M. Woodroffe	1949–1956	7
19	*Edward Godson Gatherer	1957–2011	54
20	*Lionel D. Burke*	*1961–1962*	*1*
21	*Dr. Eustace St. Orban M. Moore*	*1990–1992*	*1.5*
22	Allan Jones	2011–present	

Nevertheless, the dedication and astute service of the leaders of St. Simon's and St. Saviour's stood out, as they petitioned the Vestry for assistance for the improvement and upkeep of their chapels at almost every Vestry meeting.

Commendations for legacy based on information available

1. Canon Edward Godson Gatherer has given his lifetime in faithful and dedicated service at St. Andrew's and in astutely maintaining, enhancing and preserving its plant.
2. Rector Inniss Milton Alleyne (1898–1925) acquired at least 18 acres 38 perches of glebe land for St. Andrew's.
3. Rev. William Harvey Read refurbished the old organ, redecorated the Church by installing reredos, new benches with rails and tiling the floor. He supervised the rebuilding of the St. Andrew's rectory.
4. From the sparse records found, credit should be accorded to Rector John Hutson, who was incumbent during the laying of the cornerstone and dedication of the present Church in 1846. While it was not determined when Fr. Hutson retired or vacated St. Andrew's, during his cure we know that he was assisted and succeeded by Rev'd. John Glasgow Lewis. Sometime during Rev'd. Hutson's and Rev'd. Lewis' ministry, over 700 people reportedly attended St. Andrew's. These clerics oversaw the rebuilding of the existing Church. Fr. Hutson also had the assistance of two curates R.J. Rock and M.G. Clinkett, who served at the chapels of St. Simon's and St. Saviour's.

Gatherer at a glance

Edward Godson Gatherer was:

1. Born 28 January 1922,
2. Ordained Deacon 6 August 1951 on the Feast of Transfiguration at St. Michael and All Angels Cathedral,
3. Ordained Priest, 21 December 1952, by Rt. Rev'd. Gay Leslie Griffith Mandeville on the Feast of St. Thomas,
4. Appointed Priest of St. Ann's Church, 1 June 1953,
5. Appointed Priest of St. Andrew, 1 May 1957,
6. Attended 2 Lambeth Conferences,
7. Performed over 100 weddings on beaches and in hotels in Barbados,
8. Held Agape Love feasts,
9. Took young people to camps at home and overseas (St. Vincent), and was
10. Responsible for causing the rewriting and validation of the Constitution, Canons and Regulations of the Diocese of Barbados.

The Doors Remain Open (1990s–2011) Phase 2

Credit is due to the incumbents of St. Andrew's and especially Canon Gatherer, who has done a stellar undertaking in enhancing and preserving the Church and its grounds, especially over the last 54 years. A senior priest daring to speak on behalf of other senior clergy said that:

> Because of the strength of his colossal contribution to the St. Andrew's and the Anglican diocese of Barbados, Gatherer should have gotten more than a canonry and furthermore, its bestowal should have happened long before, so as to avoid it appearing as a mere good-bye-kiss or begrudging token gesture.[33]

It is reported that long before his conflict with Bishop Gomez, due to his "hard work in the parish" senior clergy had approached bishops prior to the incumbent, recommending that Rev'd. Gatherer be appointed Canon. Fr. Gatherer also deserves due recognition for, at least, impacting, helping, and moulding (list not exhaustive):[34]

- 3 priests—Rev'ds. Hugh Sandiford, S. Lowe, Joel Cumberbatch, to name a few,
- 1 dean—Dr. Frank Marshall, CBE,
- 3 canons—Canon George Knight, Canon Seibert Small and Canon Wilber Austin, USA and
- 1 bishop—Bishop Dr. Wilfred Wood, KA.

Albert Pike so well expressed it: "What we have done for ourselves alone dies with us; what we have done for others and the world remains and is immortal!" Indeed, Fr. Gatherer's unselfish service in St. Andrew will long live on! Objectively, in looking at the broader picture of this priest and his ministry, one cannot but see the legacy of his dedicated service and sacrifice indelibly engraved in the annals of St. Andrew's Parish Church and the parish in general.

Why should not Canon Edward Gatherer be promoted to the St. Andrew's Parish list of honourees and, furthermore, be given a significant national honour for rendering 60 years of social, community, and pastoral service to Barbados, the parish of St. Andrew, and to St. Andrew's Parish Church in particular? A posthumous award or recognition would not suffice.

Notes

1. *English Standard Version Bible*. A publishing ministry of Good News Publishers. http//www.crossway.org Accessed 7 May 2013.
2. *Ibid*.
3. The present Church dates back to 30 November 1846, when the dedication of the corner-stone for rebuilding was performed by Archdeacon Charles Lawson.
4. Interview with Architect Doug Luke, 28 October 2009.
5. *Ibid*.
6. J.V. DeGraff, *et al*. 1989. Transcribed by Nicholas DeGraff, University of California at Santa Cruz. "Landslides: Their extent and significance in the Caribbean", in E.E. Brabb and B.L. Harrod (eds), *Landslides: Extent and Economic Significance*. (Rotterdam: A.A. Balkema, 1989) 51-80. *Landslides in Barbados - University of the West Indies*. www.mona.uwi.edu/uds/Land_Barbados.html
7. Prof. Stephen A. Nelson. "Slope Stability, Triggering Events, Mass Movement Hazards" - Tulane University. Jul 9, 2012 – Natural Disasters, EENS 3050. http://www.tulane.edu/~sanelson/Natural_Disasters/slopestability.pdf. Accessed 29 August 2011.
8. J.V. DeGraff *et. al, op. cit*.
9. Interview with Henderson Catwell. 8 November 2012. Catwell, worker with the Soil Conservation Department, revealed that numerous landslides occurred in the Scotland District following heavy rains and causing collapse of buildings in Parks and Fruitful Hill, Goat Hill and Cambridge, St. Joseph; in Babylon, King Street, St. Simons; and in Mose Bottom, Baxters, Boarded Hall and White Hill, St. Andrew, the latest occurring June 2012. In the latter area, the Ministry of Housing has identified at least 160 houses which had been affected by slippage.
10. W. G. Hutchinson. Vicar of St. Philip-the-Less Church, Boscobel, St. Andrew. "Terrible Landslides in Boscobel. Hundreds of acres silently disappear". *Barbados Advocate Parish Publication*—St. Andrew. *The Barbados Advocate* newspaper, 4 October 1901 (reprinted in issue of 15 December 1996).
11. *Ibid*.
12. Interview with Brian Claxton, 20 December 2009. Engineer Claxton kindly shared some of his engineering evaluations of buildings with problems in the Scotland District.
13. It is disconcerting at times, when you visit some urban and suburban churches where there has never been ravishes of subsidence and structural problems, as are common in the Scotland District, to find broken windows or some falling off, missing glass, premises with overgrown grass and shrubs, patches of or unpainted walls, broken or defective pews, defective lighting, where only a little care and effort would make a difference.

    It never ceases to amaze me why leaders of some churches fail to see what a can of paint, pulling a few weeds, restoring a pane of glass, putting a nail or two in a board, restoring a light bulb, replacing a rail, filling a small pothole in the driveway, 'sticking back' the pages of a few hymn books, and removing cobweb would do to enhance the church plant. And often these small chores do not need significant, or any monetary expenditure (often, only a little devotion)!

What does this require? A bit of common sense, imagination, love for the plant, a pair of spectacles, training, what? Ask Fr. Gatherer!

14. *The Visitor*, 15–18 June 1987.
15. Interview with Winston Alleyne, 12 December 2009.
16. Engineer Brian Claxton, 20 December 2009.
17. Interview with Stephen Griffith, 7 September 2012.
18. Bishop Gomez's Report to the Annual Session of Synod, *Synod Journal* 1991, 7.
19. *Ibid*. "Barbados Diocesan Trustees—1991, St. Andrew's Rectory", 12.
20. Interview with Everton Bovell, 11 October 2011
21. "Road Project Ends November". *Daily Nation*, 22 April 1998.
22. Interviews with Cheryl Hurst and Cyrillene Harding, 16 March 2010.
23. Dean Emeritus Harold Crichlow, GCM. 1992 Sermon at the Commemoration Service for Rector Gatherer's 35 Years' Service at St. Andrew's Parish Church.
24. David Burke and Sons, Organ Builder. Edited and unpublished notes. Accessed 20 October 2010.
25. Credit is given to Mr. David Burke, Burke's Pipe Organ Service through whom much of the information on the organ was obtained via interviews and discussion.
26. The Church Commissioners, England, were responsible for maintaining church buildings and furnishings in the UK.
27. Fr. Gatherer entreated the management of Sagueney Shipping Service, which often travelled to Barbados empty to collect cargo (sugar), to ship two refurbished pipe organs to Barbados free. The management accepted an offer that, in return, any time they wanted to vacation in the island, Fr. Gatherer would accommodate them free of cost in St. Andrew. Accordingly, Sagueney readily shipped the organs—one for St. Philip's Parish Church and the other one, along with a console, for St. Andrew's.
28. The Clearing House no longer exists at Harrisville. Others may be found in other states, e.g. Massachusetts.
29. Interview with George Beckles, 26 July 2011.
30. Maxwell, Patrick and Stanton Jordan. 20 October 2012. These interviewees revealed that in the early days, in the absence of electricity, young men (organ blowers) would 'pump the pipe organ' i.e. inflate the bellows, through moving a long wooden arm or handle attached to the bellows up and down. Inflating the bellows supplied air (forced air into) to the pipes for producing sound when the organist pressed keys on the manual or pedals.

In the 1940s, the Vestry Minutes revealed that the organ blower at St. Andrew's was paid a fee of $45.00 per month for pumping the pipe organ for church services, practices, funerals and weddings. By 1954 he was paid $82.00 per month.

It was reported that these workers looked forward to performing their job with pride and pleasure.

31. Interview with Deborah Turney, 29 August 2011.

32. The majority of this information was extracted from Undine Whittaker's unpublished notes, viewed 9 December 2009.
33. Interview with Rev'd. Laurence Small, MBE, 4 December 2012.
34. Interview with Simeon Belgrave, 9 February 2013.

CHAPTER EIGHT

Parishioners of note who attended St. Andrew's Parish Church

Hugh Worrell Springer

Hugh Worrell Springer (1913–1994) was born in St. Andrew, and as a little boy attended St. Andrew's. He was educated at Wesley Hall Primary School under Headmaster A. Rawle Parkinson, and later at Harrison College. He achieved an Island Scholarship in 1931 which allowed him to attend Hertford College in Oxford. There he gained a B.A. degree in 1936, and an M.A. in 1944. He studied law at the Inner Temple, London, and was called to the Bar in 1938.

A few of his distinctions include:

Hugh, the lawyer, practised at the Bar in Barbados, 1938–47. He was organiser and First General Secretary of the Progressive League between 1940 and 1947, during which time he established an economic arm that became the Barbados Workers Union (BWU). He was the BWU's First General Secretary.

He was regarded as an organising genius in the labour movement, and authored *Reflections on the Failure of the First West Indian Federation* (1962). He served as Commonwealth Assistant Secretary-General, 1966–70; Secretary-General of the Association of Commonwealth Universities, 1970–80; Senior Visiting Fellow, All Souls College, Oxford 1962–63; Acting Governor, Barbados 1964, and finally, Governor-General, Barbados, 1984–90.[1]

Hugh Worrell Springer was a classical scholar, professor in classics, educator, writer, regional and international publisher, lawyer, outstanding administrator, politician, leader of organised labour (General Secretary), parliamentarian, member of the Government and National Hero.

What else could be expected of this consummate Barbadian who excelled in every area of endeavour?

For him, it was not enough to advance only in Barbados. In addition to serving his country with distinction, he also ventured further afield. Between 1947–63, he lent regional assistance in accepting the position of Registrar of the University College of the West Indies, Barbados, then went on to become the Registrar of the University of the West Indies, Mona, Jamaica. In 1963–66, he was Director of the Commonwealth

Education Liaison Unit, Commonwealth Assistant Secretary-General, and Secretary-General of the Association of Commonwealth Universities. His long and distinguished academic career and public service marked Sir Hugh among the greatest Barbadians of all time. As a highly accomplished citizen of Barbados, he remained passionately committed to making a difference.

In 1942 he married Dorothy Gittens, and they had three sons and a daughter. Sir Hugh was the third native Governor-General of Barbados following Independence in 1966. He served for six successive years, 1984 to June 1990, when he suffered a stroke.[2] He died in Barbados on 14 April 1994.

Both St. Andrew and St. Andrew's Parish Church profoundly note and honour their association with Sir Hugh Springer, GCVO, KA, CBE, OBE.

George Livingston Blackett[3]

George Livingston Blackett grew up in St. Andrew's. He was a student of the Alleyne School, which in those days "was not a first grade school as it did not enter students for the Higher Cambridge certificate".[4]

H.B.W. St. John, Headmaster of the Alleyne School, "spotted Blackett as a bright boy, and obtained permission from the Education Board to prepare him for an Island Scholarship, which he sat in 1931".[5] In those days, only one such scholarship was offered annually, and the student who performed best did not necessarily obtain it.

One of his contemporaries, Hugh Springer, who was also born in St. Andrew, attended Harrison College at the time. It was believed in some circles, even though not confirmed, that Blackett received a higher mark than Springer; nevertheless, Springer was awarded the Barbados Scholarship.

Blackett went to Belize where he was appointed teacher, later principal, and eventually the Director of Education. He was subsequently ordained as priest and rose to the position of Dean of the Cathedral of Belize.[6]

Dean Blackett retired in 1978. Only months after retirement, Bishop Sylvester of Belize and his wife succumbed to a fatal car accident in December of the same year; consequently, the See became vacant. The retired Dean reportedly came out of retirement and declared his availability to be appointed bishop to succeed Sylvester. Unfortunately, he was not chosen.

This accomplished Barbadian, now deceased, who excelled in every venture of his life, was nurtured in St. Andrew's Parish Church.

Darry Atfield Foster, Member of Parliament

Darry Atfield Foster of Belleplaine, St. Andrew, with his family, attended St. Andrew's Parish Church. He became a member of the Vestry from age 23 years, and served from 1920 to 1958. He was the parliamentary representative of St. Andrew during 1946–1951.[7]

Darry 'helped to overhaul the Vestry'. During those times (early twentieth century), there were high incidences of food and waterborne (communicable) diseases—diarrhoea, dysentery (caused by a bacterial, parasitic, or protozoan infection), typhoid (bacterial disease transmitted by the ingestion of food or water contaminated with the faeces of a person usually infected with *Salmonella typhi*) and other gastro-intestinal (parasitic) diseases.

Some novel environmental interventions in St. Andrew over which he presided saw the introduction of the waterborne system (use of water closet),[8] which was to replace the dry conservancy (use of bucket/pit latrine) method of excreta disposal[9], as the Barbados Water Authority's running water reached St. Andrew during late 1949 and early 1950. He spearheaded the upgrading of storm water drainage in the parish. With the absence of culverts along the roadside, workers had 'to provide deep, graded trenches beside the roads to receive and channel storm water to watercourses and gullies'.[10] Land reclamation and draining of stagnant water collections substantially reduced mosquito breeding foci and helped to control the malaria scourge of those days. Improving storm water drainage and excreta disposal strategically impacted the sanitation in the flat districts, striking a two-pronged attack in reducing both vector and waterborne diseases. He also oversaw the Poor Law Board which increased the old age pension from 48¢ to 50¢ per week.[11]

Following his death in March 1951, while serving as an elected member of parliament, his daughter, Mrs. Ermyntrude Bourne, contested the bi-election created by the vacant seat left by her father and won.

Dame Edna Ermyntrude Bourne, DA

Women in Barbados acquired the right to vote and become members of either House of Parliament in 1944, as long as they had the same qualifications as men. And so, Mrs. Edna Ermyntrude Bourne, Belleplaine, St. Andrew contested and won a Barbados Labour Party seat in the December 1951 General Election, following in the footstep of her father who predeceased her earlier that year. Having been returned to the House of Assembly as the elected member for the Parish of St. Andrew, she became the first female elected member of the House of Assembly under adult suffrage. She represented her Parish until 1961.

In her honour, the East Coast Road, which was officially opened by Her Majesty Queen Elizabeth II of England on Tuesday, 15 February 1966, was renamed the Ermy Bourne Highway on 23 August 2006.

MP Bourne received the distinguished honour of Dame of St. Andrew in the November 1995 National Awards of Barbados.

Sir Conrad Hunte

Conrad Cleophas Hunte, famous right-hand batsman and right-arm medium pace fast bowler, was born in Shorey Village, St Andrew. In his youth, he and his family attended St. Andrew's. He grew up playing cricket in the village, and at the Alleyne School, where he was educated. Hunte came to national attention in 1950–51, after scoring 100 at age 18, in the match when the annual Barbados Cricket Association played against the Barbados Cricket League. His big break, however, came in 1955–56, when Barbados played against E. W. Swanton's XI. On that this occasion he made 151 and 95 runs.

During the Pakistan tour of the Caribbean in 1958, Conrad emerged as an opening batsman of high calibre, scoring 142 runs on his home ground at Kensington Oval. In the third Test Match of that series later in Kingston, Jamaica, he made 260, while batting with Garry Sobers in a record-breaking partnership of 446, after which Sobers went on to achieve his illustrious world record of 365 not-out on 1 March 1958, only later to be broken by Brian Lara's 400 not-out in the fourth Test innings against England in Antigua in August 2004.

In his heyday, 1958 through 1967, Hunte played in 44 test matches, accumulating 3245 runs with a batting average of 45.06, even though he played with different opening partners. As a consummate batsman, he scored eight centuries, securing a century against every country he played.

After his defining moment in 1961, he began ministering as a committed religious person, to the underprivileged and oppressed, and to work at promoting harmonious human relations and moral rearmament. He unashamedly shared his convictions with his colleagues.

In 1997, Hunte was awarded Barbados's highest honour, the Order of St Andrew. He died of a heart attack on 3 December 1999, at age 67, after playing tennis in Sydney. Sir Conrad was one of the greatest West Indian batsmen of his generation.

For years, the Shorey Village Cricket Ground, St. Andrew, was popularly called The Conrad Hunte Cricket Ground, and its Pavilion is known as the Conrad Hunte Pavilion. These, even though unofficially designated, have been appropriately named in honour of the outstanding West Indian batsman—Sir Conrad Hunte (May 1932–December 1999).

Mrs. Erma Rock

Mrs. Erma Rock was proprietress of the Rocklyn Bus Company (Rocklyn), St. Andrew, and a member of the Vestry of St. Andrew for many years. Her company was one of not less than eight private bus companies licensed by the Director of Transport to operate in Barbados. With the genesis of Rocklyn, Barbados' only train service from Bridgetown to the terminus in Belleplaine, St. Andrew, fell into obsolescence and ceased operation in 1937.[12,13] A picture of Barbados's Baldwin locomotive (tank) engine, 1898[14] may be viewed at Figure 31. Remnants of the terminus which comprised one of 98 railway bridges are still evident in Belleplaine (Figure 14).

Figure 31: Baldwin locomotive (tank) engine, 1898

Parishioners of note who attended St. Andrew's Parish Church

The eight buses (Figure 32), which provided transportation from Belleplaine to Bridgetown, mainly operated at peak times in the morning and evening. A mid-afternoon service was added in later years.

Figure 32: Fleet of Rocklyn buses

With a highly motivated staff that took care of the buses, Rocklyn Bus Service was generally efficient. The proprietress was humane, business-like, approachable, affable and, in every way, a woman who showed and received respect.[14] In addition to overseeing Seniors, Parks and Cambridge Plantations, Mrs. Rock built, sold or rented solidly fabricated timber houses mainly for the people of her parish. Not as a politician or towering leader, but as an ordinary member of St. Andrew's Parish Church, Mrs. Rock served her parish, the Vestry, and her generation with wisdom, dignity and kindness.

A. Dacosta Edwards, MP

Although Dacosta "Joy" Edwards was not a parishioner, his presence and work in St. Andrew, and the number of religious concerts and performances he sponsored in the parish at the Parish Church and other churches, qualified him for more than passing attachment to St. Andrew's and for inclusion in this work.

In addition to serving as Member of Parliament for St. Andrew (1961–1967), Dacosta Edwards distinguished himself as a business man who built for, sold or rented houses to people in St. Andrew and beyond. As founder of the Glee Club (refer to Appendix 2), a large combined choir, he endeared himself not only to St. Andrew's Church, when his choir performed at concerts, Service of Songs, harvests, etc. to glowing tributes, but throughout the churches of Barbados and the organisations he visited.

In serving the nation, Edwards' Federal High School, in Bridgetown, provided education free, or at a reduced cost, to scores of the underprivileged and poor of Barbados.[15] For his national contribution to Barbados, and in his honour, the St. Andrew's Primary School was renamed the A. DaCosta Edwards Primary School on 22 June 2011.

Rev'd. George Harris Dickenson

George Harris Dickenson arrived from St. Andrew. It was reported that Rector William Harvey Read adopted him, and sent him to Codrington College, where he trained for the ministry.[16] On graduating, he served at the Cathedral of St. Michael and All Angels as Assistant Curate with responsibility for All Souls', and later St. Cyprian's, churches and completed a period of ministry in Antigua. He served at St Philip-the-Less Church (1950–1951) and St. Joseph's Parish Church (1962–1969). It was reported that he also served at All Saints Church and St. James' Parish Church.[17]

The Venerable Rev'd. James Levi Springer, GCM (1935-2013)[18]

James "Jimmy" Levi Springer was born, educated, and also worked in St. Andrew. He grew up in St. Andrew's Parish Church, having served as Sergeant Major Instructor in the Church Lads' Brigade (1950–1957), Leader of the Anglican Young People's Association (AYPA), and as a Licensed Lay Reader from age 20.

On leaving Codrington College he was ordained Deacon in 1960 and priest in 1961. He was the first Headmaster of St. Cyprian's Preparatory Boy's School (Cathedral School) during 1961–1965. He married Nancy Clairmonte on 18 July 1964.

In continuing his work in education, Rev'd. Springer taught Sociology at UWI Cave Hill, and Sociology and Pastoral Care at Codrington College.

Rev'd. Springer led the rebuilding programme of St. Leonard's Church (1981–1985). He sat on several national boards and commissions. He was "Talk-show Host" on the VOB Radio programme "Tell It Like It Is". Not only was he an avid writer on a wide range of church issues, he was also a respected newspaper columnist. In 1991, he was appointed an Independent Senator by the Governor General. For his service to the Church and Community he duly deserved his Gold Crown of Merit in 1992.

Rev'd. Springer was the first black Rector of St. Leonard's and he served for 22½ years. He was elevated to Canon in the Stall of St. Basil, Cathedral Chapter in 1975, became a Rural Dean of St. Michael in 1991 and Archdeacon in 1993. He served on various advisory and pastoral missions at the Diocesan, Provincial and regional levels.

Canon Springer died on 21 October 2013 and at his funeral on 31 October 2013, Archbishop of West Indies and Bishop of Barbados, The Most Rev'd., The Hon. Dr. John Holder praised him for his hard work and dedication in serving the Church of Barbados as Priest from his ordination in 1961 to his retirement as Archdeacon of Barbados.

George Winston Beckles

George Beckles of Belleplaine was educated at the St. Andrew's Boys' and the Alleyne School, St. Andrew.

After completing his tertiary education, he spent 36 of his 40 years in the teaching service at the Alleyne School, where from 1992–2001 he was appointed Principal. His remit of social activities in part included being President of the Alleyne School Alumni Association, and singing with, and supporting several choral groups and choirs across Barbados.

In supporting the St. Andrew's Parish Church, Mr. Beckles was a chorister under organists Messrs. Charles Vaughan, Louis Marshall, Geoffrey Yarde, Livingstone Bowen and Arlington Brathwaite. He was a Sunday school teacher, Sunday school superintendent, and a member of the Parish Church Council.

Response of parishioners who lived overseas

Although this work only interviewed a few returning nationals or persons living overseas that were connected with the St. Andrew's Parish Church, it was clear to the writer from the number of persons who attended church on their return on holiday, from the many who came to pay tribute at Canon Gatherer's retirement, that St. Andrew's had a profound impact on persons who had an earlier affiliation with it. From discussion with persons on holiday, or who had retuned on business, or for funerals, it became clear that many people nurtured in St. Andrew's Parish church went on to become persons of distinction around the world. The fact that many such persons returned to visit or attend the Church, and express appreciation, some of whom took great pleasure in presenting offerings and gifts, donating vestments and other assets during their visits spoke eloquently of their attachment to and of the benefit they received from this Church.

Other Persons

While time and space will limit mention of all the deserving persons with stellar connection to the St. Andrew's Parish Church, and who particularly made significant contributions in the parish, regard is paid to Homie Corbin, MP, McDonald Smith, and village shop keepers Delbert Lynch, Edmond Bourne and Siebert Small.

Notes

1. "Sir Hugh Worrell Springer". 1913–1994. . . In 1998, Springer was named one of Barbados' National Heroes thus. . . http://www.independent.co.uk/news/people/obituary-sir-hugh-springer-1433334.html Accessed 7 April 2013.
2. "Caribbean Elections". Sir Hugh Worrell Springer. Accessed 7 April 2013.
3. Interview with Rev'd. Laurence Small, MBE, 20 November 2013
4. ___, 4 April 2013.
5. *Ibid.*
6. 2011 Journal of the One Hundred and Forty-First Annual Meeting of the Synod of the Church of Jamaica and the Cayman Islands in the Province of the West Indies.
7. Interview with Darry Foster's son, 94-year old John Foster, retired Chief Public Health Inspector, 26 November 2013.
8. No doubt this novel sanitary improvement was encouraged by Darry's son, John Foster, who was a Senior Public Health Inspector of St. Andrew.
9. The dry conservancy system comprising the bucket/pit latrine or outdoor privy was usually an outdoor room for the deposition of human excreta. It contained a seat, from which a user would defecate into a bucket or pail. The bucket was usually emptied by the local authority and the contents buried.

    This system, which was widespread in the island, was fraught with environmental problems resulting from poor basic sanitation and hygiene practices and user neglect—buckets being overfilled and spilling of faeces—providing ready habitats for flies, roaches and other vermin, coupled with the concomitant proliferation of diseases.

    Later, disused 55-gallon metal drums replaced the bucket/pail containers which comprised a more modern environment sanitary pit latrine in the absence of a waterborne system.
10. John Foster, 26 November 2013.
11. *Ibid.*
12. Sylvan Catwell. *The Brethren in Barbados: Gospel Hall Assemblies, 1889–1994.* (USA, Michigan: McNaughton & Gunn, 1995), 119.
13. "The History of the Barbados Railway". [PDF] - Enuii.org http://www.enuii.org/vulcan_foundry/.../The%20Barbados%20Railway.pdf. Accessed 10 December 2009.
14. "The Barbados Railway" 1873 - 1937 - A Bajan Tour Girl Exploring ... http//www.abajantourgirlexploringbarbados.blogspot.com/.../barbados-railway-187... Accessed 7 April 2013
15. Interview with Berkeley Knight and Bertram Murray, 21 January 2010.
16. Interview with Gwendolyn Grecia and Gwendolyn Gibbons, 21 January 2010.
17. Rev'd. Laurence Small, MBE, 22 November 2013.
18. *Ibid.*
19. Extracted from an unpublished, undated typewritten copy of the Resumé of Senator The Rev'd. Canon James Livi Springer, GCM, 22 November 2013

CHAPTER NINE

Attractions and Places of Significance within 10 minutes drive from St. Andrew's

A look around Barbados from Mt. Hillaby, St. Andrew, the country's highest natural elevation, which peaks at approximately 1160 feet (353.5 m) in the southern part of the parish is a rewarding experience.

If you fancy a wild, woody hike in St. Andrew, check out Turner's Hall Woods. Get the feel of an enchanting equatorial forest with large cedars, fustic, bully and locust trees. Nestling in the higher elevation of this parish, Turner's Hall is one of Barbados' oldest natural reserves or parks. And try not to miss its Boiling Spring. Drilling in the area produced 250,000 barrels of crude oil. Earlier exploration at Cattlewash in the parish in the 1860s revealed oil at 100 feet depth, but in less than commercial quantities. Whether you fish in Long Pond or patronise Bajan one-of-a-kind pottery in Chalky Mount, you won't forget the experience in St. Andrew.

The coastal area of St. Andrew is not only a stunning attraction, but it constitutes one of the most breathtaking coastlines you will encounter. Opportunity exists for once-in-a-lifetime picture-perfect camera shots of St. Andrew and its rugged, but uniquely beautiful coastline from Cherry Tree Hill, St. Peter, or Chapel Hill and Bathsheba, St. Joseph, for choice gifts to cherished friends and for creating postcards.

What about planning a picnic on a bright sunny day, or simply eating lunch or a snack beneath the trees on the East Coast, or climbing the hillside of Barclays Park (Figure 33), which was opened by Her Majesty Queen Elizabeth in 1966. This is a

Figure 33: Picnic at Barclays Park

memorable site for a picnic and presents the opportunity to wade in the rock pools off this Park.

Enjoy the expansive view of scenic Cattlewash (where cattle once used to bathe), or the pounding milky Atlantic waves of the rugged East Coast.

If you are not feeling well, or you simply want to hide away, or perhaps just surf, visit Bathsheba where missionaries and soldiers from Guyana, South America, and England recovered from malaria and other illness in the early nineteenth century.[1] While enjoying a home-made Bajan beverage or local rum punch, take a Bathsheba bath in the salubrious waters of the life-giving pools of seawater and come away revived.

There are lovely beaches on the East Coast, some with strong currents; if you decide to take a swim, for your safety follow the directions given by the National Conservation Commission and choose those beaches recommended in order to avoid dangerous 'under currents'. If you like walking, start from Walker's Beach; move on to Lakes Beach, and then on to Morgan Lewis Beach; or from Walker's Beach, you may proceed to St. Andrew's Parish Church for an engrossing trek through its well-maintained graveyard and historic sanctuary. The more daring may also want to trudge through the original, now wooded, graveyard of St. Andrew's Parish Church (Figures 34 and 35). A search for Vaughan's 1733 tombstone, or even trying to decipher the inscriptions on ancient tombstones can be an engaging occupation for an afternoon.

Figure 34: Entering the original graveyard

Attractions and Places of Significance within 10 minutes drive from St. Andrew's

Figure 35: Wooded graveyard at Top

Places to be wary of

Magnetic Hill, Morgan Lewis

How would you like to risk your car in the Morgan Lewis area? You may drive down this road, but do not stop or and leave your car in neutral on the trip down Magnetic Hill. That is, if you do not want to risk it automatically rolling back up the hill.

On that crucial spot in Morgan Lewis, cars reportedly don't coast downwards; incredibly, they just roll back up the Hill.[2]

Cock's Crow Rock, Cleland

You may visit the location by choice; but if you wish to avoid having your car or vehicle shut down (stall), you should bypass travelling to Cock's Crow Rock. You will be startled to learn that cars, trucks, motorcycles and even buses hardly escape the repairman for daring to venture past this Rock.[3]

Adventures

For an adventure through St. Andrew woodlands, choose whether you want to hike on foot or ride on horseback. For the mature and daring, why not go quad biking with ATV Quest? Do you want an up-close encounter with Barbados' green monkeys? Then take your party or family to the Barbados Wildlife Reserve and enjoy the turtles and other interesting wildlife exhibits.

Potters can be observed at work while you shop for exquisite gifts, hand-made from Barbados' unique clay. Visit the Chalky Mount Potteries, where artisans have 'thrown pots' for over 300 years. In addition to exploring the variety of Barbadian pottery, you will be intrigued by the rugged elevated Chalky Mount cliffs, the beautiful view of the East Coast, St. Andrew, and the very picturesque green highlands of St. Peter and St. Joseph.

Farley Hill National Park

Farley Hill National Park contains a superb collection of exotic trees and the shell of a luxurious plantation house (Figure 36), once the finest mansion in Barbados. Only the stone walls remain after the 99-window mansion was destroyed by fire. The Park is used for national festivals, including Jazz and "Reggae on the Hill", for picnics and excursions, and basically as a picturesque, cool, breezy recreational amenity, especially when you sit out on the eastern elevated slopes.

Figure 36: Remnant of Farley Hill Plantation House

St. Nicholas Abbey

In addition to the Alleyne School, there is the opportunity to visit another property that belonged to Sir John Gray Alleyne, St Nicholas Abbey, St. Peter (Figure 37), one of three unique Plantation Great Houses and Jacobean mansions in the western hemisphere.

Reportedly built in 1658[4], in style and construction dating back as far as the Tudor times of James I, this mansion and property, styled as worthy to be one of the Wonders of the World with its lovely mahogany, cabbage palm and avocado trees, has many relics and showpieces that attract visitors year-round.

Figure 37: St. Nicholas Abbey, St. Peter

Sand Dunes Restaurant

When you want a cold drink, light snack, or a great Bajan lunch while in St. Andrew, stop in at the brightly-painted roadside Sand Dunes Bar & Restaurant (Figure 38), on the Ermy Bourne Highway (East Coast Road), which is open daily from 9:00 a.m. to 9:00 p.m. It is the perfect stop for locals and visitors alike, where there is always a warm and friendly atmosphere. Enjoy breakfast or its evening one-of-a-kind fresh-off-the-grill meals—the Friday evening lively session, and Saturday can't-miss Puddin' & Souse, a famous Bajan delicacy.

Morgan Lewis Mill

Morgan Lewis Mill, St. Andrew, restored in 1996, is one of only two mills in operation in Barbados worth a 'drop-by' to revisit the mainstay industry of the island's history (Figure 39), and reputedly the Caribbean's largest and only working windmill.

Figure 38: Sand Dunes Bar & Restaurant, East Coast, St. Andrew

Figure 39: Morgan Lewis Mill, St. Andrew

Notes

1. Sylvan Catwell. *The Brethren in Barbados: Gospel Hall Assemblies, 1889—1994*. (USA, Michigan: McNaughton & Gunn, 1995), 119.
2. Interview with Richard Hoad, 15 March 2013.
3. *Ibid*.
4. Larry Warren. Undated typewritten note, accessed 5 November 2013.

CHAPTER TEN

Graves and Inscriptions connected with St. Andrew's Parish Church

Graves' Inscriptions from Monumental Inscriptions

The majority of the inscriptions (except those noted in blue) have been extracted from *Monumental Inscriptions of Barbados* by Major Henry A. Thorne, *Archer's Monumental Inscriptions of the British West Indies* by Captain J.H. Lawrence Archer and *Monumental Inscriptions: Tombstones of the Island of Barbadoes* by Vere Langford. Oliver noted that some of the inscriptions were not decipherable due to omissions or fading of the letters, and so, sometimes clarifying notes were added. As there was no intention to edit the work of these authors, the undecipherable extracts were reproduced as noted. Inscriptions in blue were actual sightings observed by the writer in the overgrown original graveyard, and in St. Andrew's Parish Church and its graveyard. Following the Inscriptions at Table 8 are a few photographs of the slab and inscription of John Food's grave, and a grave slab with undecipherable words found at the entrance of the graveyard (see pages 191–192).

Most of the inscriptions, plaques, and tablets were not actually visible at the time of writing as they were defaced, removed during refurbishing of the Church, covered by carpeting, or removed during the regrading of the graveyard. Others in the disused burial ground (off Benjamin's Sandhole), the original graveyard, had been covered by debris, vines, accreted sand and bushes while others have been defaced with time or vandalised. Following carpeting and tiling of the Church, many of the inscriptions were no longer visible.

Table 8: Inscriptions of St. Andrew's Parish Church

Inscriptions in the Church	
On a white marble slab in floor of the Sanctuary on left side of the Altar:— Sacred to the Memory of FRANCES BOOTMAN daughter of FRANCIS & REBECA BOOTMAN Born October 29th A.D. 1787 who departed this Life July 13th 1819 Aged 30 Years A Dutiful Child, a Kind Relation; and a Benevolent Heart C. Rossi	*On a white marble slab in floor of the Sanctuary on right side of the Altar:—* A friend causes this stone to be erected to the memory of JAN ANN THOMPSON *Freed Coloured Woman* and her Three infant children as a mark of Esteem and Gratitude for the Faithful Services of the former who departed this life January the 27th 1810 Aged 75 years C. Rossi
White marble on south wall of the chancel In Memory of ROBERT Infant son of Col. Ross, R.E. And of ALETHA EMMA his wife Born May 5, 1864 Died October 17, 1864.	*On a grey marble slab in the floor of tower or entrance (west) porch:—* Here Lyeth Interr'd ye Body of Mrs. MARY MORRIS ye Daughter of Majr ROBERT MORRIS born ye 14th Day of March 1694 Married to JAMES DO . . . N ESQR the 7th of February 1713 Departed this life ye 12 Day of July 1720.
On a grey marble slab in the floor of tower: To the Memory of *ELIZABETH MARY* Daughter of *SAMUEL MAYERICK* Esquire and Wife of *ANTHONY GREGG M.D.* (erected by husband) (died) on the 23 Day of Octr 1790, Aged 49 Years (?4).	*Party under the steps to the pulpit:* To the . . . JACOB HINDS and . . . Who departed this . . . the former in September 18. . . Aged 68 the latter July the 10th 1806 Aged 58 Years *Their affectionate Son JACOB HINDS has caused to be erected this Marble as a lasting tribute to his affectionate and tender Parents*
East window: IN MEMORIAN COLERIDGE HUDSON	

Graves and Inscriptions connected with St. Andrew's Parish Church

Inscriptions in the Church (cont'd)	
In the chancel floor near the communion rail: Here Lyes Interred the Body of TURPIN WILLOUGHBY Who Departed This Life March The 2, 1741 Aged 61 years.	*Floor of northeast of nave:* Here lies: the Body of ANN POOLE Who departed this Life The . . . day of January 1740 Aged 56 Years.
(On two halves of grey marble in the floor. On the upper half): Here lieth the Body of MARGARET RUDD . . . *(several worn away lines*)* . . . 52. Here alfo . . . Body of . . . DAVID RUDDER Esq. . . . v Elizabeth Rudder Who departed this life *the second half has poetry.)* * *Archer gives "Daughter of David & Elizabeth Rudder, died June 16, 1752 . . . Also David Rudder her father died April 17, 1753."*	*In South aisle:* Here lyes the body of Mrs. Lucy Johnstown—departed this life 9th 1680 being about 22 years *In the S. Aisle:* Here lies the Body (of the) Rev. William Thomas Rector of this Parish who died Dec. 20, 1801, age 46 years.
Inscriptions in the Church Graveyard	
On a marble headstone: In memory of Samuel Maynard Alleyne eldest son of S. M. and S. A. Alleyne he was born 25th August 1808 and drowned while bathing at Bathsheba May 29th 1847	*Cross:—* This sepulchre Belongs to the REV. JOHN DUKE In which is deposited the. . . . . . JOHN BBADSHAW M.A. B.M. T.C.D. (fOR 17 TEARS RECTOS OF THIS parish) I. . . and MARY JANE BRADSHAW (erected by children)

Inscriptions in the Disused Burial Ground (Graveyard of Original Church) off Benjamin Sandhole	
Headstone Sacred to the memory of Francis Bootman, daughter of Francis and Rebecca Bootman. Born October 29th 1819 age 30 years.	*On a semi-circular grave stone partially covered with sand and lying beneath a cashew tree* Here lies the body of John Foord, Gent. who was B—1617, and died—. *(He was probably an ancestor of Thomas Ford, Esq. of Barbados, great grand father of Sir Francis Ford, created Baronet in 1793.*
Fragment on broken stone VAUGHAN, 1733	
Inscriptions on headstones in the Church grave yard	
In loving memory of Sir Conrad C. Hunte Knight of St. Andrew West Indies Cricketer 1932–1999 Rest In Peace	In Loving Memory of Erma Rock Beloved Aunt Sister and Friend Who went away with Jesus On 1st July 1980 May she Rest In Peace

Figure 40: Clearing slab of John Foord's grave

Figure 41: Inscription on grave of John Foord... B—1617

Figure 42: Tombstone of Sir Conrad Hunte

Figure 43: Slab of grave found near entrance of original graveyard

Figure 44: Tombstone of Rev'd. John Hutson

Figure 45: Tombstone of Erma Rock

CHAPTER ELEVEN

Canon Gatherer and Retirement

Retirement

The time comes when a hard-working, committed person will retire. This happens despite how much one loves the job. Stay long enough in church work and your time will come. Working 'wears down the spirit, soul and body', especially when there is not proportionate appreciation in return for effort expended.

It is interesting to sit in the 'departure lounge' (just where the writer sat in writing this manuscript) listening to persons who would like to occupy your position, or who can no longer tolerate your holding the position, and cannot wait to have it for their friend or family member. Invariably, some impatient people come up to you to ask:

1. When are you retiring?
2. When are you going to begin to enjoy your big gratuity?
3. Why don't you vacate this job and provide opportunity for some younger, unemployed person?
4. When are you going to spend some more time with your family?, and the litany of queries goes on.

Recently I overheard a report concerning a very senior professional in Government, who sharply retorted to the promptings regarding retirement by saying that he never begged for a job, and he would not give up his lawful profession and go chasing after another.

The conscientious professional is to be applauded for his answer. Reportedly he generally turns in a commendable performance for which he duly commands respect. The Chief Executive Officer in question serves in a distinguished office that several admirers would like to have. But he earned his right to acquire and keep his position. Similarly, prospective executives and employees need to earn their right to legitimately acquire the profession or vocation of their choice, and lawfully keep it until they choose to retire, or are made aware of a legal limit to their tenure. This is the most equitable way for all concerned.

The benefice of St. Andrew's is an attractive one for which several leaders and aspiring leaders understandably yearned. Many persons look forward to serving in the beautiful parish with its salubrious coastal breeze, an attractive church, a lovely pipe organ, and the place where many weddings and funerals are often held. Some aspirants could not wait to assume the envied incumbency. A number of people opined that it was time for a younger person to take the rectorship and 'do the job better'. Others quibbled that a 'more experienced cleric was preferred', while still some suggested a more charismatic, more energetic, more caring, more people-oriented person should assume the position. Of course the list went on and on.

Eager enthusiasts (not the Eager Eleven)[1] who could not wait reportedly surged ahead and asked the incumbent for his job, to put it mildly. Some friends and well-wishers or impatient persons urged him to find another cure. Others suggested that he engage in alternative ministry, while another attempted to axe him.

What is this thing about retirement?

The Anglican Church Act 1969, the Constitution, Canons and Regulations of the Diocese of Barbados, together with the deliberations related to the *Gomez* v *Gatherer* confrontation, have quite comprehensively addressed the matter of retirement of clergy and other diocesan staff. Regulations E3 of the Diocesan Pension Fund in part state:

1. There shall be a Fund to provide pensions for the clergy and other diocesan employees, their widows and orphans, which shall be vested in the Barbados Diocesan Trustees.
2. The Fund shall be managed by the Trustees in accordance with rules made by Synod and administered in accordance with regulations made by the Trustees and approved by Synod, which rules and regulations shall be printed and appended to these Regulations.

Indeed, abundant comment on the subject can be found in circulating literature. But could there not be a more humane approach to retirement in the interest of all concerned? The real issue is not physical facilities, or providing retirement villages, or having an enviable stipend (from the church and government), but simply adequate provision to help clergy to retire gracefully and to live in dignity thereafter. Moreover, in realising that they work hard in helping so many people to live, marry and die, we need to ask:

1. What is done for clergy during the period that predates dying? How tolerable is the twilight age when you are no longer able to serve, and few people are willing to remember you, far less to serve you?

2. How can we help to promote the dignity of clergy upon retirement, by guaranteeing them a reasonable income, and support to live on and maintain their dependents?
3. What about an organised method of keeping in contact with retirees, socialising with them, and meaningfully tapping their vast life experience and other essential resources?

Bearing in mind that the cost of living generally outpaces the income available for a certain standard of living, and adversely impacts the quality of retirees' lives, there is need for a strategic plan that would change the retirement dispensation, not only in the Anglican Church, but for the benefit of clergy of every denomination.

The church needs a continual assessment of its retirement services. It is timely to call on all who have an interest in strengthening democracy and service delivery to examine the current retirement proposals with a view to consolidating the hope and comfort of leaders and workers who ministered so faithfully to the cure of souls. Albeit, one must not miss the opportunity to commend the Anglican Church for providing pensions and other services to retired personnel, and to spouses of retired/deceased leaders, and their dependents, where possible. In the quest of justice and sheer love, this is a strong plea for all denominations and organisations to properly support their retired clergy and other staff who serve in church.

Nor is it ever too early for clergy and staff (in service) to make wise financial investment(s) towards their retirement! Some might argue that this is a difficult matter to consider when one is operating on a shoestring budget; but the more meagre one's budget, the more important it is to invest for retirement. All of us, including clergy, should embrace opportunities to prepare and invest wisely, no matter how small our budget. Perhaps, one can be greatly helped in this undertaking by seeking the assistance of a knowledgeable financial adviser.

Profitable financial instruments

At two recent lectures on Financial Instruments[2] and Financial Stewardship and Prudent Investment[3] that I attended, it was interesting to hear the presenters discuss the various offerings available, while encouraging listeners to avail themselves of attractive financial services. Presenters were at pains to point out the need for the audience, especially in the current, gripping economic recession, to be entrepreneurial (provide a service or product at least to make some additional income), and to be astute in shopping for a suitable financial instrument in which to invest, while making sure to diversify savings and investments (don't put all in one basket).

Similarly, leaders/clergy and workers alike are encouraged to invest in securities or investment instruments issued by Government. These include fixed income securities and variable dividend securities—tax certificates, bonds, debentures, and notes—which are reputedly secure investment instruments. In order to whet one's interest, note some offerings:

Tax Certificates:. These secure instruments are highly recommended; they pay attractive interests.
Saving Bonds:. These robust instruments can 'come in handy' for emergency use.
Debentures:. These secure long-term investments can be used for pension purposes, or to save for a proposed property purchase.

One can invest at higher interest rates by becoming owners of stocks, shares, or equities on the open market.

Along with Government, there are numerous commercial institutions with available financial instruments, including banks, credit unions, insurance companies (insurance: the appropriate type can provide savings and offer security and wage replacement in emergency), to mention a few.

However, a word of caution is timely—the higher the interest sought, the greater the risks incurred; conversely, the greater the security sought, the lower the interest to be earned.

Notwithstanding the fact that financial investments make good sense, especially when done early in life, **one should always err on the side of caution and wisdom in making investments, which supposedly yield very high interests,** as many Ponzi schemes and other high-risk enticements abound.

If leaders want to exemplify good stewardship and be an example to persons they lead, prudent engagement in financial investment, which could redound to their personal benefit in the short and long term, while providing a solid basis for teaching and ministering to others, is a way to go. Accordingly, the abovementioned instruments are commended for the consideration of clergy, diocesan and other staff. And where their primary ministry will not be compromised, employment (e.g. teaching, agricultural pursuits) 'on the side' can help greatly.

Speeches and an Edited Sermon presented at Fr. Gatherer's Retirement Commemoration Service, 27 March 2011

The Bishop's Message was read

It is with a sense of gratitude and appreciation that I, on behalf of the entire diocesan family, extend sincere thanks to Canon Edward Gatherer for his many years of ministry in this diocese.

I am sure that there are many persons in this parish and in the wider diocese whose lives have been influenced during his 60 years of ministry.

His approach to life and to ministry made it easy for anyone to approach him and seek his assistance. His love for children and his great concern for their welfare will stand as one of the significant contributions of his ministry.

He will be leaving behind in the congregation at St. Andrew and the wider community many persons who will remember him fondly as their priest. We thank God for all the blessings He has bestowed upon many persons through Canon Gatherer.

We have bestowed upon him the title of Honorary Canon in recognition of his ministry among us. This is only one way of appreciating his contribution to the ministry of this diocese.

We wish him God's richest blessings as he retires from active parish ministry. May his years of retirement be restful and rewarding!

+ John Barbados

An Affirmation of the Reverend Canon Edward Gatherer by the Very Reverend Dr. Frank B Marshall, CBE

'Father Ed', as he came to be lovingly affirmed among not a few in Barbados, was born in the island of St. Vincent. He offered himself to be trained for the Ministry of the Church and entered Codrington College in 1946, a year after I was born. In 1951, August 6, on the Feast of the Transfiguration, he was ordained a deacon at the Cathedral of St. Michael and All Angels, and was elevated to priesthood on the Feast of St. Thomas, December 21, 1952.

Father Ed served as Assistant Curate—firstly at the Church of St. Mary and subsequently at the Parish Church of St. Joseph, prior to his appointment as the Vicar of St. Anne and St. Bernard in 1953. Fr. Gatherer's period of incumbency was one in which he carried the nick name of "Pop", which was clearly related to the image he portrayed as a 'father', especially among young children, for whom he had a deep sense of care and affection. There was much to encourage the Youth, not least the Church Lads' & Church Girls' Brigade, among whose leaders was a certain youth, now the Rt. Sir Wilfred Wood, friend and protégé of Father Ed.

Many of these young folk in the Parish reached out to Father Ed with trust and appreciation, finding him to have been to them a most gentle, caring and inspiring personality; so much so that even today a significant number of those who now live abroad seek him out on their trips back home. Indeed, from abroad have come some of his former parishioners to join in this hour of honour and affirmation of him.

Father Ed accepted the rectorship of St. Andrew's Parish Church in 1957, where early ministry had its joys, but also increased in its challenges over the years. We need not delude ourselves, in that the Church can be quite a political ferment: many of the issues surround the personal aspirations and ambitions of members, which are not simply a matter of arrogance on the part of leadership.

While local government lasted during his incumbency, Father Ed was also Chairman of the St. Andrew's Vestry.

Father Ed wishes to be thought of as modest and seeking only to do the work of the Lord. We recognise that which in more fruitful times have been reaped from his ministry, and affirm his contribution to our diocese, this Parish and community.

Father Ed's love for the young was also in evidence at St. Andrew; particularly is this to be noted in the context of the schools. I have heard members of Chalky Mount Mixed School recall how he visited, how he would invite the Brownie Pack to Church Service and give them a tour of the Church, followed by a treat at the rectory from time to time. I myself am a product of the Church of St. Anne and St. Bernard, and I know how treasured Father Ed was within my community and among our families.

I recall my conversation with Fr. Edward Gatherer at the rectory here in Belleplaine in 1989 on the subject of his retirement, and the opinion I had tendered him, upon being asked by him. I had answered then, "Father Ed, you have had a long ministry—difficult in parts—and if I were in your place I would not want to spoil my evening. I would retire and look forward to sharing my ministry elsewhere in the diocese."

I had envisioned the exercise by him of a ministry to schools, probably facilitated in an associate ministry with the suburban parishes of St. Stephen and St. Leonard. For, as implied earlier, I have always been touched by the persona and gift of Father Ed in relation to the young.

Let me say further, I consider that Father Ed has generally been a man for peace, even if seemingly stubborn to some. I will never forget the passion with which he pleaded in the presence of the clergy assembled in the Chapel of Bishop's Court in 1982, pressing upon the Archdeacon of the day that he should withdraw from the Court an action which he had entered against the Dean of that period. With Bible in hand, the goodly Fr. Edward Gatherer argued the inappropriateness of the brother going to court against the other.

It seems ironic that Father Ed would be the centre of a pastoral and legal issue within a decade thereafter. Without seeking to resurface that matter, I will concede that the diocese was somewhat hard put by a transition from one condition to another—from established to disestablished, from dependent to independent status—and probably had not the clearest perception, vision, and certainty of the road which it proposed to take.

The period of our disestablishment/disendowment will need to be thoroughly researched, relative to the legal, political, sociological, and ecclesiological factors then at play. But, let me say that the church was, as it were, leaving the side of one groom for a new groom; but yet needed to determine its true spouse and the organisation of its household. That lack of fullest visibility was probably the cause of the accident between Father Ed and the administration of this Church, with its ensuing consequences.

It has been the pleasure of our Bishop to confer on Father Ed the status of Honorary Canon. In this is celebrated his contribution to our diocese and in particular to St. Andrew. In an honest appreciation of him we will not allow the constitutional issues of twenty-two years ago to diminish his stewardship, which had been quietly exercised, and a manifestation of which has been evident in his stewardship and care of the environment and the ambience of this historic Church of St. Andrew. We wish him well!

Canon Edward Gatherer, the Lord bless you and keep you. The Lord make His face to shine upon you and be gracious to you; the Lord lift up His countenance upon you and give you peace, now and for ever! Amen. Fare you well!

Excerpt of the Early Ministry of Rev. Edward G. Gatherer of St. Andrew's—Canon Lionel D. Burke

Among the priests in the Diocese of Barbados who understand the implications of, and don the title of endearment, "Father", accorded to priests by members of the Catholic Church and also by others, the Reverend Edward G. Gatherer stands out. It would seem that for him, "Father", in this context, represents a pastoral relationship, as strong as, or sometimes stronger than that of a biological father. The man whose personality and influence have become inextricably interwoven in the life of the parish of St. Andrew is Father Gatherer—known by all.

Our periods of study and preparation for the priesthood at Codrington College overlapped. Being senior to me, Edward was ordained ahead of me; nevertheless, we had already made our impressions, the one on the other.

Father Gatherer became Rector of the St. Andrew Parish Church in May 1957 as a relatively young priest. But he was obviously well aware of his responsibility to God and to God's people, and also of the gifts he had, and those he needed for this work. As one of our Ember Hymns put it in a prayer to God—

> Wisdom, and Zeal, and Faith impart,
> Firmness with meekness from above:
> To bear Thy people in my heart,
> And love the souls, whom Thou dost love.

Thus, both himself and his gifts, he seemed to have dedicated totally to God and to God's people.

In 1960, I was Rector of a cure of three substantial churches in St. Kitts—St. Mary, with Christ Church and St. John—when I received a letter from Fr. Gatherer, who was charged with responsibility for filling and managing any vacant cures within the civil parish of St. Andrew during the first six months of vacancy, after which the responsibility fell to the Bishop. The churches of St. Simon's and St. Saviour's were both vacant, and I was offered the choice of either. I chose St. Saviour's.

On arriving in Barbados during May 1960, I was inducted and instituted as Vicar of St. Saviour's. With the leadership of St. Andrew's and St. Saviour's filled, that of St. Simon's remained vacant. Fr. Gatherer arranged for himself and me to share the pastoral work at St. Simon's. That was not all we shared: we seemed to have shared a similar style of ministry, and were soon managing the three churches and the out-Station at Hillaby.

This twin-ministry of ours was further cemented when Fr. Gatherer, mindful of the need for and the wisdom in keeping abreast of Pastoral and Theological research, arranged to go to Kings College, London, for a period of study. It was my happy privilege to assume responsibility for the whole parish, with kind help from Fr. Lloyd Clarke—now Canon Clarke—who celebrated monthly mass at Hillaby, Turner's Hall, St. Andrew.

On Fr. Gatherer's return, after a year's leave with the benefits gained from his studies, each church in St. Andrew now had, in effect, the services of two priests— Rector Gatherer and me. The St. Andrew's Parish became one church family under two priests.

This concept and practice of unifying and effectively enlarging the churches' families was carried on, even when I was transferred from St. Andrew's, St. Simon's, and St. Saviour's to All Saints, St. Peter. We continued to practise as much 'twinning' as was practicable between St. Andrew's churches and All Saints, with Sunday schools meeting for fellowship occasionally half way at Farley Hill, long before that property became a National Park, or at Six Men's Beach, St. Peter.

One of Father Gatherer's special gifts was attracting and ministering to children; in so doing, this was itself a ministry to the parents, who seemed to beckon him: "Love me, love my child. Love my child, love me".

The St. Andrew's Parish Church, under Fr. Gatherer, continues to be one of the most attractive, well kept, and cared-for church sites in our diocese. This could very well be reflective of the love, enthusiasm, and care for the people of that parish.

Faithfulness to duty and obligation are among the noble characteristics that any individual can endeavour to cultivate. And Fr. Gatherer set a splendid example of these gifts in his relationship to this parish and God's people.

Figure 46: Clergy and friends at Retirement Service

The St. Andrew's rectory, which was built around the same time as, and in similar style to, the Parish Medical Officer's residence, was unfortunately allowed to fall into disrepair. Notwithstanding how the adverse effect of this ill-fated loss was felt, the pastoral care and administration of this parish remained unaffected, as Fr. Gatherer travelled faithfully from his home in the neighbouring parish of St. Joseph to be with his church family in St. Andrew. Such devotion and diligence seem to radiate not merely from a sense of duty, but from a heart of love.

May the Almighty Father continue to bless and strengthen Fr. Gatherer and his cure, and make them and their work more and more acceptable in His sight!

Canon Lionel, D. Burke, BA, LRSM
Precentor of St. Michael and All Angels

Edited Farewell Sermon by Canon Wilbourne Austin

Let the words of my mouth and the meditation of my heart be acceptable in thy sight, O Lord my strength and my Redeemer! Amen.

. . . I extend a warm welcome to each and every one of you. Without you, Father Gatherer, we would not be here at this time. So I thank you for bringing us all together here this evening, and I say welcome to you, Father Gatherer, as well.

I think before I begin my message, I ought to say this. I have a few requests. Please refrain from looking at your watch during my message. I promise not to keep you more than three hours. I'm just kidding; but please remember that Father Gatherer (Figure 46) served this community over sixty years. It is difficult to encapsulate a life of that many years into just five minutes. . . .

When I received the invitation to speak at Father Gatherer's retirement, I have to admit that I felt a little like how I believe Moses felt when God commissioned him to plead the cause of the Israelites before the Pharaoh. At the same time, I also recalled what God's response was to Moses; so I have faith that God will guide me through this evening.

I bring you greetings from my congregation, St. Stephen's Episcopal Church in Bloomfield, Connecticut. Father Gatherer, they asked me to wish you God's continued blessings on your life, and they hope they get the opportunity to meet the gentleman they've heard so many good things about.

As I was preparing my message for today, and trying to think about what I was going to say, a passage of Scripture kept coming into my mind, and I thought it might be appropriate for today.

The passage is taken from the Book of 2 Timothy 4:7: "He has fought the good fight. He has finished the race. He has kept the faith."

Father Gatherer would most likely think it presumptuous of him if he were to say these words about himself. I, however, can say this about him. . . .

As I say this about Father Gatherer, I have to ask myself, could someone say this about me? If the answer is no, then I need to work towards that goal. It is a goal for which to strive, and I should examine my life to see what things need to be changed for it to be said that I truly fought the good fight, finished the race, and kept the faith.

. . . I have a Barbadian friend in Connecticut who comes out with all sorts of sayings that make you laugh. When you think of them, though, there is a lot of truth in them. One of her favourites is, "Some people are called and some jump up and come."

Father Gatherer came to Barbados and specifically to Codrington College to be trained in the priesthood. Upon becoming a priest, he opted to remain in Barbados. I do not know if that was his intention when he left his home in St. Vincent, but based on the work he has accomplished here in Barbados and specifically in this lovely parish of St. Andrew, I would say that God led him here. He did not jump up and come. In my humble but accurate opinion, I believe that he was called by God to this part of God's vineyard. I am happy that God sent him to us.

From the first time I met him, I can truly say that I have had the greatest respect for Father Gatherer. You know, sometimes you lose respect for someone? In my case, the respect I have for Father Gatherer has only grown stronger over the years. Never once have we had a misunderstanding.

One of the things I have always admired in Father Gatherer is summed up in something a friend says frequently. He often says that "one has to stand for something or one will fall for anything." I have found Father Gatherer to be the epitome of that saying.

You see, years ago I was privileged to be employed at the Alleyne School and during that time, Father Gatherer was the Chairman of the Governing Body of the school. I mentioned earlier that I have always had a great respect for Father Gatherer. Well, I admired how he conducted himself at the meetings of the Governing Body. He was no push-over. Never rude, but in his soft-spoken way, he got his point across.

I had not heard the standing for something quote at that time. But looking back now, I wonder if Father Gatherer had heard that then. I think my answer would be, probably not. He was simply a principled man and that was how he was all along.

It is said that we are the product of our environment. I also know we are living in modern times, but I find it difficult to stray from my old upbringing. That is who I am. Please understand what I am about to say. A perfect man I am not. My family is not the perfect family, and that includes my four daughters. They are now all women, but in their younger years, I have had occasions where I have had to put my foot down. I can recall that when our second daughter, June, was fifteen, one day she said to me, "Dad, I hate to admit this, but you are always right." Can you imagine a fifteen-year-old child admitting this, and actually saying it to you?

Now I ask you a question. Could my daughter have said that if I had allowed her to go without any correct direction? What I am trying to say is that we have to stand for something, even though our decision may not render us popular. We have a choice—popularity or having the willpower to stand up for what is right.

Father Gatherer will be remembered for being resolute in what he believes to be right and I pray that all of us will take a page out of his book.

Where are we today as a society? Are we standing for something or are we falling for any wind that blows? I know that's another sermon in itself, but I also strongly feel that it is something to which we ought to give some thought.

In the Book of Daniel, chapter, 3 we find a prime example of standing one's ground. It is the story of the three Hebrew boys, Shadrach, Meshach and Abednego. For refusing to serve any god other than the True and Living God, the king ordered that they be thrown into the fiery furnace.

... My sisters and brothers in Christ, how important is it for us to stand firm and not be tossed about with any wind that blows! That's why this evening I can stand here before you and speak without reservation about the gentleman Father Gatherer, I know.

... I cannot help but think of his faithful service to this parish. During his sixty years of service, he has touched the lives of thousands of people in one capacity or another.

He certainly touched the lives of our family in a big way. Everyone has his or her story about Father Gatherer. I can't tell yours, and even if I knew it, it would not be my in place to do *so*. I can share a little of mine with you. My wife, Mary, and I still recall the counselling sessions we had with him and our wedding ceremony in 1965. We thank him for blessing our marriage and for baptising three of our four daughters.

Father Gatherer was the one who performed the service of burial for my wife's grandmother and step-father, and we thank him.

I can recall one summer when he took some Sunday school children, including our daughter Nan, to St. Vincent. The year was 1979. I remember that well, because there was a hurricane warning and Mary, my wife, who was pregnant at the time was worried . . . that she would not see her child alive again. The story has a happy ending. They returned safely, and to this day Nan still talks about the wonderful time they had on that trip. It was because of Father Gatherer that Nan added to her list of travels.

I am so happy today that our priest, our spiritual leader, our friend, is being honoured this evening. There is a saying that goes something like this: "Give me my flowers while I can smell them."

Father Gatherer, this evening's gathering serves as an opportunity to show you how deeply people care for you.

. . . You have fought not just any fight; you have fought the good fight. You have fought to lead people to Christ. We all know the song, "Will there be any stars in my crown?" Well I heard a preacher say once that there will be no starless crowns in heaven. I know that your crown will be star-studded.

Father Gatherer, you have finished the race. . . I know a little bit about you. You may no longer be the Priest of St. Andrew's Parish Church. But you will always be one of God's faithful followers.

I cannot see you doing anything but continuing God's work in another setting. I know you will continue to work in the vineyard of our Lord until you can no longer do His work, and I pray that I turn out to be half the Priest you are. Father Gatherer, you have kept the faith. Your faith in the God we serve cannot be questioned. You were not one who got up and went. You were called by God. Your faith has brought you thus far and your faith in Almighty God will lead you on.

I am so glad. . . . I am so blessed to have had the good fortune of having my life shaped in great part, by you. God in His wisdom sent me to St. Andrew to be guided by you. And in the meantime, I got a wife. I don't know if I realised that before, but is that not how God works? How often do we say, "God works in a mysterious way?" I wonder, do we truly know the weight those words carry?

. . . This evening has given me an occasion to look deeply inside of me; to remind me what is important in life. This evening has given me another opportunity to understand what I believe God has called me to do. I know that I must fight the good fight. I have recommitted to finishing the race I have begun. I pray, especially during this season of Lent, that I will be faithful to the work God has for me to do.

Father Gatherer, I have to thank you for this evening. I thank you for blessing not my life only, but the lives of all who are assembled here, and all the other lives that are here in spirit. Everyone here joins me in praying that God in His mercy will continue to shower you and your family with His goodness. We pray that God in His loving kindness will grant you great health all the days of your life. We pray that God will give you the strength and the courage to hold on to His unchanging hands. We thank you for your faithful service to God and to His children you have led all these years.

And now, may the Lord bless and keep you; may the Lord make His face shine upon you and be gracious unto you; may the Lord lift up His countenance upon you and give you peace now and for evermore! Amen.

Canon Edward Godson Gatherer's Farewell Message

My Dear People

I extend a very warm welcome to you today at St. Andrew's Church, and I thank you for joining us in this act of Thanksgiving to Almighty God for His many blessings.

Almost sixty years ago, on the Feast of the Transfiguration—6th August 1951—I was ordained a Deacon in St. Michael's Cathedral by the Rt. Rev. Gay Lisle Griffith Mandeville. It was indeed a Red Letter Day in my life. Little did I think at that time that almost my entire ministry would be spent in one position. For me, it has been a great joy and a privilege to serve the people of St. Andrew for so long a period—though others might see it differently.

Figure 47: Canon Gatherer's final 'Thank you' at his retirement service

I believe that most of us here today can make a long list of the things for which we can, and ought to thank God. And if we are in the habit of complaining, there are also lots of things to complain about.

Today I just want to thank God and to praise Him for everything—the good and the bad, the joys and the sorrows, the pleasures and the pain—all those experiences which make us what we are, and equip us for our role as servants in His Kingdom.

I trust that you will continue to pray for me as I do for you. Pray, as St. Paul says (Phil. 1:20) that I may never fail in my duty, but at all times and especially just now, I shall be full of courage, that with my whole being I shall bring honour to Christ whether I live or die.

May the Lord bless you richly as you continue to serve Him!
Yours faithfully,
Father G.

Notes

1. The 'Eager Eleven' referred to eleven members of the Democratic Labour Party of Barbados who in 2012 reportedly called a secret meeting to discuss/address the leadership style of their party leader, the Prime Minister, about which they were uneasy, if not impatient. The meeting was aborted as one of the disaffected members of the Eleven, who was apparently a bit more loyal to his Prime Minister, leaked the secret proposal to the Prime Minister, who later threatened that 'all heads would roll'. Nothing apparently ever followed the Prime Minister's threat.
2. Globe Event Planners. Lecture on "Financial Instruments", held at the Grand Salle. January 2013.
3. Marcia Goodman. Lecture on "Financial Stewardship and Prudent Investment", held at Ellerton Gospel Hall, St. George, 29 January 2013.

CHAPTER TWELVE

Edited Excerpts of Tributes to the Rev'd. Canon Edward Gatherer contributed by relatives, members and friends

Father Gatherer's work at St. Andrew's Parish Church will long be remembered. His ministry among the youth—children and young people—was highly valued (Figure 48). Even in his senior years and feeble days, it was celebrated. During his fifty-odd years of ministry, children stayed by his side and he continued to serve and minister to them, and they took time out to acknowledge him as their true spiritual leader and father.

Figure 48: Fr. Gatherer serving / blessing children

Young people and the Sunday School poured out their heart-felt appreciation and gratitude at his retirement service

Edited Excerpts of Tributes to the Rev'd. Canon Edward Gatherer contributed...

Sarah Elizabeth Hurst

Figure 49: Sarah E. Hurst

The Reverend Edward Godson Gatherer has been a respectable man as I remember. He baptised and confirmed me in St. Andrew's Parish Church.

The Rector is someone who, personally, I think is very close to God. When I heard he was retiring, it came as a shock to me, as I am sure it did to many people. I can appreciate that he has made a decision with which he is pleased. I am convinced that the Rector dedicated his life to the St. Andrew's Parish Church's congregation and to God.

I know God is most pleased with the work that he did around the church and in other areas. He has encouraged young adults and children to do according to God's will and that is the way they should be brought up.

The Rector and I get along fairly well, and our relationship is quite heart warming.

Every best wish to him, and I hope that the good Lord will spare him life for many years to come!

Alala Moore (8 years old)

Figure 50: Alala Moore

Father Gatherer was like a father to me; he was kind, loving, generous, helpful and caring. He loved everyone. He stuck up for us. And I think he would make one of the finest fathers in the world.

He would share the Word of God with us and make lessons very exciting. He would teach us things we never knew. He always knew what to do, when something was wrong.

May God add years to his life and life to his years!

Happy retirement, Father Gatherer!

Thea Graham

While I was not very close to Fr. Gatherer, I did have some fun times with him. I will never forget the day we were at a Sunday School Christmas party at the St. Andrew's Parish Church, having lots of fun when Father Gatherer exited the vestry with a cooler. We asked him what was in it and he said it was ice-cream. Everyone got excited. When I saw the smirk on his face, I knew he was up to something and I told him it was not ice-cream.

When he opened the cooler, we saw something. All of us went "Yuk! What is that?" We did not know what it was at the time. He told us it was honeycomb and he rubbed some of the honey on some of our mouths. We liked the taste.

He did not tolerate foolishness. I remember one Sunday morning before church started, some people were talking and laughing, and he came out of the vestry and spoke to them about it; and I admire him for it.

Father Gatherer is a really nice person. I just want to say, "Thank you Father Gatherer for the fun times we spent with you!"

Leandra Murray

I want to thank Father Gatherer for all the good work he has done. I thank you for the great service you gave to the people at St. Andrew's Parish Church. I hope that you have a wonderful retirement!

Rashan Howell

Dear Father Gatherer, thank you for being the Rector of our church and I would like to wish you a happy retirement!

Shaquille Harris

Thank you, Father Gatherer, for the 53 years you spent as an ordained Minister of St. Andrew's Parish Church. Please enjoy your retirement!

Family

Carmen Conety and Elaine Connell

Fr. Gatherer was no less beloved by his family throughout his life. In remembering him his sisters—Carmen Conety and Elaine Connell—took time to note:

Reverend Father Edward Gatherer's attachment to the Anglican Church dates back to his early childhood days in Georgetown, St. Vincent. Whenever there was a service in the Holy Trinity Anglican Church, he was present. His fondness for and close association with the then Georgetown Anglican priest, Father Feddowes, caused his siblings and intimate friends to nickname him Father "Feddowes". As a young boy doing the Lord's work, at times he accompanied Father Feddowes on his preaching engagements to Union Island, one of the Grenadines. It was clear from this early attachment that Edward was destined to become a priest.

As a priest, Father Gatherer's actions showed his inherent concern and love for children, the elderly, the afflicted or disabled, and his immediate family members. His love for children, especially when in need, was exemplified by his fostering care for Cheryl "Cherie" Hurst as a teenager. He took her into his home and saw her through

Edited Excerpts of Tributes to the Rev'd. Canon Edward Gatherer contributed...

to adulthood. His love for Cherie was reciprocated. She was heard to say: "After God is Father Gatherer." Now she takes care of him attentively and has assisted him in his parochial duties at St. Andrew's.

During his years as Rector, his delight in bringing joy to his Sunday School children was obvious. He organised for them lunches at the rectory, picnics at beach resorts, and overseas trips to St. Vincent.

Father Gatherer's affection for the elderly was marked by his regular visits to 'Mother Bradshaw' at Bathsheba. They doted on each other. She was like a mother to him. The Rector's brotherly love for the disabled was evident, for example, in the attachment formed with a crippled young lady in distant Germany. Whenever he was able, he visited her to offer cheer and comfort.

To his siblings, Edward has always been a dear brother whose concern for their welfare is treasured. He brings fun and laughter to all family gatherings. As a favourite of his remaining sisters, Carmen and Elaine, he endears himself to us and readily makes his home a welcome hearth whenever we choose to visit him.

May he enjoy continued peace and happiness in his retirement!

Friends and Church Members

Olga Russell

Tampa, Florida

Sincere Greetings and God's richest blessings on your retirement from St. Andrew's Church after almost 54 years of service!

What a blessing! God gave you the gifts of time and talent, and you have used them in his honour. Now, God has new plans in store for you. May you find new ways to let your light continue to shine in your retirement years, and may this time in your life hold more blessings for you!

Father, I want to thank you for the spiritual guidance you provided my family and me, as we took our spiritual journey. We continue to raise our families in the fear of the Lord. I will never forget the teachings of the Mother's Union and the Church Girl's Brigade at St. Anne's Church under your guidance and teachings.

Figure 51: Fr. Gatherer in Bishop's Certificate Awards Ceremony

We always enjoyed your sermons both at St. Anne's and later at St. Andrew's Parish Church.

You have been with our family through baptisms, confirmation, and the marriage of one daughter in July 1978. You have been our mentor. It is always a pleasure to see you and to fondly remember the good old days.

Congratulations and may God continue to bless you, and guide you as you enjoy your "rocker" years!

God's Blessings!

Simeon Belgrave

I first met Fr. Gatherer in 1958 when he paid a visit to my home. That day, he and I engaged in a lengthy discussion about the birth and history of the Anglican Church. He subsequently invited me to attend church, but I was not ready to heed the call.

Figure 52: Simeon Belgrave

I can say that he has changed both the physical structure and spiritual outlook of the Church here at St. Andrew. When he first arrived, the stained-glass windows were broken and the space was boarded up. He immediately set to work and contacted the best restorers of stained-glass windows in England to have them restored. To accommodate the elderly parishioners, he removed the numerous steps and installed the paved driveway, so that these members could have easier access to the Church, and anyone could drive up to the door.

Father Gatherer transformed the graveyard from a bushy area overrun by weeds and shrubs, to a beautiful, well-manicured resting place, truly making it God's Acres.

Due to the propensity for erosion in this parish, every year he carried out maintenance to ensure that the physical structure of the Church remained safe and secure. He did this while sacrificing his lodgings at the rectory.

On the spiritual side, he organised such groups as the Mother's Union, Church Army, and Anglican Young People's Association to provide opportunities for parishioners to meet and have fellowship with each other. He also sent young members to Diocesan House to be trained as Sunday School teachers under the tutelage of the late Canon Harold Tudor.

Father Gatherer was more than a Rector to St. Andrew; he was a social worker, a counsellor, an ambulance driver, a tour guide and much more, not only to the people of this Church, but also to anyone who needed his assistance. His stewardship transcended the Anglican faith and embraced all persons. He truly is allegorically named, for Edward means 'rich guardian'; while 'Godson' speaks for itself, as does 'Gatherer'.

Edited Excerpts of Tributes to the Rev'd. Canon Edward Gatherer contributed...

He has been a rich guardian of this church, gathering souls for his heavenly Father. A blessed retirement to you, Father!

Cheryl "Cherie" Hurst

I firmly believe that God sent me to be a part of Rector Gatherer's life. Just before I finished school, I was hospitalised. It took me a very long time to get better and, along with my family, the Rector was the driving force behind my recovery. I had practically given up, but he would not let up—he pushed me, sometimes gently, and when he felt I needed a kick, this he did.

It was a long and painful road, but he was always there. I learnt that priests can also be friends, and the kind of teachers that would motivate their charges to love and trust God. Always with a smile on his face, with radiant and loving passion, he would make it his mission to make me feel something good about each day. He has a very special gift in making me see the good and positive in everyone. This Christ-like gift is undoubtedly a result of his faith and trust in, and love for God. I am extremely grateful and thankful for this training, which has made me into the person I am today.

Figure 53: Cheryl Hurst

In 1989, when his troubles with the Anglican Church began, I am convinced that God had prepared me to be by his side to offer support. I had just returned from the Mission Field, and a very intensive and eye-opening two-year study in Human Relations in London. I highly commend him for his courage in trying, at considerable personal hardship and enormous expense, to correct what he saw was wrong in the Church to which he belonged, and which he loved. He was persecuted and harassed, but I am confident that this experience has not made him a bitter man, but rather a much stronger servant.

The Rector has worked hard in a poor and difficult parish for almost fifty-four years without complaining, and without seeking preferment. His home was always open—so was his kitchen.

I recall the many times we as children were allowed to cook and bake, although some of us had no idea of what we were doing. Whatever was the end result, the Rector cheerfully ate some and he praised us.

The Rector is the only priest with whom I was closely associated. He baptised me, and for all these years he has been a very good example in his living and in his teachings. He insisted that all things must be done decently and in order. Everything had to be done to the best of your ability, and he taught us to read the scriptures with expression and reverence. By the time we were given the opportunity to read in church, we knew the passage without looking at the Bible.

The Rector is a true man of hope, faith, and love. No one or nothing was beneath him, and I marvel at the calm, cheerful, and prayerful way he carried himself. I pray that God will continue to keep His arms around him, and that the Rector will keep holding on and never ever let go!

May God continue to bless, guide and inspire him always!

Magdalene "Maggie" Kellman

Father Gatherer

Life is filled with special blessings. On a day 50-odd years ago, my family and I met you for the first time. My memories of you then were that the Lord had wonderful plans for you, as we travelled together to different places. I would like to thank you for your teaching, thoughtful deeds, and friendship over the years.

You went through some trials and tribulations, and you overcame them with God's help, and a few faithful friends who believed in you and the truth. You have always had a soft side, and showed compassion for the things people go through. One episode, which I vividly remember, is that regarding La Soufriere, when you returned to your homeland to give comfort to the people, especially the children of St. Vincent, where you captured their hearts with your kindness. You took me to the market where we purchased $500 in flying fish. As was your normal generous self, you paid for the fish. We took them to the rectory and I scaled, boned, seasoned, and fried them; I boned by day and fried by night and packaged them for the trip.

We took them to a shelter, along with drinks and water. The decision to go on the mission was the Rector's; and we willingly volunteered, and you paid our passage.

This generosity was also extended here in St. Andrew, a parish which you wholeheartedly embraced. You took the Sunday School children on picnics. In love, you did a lot for the people of St. Andrew. At the personal level, you did a lot for the Kellman family. Ours was the first family you met when you arrived at the Church; we were your welcoming committee. When I would return to Barbados for a vacation, you would always collect me from the airport. I later became your volunteer housekeeper. We all lived as friends. If my mother were ill, no matter the hour, you would always rush to her aid.

You were a great teacher. After breakfast we attended church every morning for 7 a.m. and you played a psalm and told me to hum it; I did it twice and got it wrong. You asked my mother to hum it, and she did it without error. You are a perfectionist. There was also Hymn #8,

> "Forth in Thy Name, O Lord I go,
> My daily labour to pursue,
> Thee, only Thee, resolved to know,
> In all I think, or speak, or do."

which you made us sing every morning until we got it right.

Just as you were there for us, I had to be there for you and I took time off work in England to be there with you at the tribunal.

For over 53 years, I watched you do charity work, donating hampers to the district hospital, helping the needy, visiting shut-ins in the parish, and those at the psychiatric hospital. The list was endless.

Then there was the work at the Parish Church itself; you were groundsman, caretaker, and jack-of-all-trades. Up to five years ago you were still physically toiling to keep the churchyard in tip-top shape. We were raking leaves and you were carrying the wheelbarrow. We insisted that you were too tired and should rest. You allowed us to carry a few loads, but on the last load, you 'jumped in' and took over and commented: "See, I'm not tired. I can do it."

You have always shown that servant spirit humbly, always assuming part of the process, and not merely the preacher, who preaches alone, but the preacher who practises and works side by side with his parishioners.

The Kellman family and I will miss you dearly from the pulpit of St. Andrew's.

Cyrillene Harding

I have known Father Edward Godson Gatherer for over sixty years. Two years after his ordination he was installed as Vicar of St. Anne's Church. Four years later, he became Rector of the Parish of St. Andrew. He was a frequent visitor to our home. His respect for his religion and church was evident at all times: no more so than when my brother, who did not attend the weekly confirmation classes, was made to present himself daily to Father Gatherer to complete the required number of hours of teaching. Then and only then was he presented to the Bishop.

Kind and Considerate

Fr. Gatherer was very supportive of my musical voyage. My most formative years on the organ were spent in St. Andrew's Parish Church with him listening and encouraging me. His calm and assuring manner always allowed me to practise freely, even during his visits to our home. During these visits, he would often borrow music books and share his thoughts with me. He was a 'regular' at choir practice and always had an encouraging kind word for the choristers. His hymn selections were always appropriate for the season, and he always gave kind consideration to his choristers and organist—always sparing a thought for others.

Love and Dedication

His love for young people was unsurpassed. He spent long hours with "his children" carrying them to and fro in whatever vehicle he had. Many of St. Andrew's prominent sons and daughters received their spiritual guidance at Fr. Gatherer's knee. Picnics and outings were the order of the day. There was always a lesson to be taught. Sharing was foremost among the principles taught. There was an absolute fairness in all of his dealings with the children. However, a child was also taught to 'know his place'. Many of the children—mine included—spent several hours in and around the Church cleaning (playing), and all of them knew that the sanctuary was off-limits.

Talking above a whisper was a no-no unless reading a lesson. The vestry was his place of peace and quiet—**enter only if summoned**.

So dedicated and committed to furthering his young people was he that Fr. Gatherer organised a tour to his native St. Vincent in 1979. With the assistance of a few adults, he carried his Sunday School *et al* on an educational tour of the neighbouring island. For many of these children, it was their first overseas tour. This is just one of the many examples of his love and dedication.

Always there

Fr. Gatherer was always approachable and accessible. The rectory was always open to his people. He knew his parishioners and their needs, often before they did. His willingness to help in any and every situation was admirable. Whether it was a lift to a destination, repairs to a home, a cup of tea, or lodging for the night Fr. Gatherer was always available.

Fr. Ed—The Businessman

Father Gatherer was a shrewd business priest in many ways. Sixty slices from a 9-inch cake, gallons and gallons of mauby from one bottle of syrup, cones upon cones of ice-cream from one bucket—and the Fair was a resounding success! . . . need I say more?

Fr. Gatherer—My Priest

I have earned the right to call him MY PRIEST. He officiated at my wedding, he baptised and confirmed both of my children, and officiated at the funeral services for both of my parents. Apart from all this, Fr. Gatherer is responsible for my ability to read and play music publicly with confidence. And I know that I am not the only beneficiary of his inspiration.

In the Community

Fr. Gatherer was an ever-present figure in the community. Schools and homes he would visit, but none more often than the St. Andrew's Children's Home. These children often worshipped with us on Sunday mornings. His visits also extended to neighbouring district hospitals and homes. He was also instrumental in founding the local chapter of the Richmond Fellowship of the Caribbean—a non-governmental organisation dedicated to establishing halfway houses.

Edited Excerpts of Tributes to the Rev'd. Canon Edward Gatherer contributed...

The Golden Mile

Fr. Gatherer has worked tirelessly to ensure that St. Andrew's Parish Church has the best maintained graveyard in the island—his "Golden Mile"!

I would like to take this opportunity to thank Fr. Ed for his love, dedication, and support to my family and me throughout the years, and to wish him a joyous and peaceful retirement for a job well-done!

David Goring

I consider it both a privilege and a pleasure for me to be able to make a few comments with regard to the ministry and labour of Canon Gatherer.

One writer said, "I expect to pass this way but once. Any good therefore that I can do to any man, let me do it now, for I will not pass this way again."

In the context of this statement, there is no doubt that much good has been exhibited during the long service rendered to this community and to us by Canon Gatherer. Indeed, a sober reflection will indicate that it has been both extensive and varied.

I recall the numerous opportunities that were afforded me to serve in several capacities within the church. These impacted on my life as a young person growing up, and as an adult in a very positive and meaningful way. I personally would like to make special mention of the Bible classes—which allowed me to read, mark, understand and inwardly digest the Bible as I read it from cover to cover, and those Good Friday Services when a very heavy cross had to be borne from the church to Belleplaine Community Centre, or St. Simon's. This especially demonstrated, in a meaningful way, the significance of the sufferings of Christ.

I admired his exceptional love for children. Every week, the children from St. Andrew's Boys' and Girls' would journey to the Church for morning devotion. If there was rain, he would go to the school. He would also visit the other schools in the parish. There were always special services at Ash Wednesday, Harvest Time, and Easter for the children.

I remembered the St. Andrew's Challenge Shield, which was competed for by Sunday Schools in neighbouring parishes. Summer camps and handicraft classes were always organised for the children. Children led by Canon Gatherer explored the rugged terrain of St. Andrew and were engaged in many hikes to the surrounding parishes; in addition he conducted overseas trips to St. Vincent, Cariacou and Bequia.

How many of you remembered that there was a Church Girls' Brigade and, as it paraded in uniform in front of the Church, motorists would come to a standstill, as they admired the performance of the girls?

His work with young people was quite outstanding. He was a man of prayer. He touched many lives that helped children to experience the goodness of God. These experiences taught the children many life skills and discipline. Canon Gatherer's commitment and dedication were clearly shown in the way he shared in the experiences himself—whether leading the way on the hikes, enjoying whatever was cooked, going to the sea, playing games, or picnicking—the children and youth were his focus, and this provided the context for the development of many life skills. For those who participated, I am sure that they would regard the experiences and lessons taught and learned as memorable.

It is against this background therefore that I join with others here and elsewhere, to express my gratitude for those enterprises, helpful measures, community input, and personal development opportunities afforded during his tenure. I take this moment on behalf of my wife, boys, and myself to wish him well for the future. May he take to heart the comforting words of King David in his confident declaration of trust in the Lord's provision in Psalm 16:11: Thou wilt show me the path of life; in Thy presence is fullness of joy; at Thy right hand there are pleasures for evermore!

Remarks by friend Rex Wason

It is with deep regret that I have been forced to be absent [due to illness] on this historic occasion [Gatherer's Retirement Service] for the Rev'd. Edward Gatherer, and words cannot express how it has affected me.

During my term of office as Hon. Sec. of the Barbados National Trust, I had the pleasure of meeting him to arrange a historic service at St. Andrew's Parish Church on St. Andrew's Day 1982. From that day our friendship has grown throughout the years, up to the present moment. That historic service in 1982, which was attended by His Excellency the Governor General Sir Deighton Ward, government officials, and many other dignitaries, was a most memorable occasion.

We have during the years, though miles apart, kept in touch by the telephone and occasional visits.

I found Fr. Gatherer a very sincere, faithful friend from whom I could always glean words of wisdom and support. He was loyal to his friends. Fr. Gatherer would show glorious moments of humour with those who came in contact with him.

When my health improves, I shall write a more detailed tribute for this honourable gentleman.

I congratulate him for the honour bestowed by the Anglican Church after 60 years of dedicated service.

I pray that he will enjoy his retirement in good health and that God will bless him.

Following a bout of illness, Rex died within two weeks of writing this tribute and was buried on 12 April 2011.

Carrol Bourne on behalf of the Husbands and Bourne families

The year 1957 was a watershed in the Church of St Andrew. The Rector G.C.M. Woodroffe was transferred to St Joseph Parish Church, and the Rev. Edward Gatherer succeeded him. The new Rector was a tall, slim younger man, quite unlike Rector Woodroffe, who was of great stature.

Rev. Gatherer was blessed with a large congregation of parishioners who loved and were committed to their church. Nestled in the beautiful plains of the Scotland District and surrounded by the hills and valleys of St Andrew, Rev. Gatherer was presented with

Edited Excerpts of Tributes to the Rev'd. Canon Edward Gatherer contributed...

---

an environment fit for a king. No wonder then that he spent 54 years of his priesthood in this parish, leaving a legacy of environmental order in, and around the Church that is the envy of many!

Rev. Gatherer was a very friendly and soft-spoken priest, who knew everyone in the parish. He visited them, and prayed for them when they were sick, regardless of their religious persuasion. Most of all, he loved children and kept them close. At times he had his challenging moments with some members of his congregation, and even with his Diocese, but through fervent prayer and persistence, he conquered. We vividly remember at church excursions Father Gatherer having to stoutly defend some who were under attack by others. Who can forget how he floored a gentleman at Foul Bay, not once but twice in succession, much to the surprise and laughter of those of us in the immediate vicinity—a test of his physical strength and prowess?

Rev. Gatherer was also a family friend—he never forsook us even though we had all left St Andrew. He maintained relationships with all of us, both here and overseas. My personal contact with him over the years has been honest and reciprocal, especially in 2005, when I was hospitalised. His regular visits and steady prayers strengthened me, and gave me the will to recuperate, through a stronger faith in the Almighty—and for that, I give him thanks.

The Husbands-Bourne family truly appreciates the sterling work Fr. Gatherer has given to St Andrew. It is not easy to have worked for over half-a-century in one location; but Rev. Gatherer is made of that sterner stuff, and we hope that he will always regard St Andrew as his home.

Thank you, Father Gatherer, for your support and moral fortitude over the years. We are the richer for it, and we hope that you will continue to be shielded by God's grace. We also congratulate you on receiving the accolade of Honorary Canon, though belated, but well-deserved.

In closing, here is a verse of Hymn 477 from the Ancient & Modern hymn book:

> The sun that bids us rest is waking
> Our brethren 'neath the western sky,
> And hour by hour fresh lips are making
> Thy wondrous doings heard on high.

Keep pressing on,
Canon Gatherer, may you see the rising sun
for many years to come,
through Christ our Lord!

Sis. Rita Gibb-Goddard and Bro. Cameron B. Goddard

"Rejoice in what God has done"

Congratulations to Canon Edward Gatherer, affectionately known to me as 'Father Gatherer'!

The Goddard family thanks you for over 54 years of service to this historic Church, St Andrew's, which is referred to in early records as ST ANDREW OVERHILLS. It was one of the new parishes created during the administration of Governor Philip Bell (1641–1650). The Church existing in 1831 survived the hurricane of that date, but the building fell into disrepair. The present Church was built in 1846.

Father Gatherer, you struggled over the years to keep this beautiful historic Church alive. You must be commended for this. During those years you served your Parish Church with dignity, humility and love—always with a broad smile. That smile will be missed.

You are a good shepherd, who travelled over lofty sand dunes, beautiful rivers, lovely vegetation, numerous cane fields, fat pork trees, sea grape trees, cashew trees, khus khus grass, almond trees and much more, wearing sandals and much more to tend your flock.

Bro. Cameron and Sis. Rita wish you a happy, healthy and blessed retirement! Never forget to smile; and may God continue to bless you!

"And now abideth faith, hope and love; these three, but the greatest of these is love." God Bless!

Marsilene Hurst, Brooklyn, USA.

Father Gatherer's motto was 'Do all things decently and in order' and to this day he lives this. Father G is the only priest that I have known. He baptised me, prepared me for confirmation, disciplined me when it was necessary, and instilled morals and values.

Confirmation class on Saturday mornings was something to look forward to. Although Father used his special strap on us when we misbehaved, instruction was very spiritual and inspiring. We had to learn the Catechism, and once a month we were given a test. Father only arranged for the Sacrament of Holy Confirmation when he believed that we were ready. We were taught from the early age to work for God without seeking something in return. We cleaned the Church, the rectory and the Church yard. During these chores, Father made sure that we had a little fun—we would sing, tell stories, and play guessing games—all to keep things interesting.

Every morning, Father led Mass, even if he was the only one present. On Wednesday nights he conducted Evensong and this was very interesting. Father would always use this time to study the Bible with us. He would ask us children lots of questions. He encouraged us to think, ask questions and to debate. The ones who were too timid to read were given the opportunity to read a lesson while being encouraged by him.

My first trip out of Barbados was at the invitation of Father. He encouraged us children to have sponsored walks, cake sales, and other fundraisers in order to help our parents foot the airfare. Father taught me how to save. He encouraged us as children to bring our ten and twenty-five cents to Sunday School. This he recorded on our cards and at the end of the year he gave us back.

I am extremely grateful and appreciative of all Father has done. He trained, guided, protected, and provided the most wonderful experiences and spiritual nourishment.

Father, you will always be in my prayers and thoughts and I will look out for you.

Edited Short Tributes

Simeon Belgrave

The first time I ever boarded an aeroplane, scaled a volcanic mountain, sailed on a yacht, drove a car, and took communion, Father Edward Gatherer was there.

He has known me all my life and has been present for many memorable occasions in my life. His gentle and calming nature has touched not only my life, but the lives of my parents, siblings and indeed many people.

I love you dearly. May your retirement be filled with many years of immense joy and peace!

Hershey Smith

I would like to record my special appreciation and thanks to Father Gatherer, now Canon Gatherer.

He it was who kindly gave me my first job as a pupil teacher at the St. Andrew's Girls' School, on 13 September 1957. For that and many more kindnesses, I will be eternally grateful.

God bless you in your retirement!

John Worrell & family

On behalf of the late Mr. and Mrs John Worrell and all the Worrell family, formerly of Airy Hill, St. Joseph, I would like to congratulate Father Edward Gatherer on his retirement, and wish him a very happy and long retirement!

Good luck and God's blessings to you! Have a great time in retirement!

Ashleigh Luke

I wish you a good and blessed retirement in which to relax and enjoy your life. For all the years you have been preaching here, may the Lord guide you, and keep you in good hands! We will all miss you.

Cheryl Audrey Morris

Rev. Gatherer:
You have left your indelible mark. We will miss you a great deal. May God continue to bless you as you set out on your retirement!

Ghandi Morris

Father Gatherer:
All God's blessing and a happy retirement!

You have been a source of inspiration and a great example of a worker for the Lord. May your coming years be filled with well deserved rest and relaxation!

Letters of Love to Father Gatherer

To My Dearest Father Gatherer

You have truly been a blessing to my family and to the parish of St. Andrew. You have been the most generous, caring, understanding, and loving person I have ever known. You have built a solid foundation in my life and the lives of so many others and for that I will be forever grateful.

I remember summer camps at the rectory, Saturday morning confirmation classes, cleaning the Church, driving around in your big blue car, and Lassie your faithful dog that would follow you to church.

I cannot mention everything because I would never stop writing, but most of all I remember my first plane trip to your homeland of St. Vincent. We had a grand time. I am sure that many others will agree with me that we have experienced many exciting adventures in our lives because of you.

St. Andrew's Parish Church will never be the same without you. No-one, no-one can ever fill your shoes. We say that Aretha Franklin is the queen of soul, Michael Jackson the king of pop, and Mohammed Ali the king of boxing. I am sure many others will agree with me in "knighting" you the *King of Priesthood*.

Father Gatherer, my family and I would like to say thank you! You will forever be in our hearts and continually in our prayers.

Father Gatherer we don't say it often enough, but we love you.

Yours sincerely,
Petra Gibbons & Gibbons/Kellman Families

Monica Marshall & Jocelind Grant, Boston, USA

Over the years, you have been a stalwart of strength and spiritual guidance to our family and we will be forever indebted.

May you be blessed with a healthy and happy retirement!

Francine, Stephen, and Charday Holdip-Harewood, Gall Hill, St. John, Barbados

Father G.

As you retire, we pray that God will continue to bless and inspire you. We know that you are a very prayerful and thankful servant of God, and we are grateful for the huge difference you have made in our lives.

Take care, stay healthy, and enjoy your retirement! You have surely earned it.

Poems

Father Edward Gatherer

Edward Godson Gatherer,
A faithful worker for the heavenly Father,
He answered the priestly call,
And sought to share the Good News to all.
Vincentian by birth,
He moved to this little corner of the earth.
At Codrington College he studied well,
For the Bible he had to tell.
For sixty plus years he was working,
Preaching, praying, mowing and forking.
He is an inspiration to many,
His work ethic better than any.
Not many would sacrifice their health,
Or even share their little wealth
To bring joy to a parishioner,
Like caring Father Edward Gatherer.
He has made his mark,
He has done his part
To raise the standard of St. Andrew
As he ministered to the faithful few.
May God continue to bless you Father G,
And shine his light upon thee!
For you have given of your best,
And withstood all the devil's tests.
God richly Bless!
By Simeon Belgrave

A Prayer for Father G

I pray that the paths you continue to walk,
And the roads you continue to travel,
Will be guiding lights showing the way, and
Shining every single day.
I appreciate your presence in my life, for you
demonstrate love in such a way,
That we know it was a divine gift given to you
to share with so many others.
May God continue to bless and guide you Canon Gatherer!
Anonymous

**"They took knowledge of them that they
had been with Jesus", Acts 4:13.**

He was like Christ in boldness;
Never blush to his own religion;
Never ashamed of the gospel;
Very valiant for his God;
He imitated Him in his loving spirit;
Thought kindly, spoke kindly,
Did kindly so that men could say of him
"He has been with Jesus."
Bro. Glyn Hurst

Edited Excerpts of Tributes to the Rev'd. Canon Edward Gatherer contributed...

Like a Tree of Kindness

You are kindness.
Kind hearts are the gardens,
Kind thoughts are the roots.
Kind words are the blossoms,
Kind deeds are the fruits.
And with age this tree gets stronger;
For age is just quality of mind,
And you still have a life filled with zest,
A quality which grows like your kindness.
For it is the love that you've shown,
No matter how the birthdays fly,
You are not old, but like a tree of kindness and
You gave us a chance to grab hold.
By Magdalene "Maggie" Kellman

The True Gatherer

Canon Gatherer
You never pretended to work;
You toiled, sweated and were a door mat for all.
You kept your focus on Jesus.
You refused to jump on any bandwagon and did not entertain gossip;
You took your directions from God.
You always had a plan—A Plan with God in mind,
And so, whatever you undertook
You and the plan were greatly blessed.
By Cheryl Hurst

CHAPTER THIRTEEN

"In the Pew"—Any Word to Heed? Any Lessons to Learn?

"In the Pew" was the place where one heard many questions being asked about church, and note, not exclusively St. Andrew's Parish Church. In general, you heard the groans and saw the tears of the dejected and listened to the inquiries and ideas regarding people's feelings and thinking about church. You met people who were 'weary, languid, and sorely dismayed' and who sought answers to issues that for a long time caused them depression—answers about church that had eluded them, and which leaders shied away from addressing: answers that leaders themselves, ourselves, seek.

Without necessarily providing answers in this chapter, the following is a brief outline of a few of the issues that arose while one was sitting "In the Pew" and from interviews undertaken during the research on this volume.

1. How can the church best utilise professionals: the retired but active members who made substantial contributions to our nation?
2. How can we get the church to address declining membership?
3. How can we more effectively use the laity in administration, day-to-day activities, and ministry of the church?
4. What is the best way to resolve a civil dispute with a member of your church? Should we revert to the law court or settle it within the church?
5. Is it really advisable to keep away from the court if you want justice?
6. How do you deal with a bigot or despotic leader in your church?
7. How do we get a leader to impartially share ministry and responsibilities in church and not with a few of his friends and hand-picked members?
8. What must be the church's response to abuse (sexual) of vulnerable members by its leadership?
9. How do you stop your leader from patronising (talking down to) her/his audience?
10. Can the church be required to conform to civil requirements that are not included in its code of practice?

Needs of Leadership in today's society

In an enlightened society where information is common commodity, and people can learn in their homes at the push of a button, church leaders need to be well trained and must understand and practise good personal relations and basic good manners. Any semblance of dictatorship, heavy handedness, or uncouthness cannot, and will not be tolerated. Coarse and unseemly behaviour is bound to be met with repudiation and disaffection on part of members. Leaders must understand this and must endeavour to treat people with sensitivity, justice, and utmost dignity. Where ingredients of self-respect and basic good interpersonal relationship are lacking, nothing but trouble, disruption, and church secession will ensue.

Church administration needs to be ever cognisant that training and retraining of its personnel in helping them perform well is mandatory and vital. Regular on-going help/training in good human relations is necessary, if we are to prevent leaders from falling into a mode of behaviour that could frustrate people.

Retraining must not be interpreted in the light that leaders have failed, or are simply inadequate, but rather as a means to keep them on the cutting edge of good performance. It equips leaders to be able to identify problems and challenges in their ministry, and enables them to be more competent in engaging with solutions and alternatives needed in resolving conflict and potential problems.

So often leaders' dilemmas become all the more overwhelming because they are unaware of an alternative path to choose, or where help is available. To confront a serious problem, and not be able to call upon resources can be devastating, not only to others, but to leaders as well. Moreover, for the church hierarchy not to provide avenues of training and recourse for leaders to avail themselves of essential help, is to fail them.

The church is often guilty of not availing itself of the opportunity to provide the best help and counselling support for its personnel at all levels. It cannot be emphasised enough that leaders have an onerous responsibility to lead rather complex and diverse groups and people in their respective congregations, and that leaders' thorough and continued preparation should not be underestimated or sacrificed.

Those in the forefront of leadership generally, but the caring leadership in particular, often become severely burnt-out. Unless there is a dedicated provision available to address this situation, we are doing our leaders and nation a disservice. Unfortunately, many leaders have never had the benefit of professional counsel or the opportunity to de-stress with professional help. Leaders' 'support therapy' is becoming common and should be seen as an essential component of church ministry. Providing essential support, at least once yearly for leaders, or as often as necessary, should be embarked upon. The church needs to take better care of its leaders for optimum benefits to accrue to the body and the nation.

Training for enabling leaders

Due to the very important and demanding ministry the church offers to society, the Training Administration Division and/or the Productivity Council, with government's approval, is well poised to consider, as part of their mission to the nation, admitting a few church leaders/personnel into their regular personnel equipping modules. This could only redound to rich national dividends, as church leaders teach or directly and indirectly impact the nation of Barbados. Good 'interpersonal grooming' and other relevant government training initiatives provided to enable the working sector could be of intrinsic benefit if shared with church leaders/personnel, who give so much support to workers of Barbados on a weekly, year-round basis.

Leaders' training must not be a one-off initiative of three or four years, when persons receive some form of qualification and are sent into a parish. It must include 'agape love', constant grooming, affirming, disciplining, mentoring, retraining, and helping persons to cope with stress on the job, as well as mundane issues. Less than adequate training can result in failure, frustration, and possible harm in a church organisation.

How about having clergy annually submit to "x" hours of continual education (refreshing/equipping) via seminars and workshops provided by the church? In this case, the requirement could be attendance and participation. Perhaps, a nominal monetary gift or other appropriate incentive could be offered.

Candidates offering themselves for the ministry are likely to perform better if they have spent prior time working with people in order to acquire experience, and to be better able to understand them *en masse*.

Poor interpersonal attitudes

Leaders with poor interpersonal (and family) relationships and ethical issues should not merely be reshuffled (sent to another parish to continue ministry or misery). People/leaders encounter problems (e.g. health, social, ethical, spiritual) from time to time and deserve to be helped, not abandoned like a wounded cub in the woods. While abandonment is practised among animals in the wild, such behaviour must not be entertained in religious or humane organisations. Pastoral help and mentoring are helpful interventions, and can be effectively utilised by leaders in supporting and assisting each other. Much more of this needs to be encouraged.

Mistakes the church can ill afford to repeat

I was called from sitting "in the pew" to assist a leader who was unable to carry through with a ceremony. I responded, permitting the leader to regain consciousness and composure. It required me to provide assistance in completing the service/marriage.

The lesson to be emphasised here is that inevitably leaders become unable to carry on. As retirement approaches, or disability occurs, we must be willing to defer to others for the glory of God, in order to avoid embarrassment and dysfunction in the organisation. Allowing leaders to continue serving when their capability has irretrievably been eroded is imprudent and unnecessary.[1]

It was disconcerting to witness a leader being coerced to sign documents in an effort to keep him plodding on in a ministry with which he was unable to cope. With his increasing age and disability, one unfortunately saw relationships in the fellowship crumble, as an assistant tried to run the organisation. Notwithstanding, in all this, resilient members remained, while weaker ones simply left the church.

Irrespective of all other reasons alleged for the resignation of Pope Benedict XVI, the spiritual leader of 1.2 billion Roman Catholics, his explanation—due to an advanced age:

> ...both strength of mind and body are necessary, strength which in the last few months has deteriorated in me to the extent that I have had to recognize my incapacity to adequately fulfill the ministry entrusted to me,[2]....

is laudable. We just must not merely plod on and on until expiry. And this must speak volumes to church organisations and leaders alike who still incorrectly maintain that a spiritual vocation is for life.

You sit "In the Pew" with diffidence and dismay, observing capable lay members who can ably assist or perform get brushed aside in preference to others who are 'buddy-friends' of the leader. Capable, qualified teachers are denied opportunity to serve and minister only because they are not 'yes-followers'.

Bishop Drexel Gomez in his Charge to the church wisely admonished "A leader who deprives himself of advice and reaction from his flock is impoverishing himself and them disastrously."[2] He went on to quote from Albert Camus: "Don't walk in front of me, I may not follow. Don't walk behind me, I may not lead. Walk beside me and be my friend."

And the Bishop further passionately affirmed:

> . . .That's the only kind of leadership that modern people understand. . . .walk hand in hand, opening the Word of God. That's the path of shared responsibility in the body of Christ.

Moreover, in repudiating a leadership style where the leader tried to lead a large community by himself while ignoring input from other capable helpers, the Old Testament firmly chided: ". . .The thing thou doest is not good. Thou shalt surely wear away, both thou, and this people that is with thee. . .," Ex. 18:17–18.[3] Such ancient and timeless wisdom still has relevance for modern leaders. And they need to heed the warning, at least, in order to avoid burn-out. Church leaders need to share responsibility not only for the sake of their health, but also for the healthy spiritual and social wellbeing of their members and followers.

In a day when so many church members are extremely well qualified in their chosen fields, it is regrettable that, in poorly-led churches, the contribution of these people is ignored.

While sitting "In the Pew", one observed numerous teachers, staunch, knowledgeable church members, ex-head teachers and senior teachers who were not effectively involved, and whose vast knowledge was not properly utilised. Why and how could a church refuse the rich benefit and resource from the collective wealth of experience of 15 retired persons who had held senior positions in the public service and business? Why and how could a leader ignore such rich diverse talent and potential in his organisation?

Challenge to church organisations

The Parochial Church Council and other organisations must not be a limp, hand-picked association of followers or leaders' friends, if they are to seriously perform the church's business in a godly manner, objectively and effectively. These organisations must be properly and democratically chosen, and must be willing to perform their duty to the glory of God and the mutual benefit of all, impartially, fearlessly and without coercion. And this is by no means a call for heavy-handed aggression or strike. Such self-serving knee-jerk reactions, which are increasingly brewing in our nation, are undesirable among a law-abiding, peace-loving society, and worse for a church organisation.

Words to the spiritual

God has endowed the church with spiritual leaders who need to take their responsibility seriously. They cannot afford to take their fellowship and communion with God lightly. If they are to communicate effectively with their members, they must first establish regular communion with God. As God's spokespersons, leaders have an onerous responsibility to live and lead a godly life first—a life through which God can powerfully bless them, and they, in turn, become a source of blessing to their followers. Nothing else will suffice!

Discourse for optimum results

In a literate Barbados, where it is hoped that there will soon be a university graduate in every household, we need to reconsider the potential of laity to contribute to church development and success. Members have unlimited access to information and are availing themselves of education. Since the church has lost its voice as 'the spokesman' for the society, church leaders should no longer feel the need to be God's exclusive prophetic mouthpieces. God continues to use godly, humble members as well, and they should be used more in preaching and teaching engagements in churches. A few quotes from the book *Mega Shift: Igniting Spiritual Power* are in order:

> God is catching us all by surprise, doing things around the world without asking anybody's permission! Churches are growing in places and styles we think should be forbidden because it upsets the status quo.
>
> The Lord is bypassing some of our most cherished heroes and using housewives, teenagers and faceless nobodies to prophetically guide the church. . . .[4]

> A vast cleansing storm is roaring toward us from abroad. . .
>
> Thousands of committed teams around the globe are producing a neo-culture of **responsible freedom**. . . It is a joyful megashift away from pastor-centered, spectator religion toward a more Biblical church where God works directly through you—and you [laity] are freed from your problems and empowered to do wonders.[5]

Consequently, members must be given greater opportunity to share in church ministry and leadership. Concomitantly, church leaders must be willing to provide greater opportunity for the laity to serve and assist in administration. They must make a way. And, in turn, church members, young and old, should realise the need for their involvement in church at this time and be willing to participate. See Acts 2:14–18:

> Then Peter stood up with the Eleven, raised his voice and addressed the crowd: ". . . It's only nine in the morning! 16 No, this is what was spoken by the prophet Joel:
>
> 17 "'In the last days, God says, I will pour out my Spirit on all people.
>
> Your sons and daughters will prophesy, your young men will see visions,
>
> your old men will dream dreams. 18 Even on my servants, both men and women, I will pour out my Spirit in those days, and they will prophesy.'"[6]

Monologue discourses are not the most effective and modern means of communication. Their days have passed. Effective teaching dictates that we use all available means (audio, visual, audience participation, interaction, etc.) to get the message across. In this regard, the laity should not be left idly by as mere onlookers; the members have much to contribute to the learning process and advancement of the body. Let the talent and gifts of the body be utilised in the church to the glory of God and for the advancement of His kingdom!

Sharing information

Because a leader is not dishonest or accused of misappropriating funds is no reason for her or him to deny a congregation the right to transparency and to know the financial status of the church to which members contribute. Failure to be open and to regularly share information on finances and other transactions of the church, and to provide regular, clear accounting reports of people's offerings and contributions, is a travesty. Without begging, people need to know, and must be allowed some say in how their financial contributions are being utilised. Timely dissemination of information also constitutes prudent stewardship.

Many persons interviewed that were connected to St. Andrew's Parish Church had no difficulty with giving regular offerings or even having extra solicitations to give, but they complained about being denied the knowledge of, or having input into, how their funds were managed. Interviewees were generally pleased that the Church plant was satisfactorily maintained, but said that they needed more information about the Church's plans, objectives, programmes, and the management of its finances.

Some former adherents promised to return to the fellowship at St. Andrew's with a change of administration, and especially to one that is caring, sharing, spiritual, and mature.

Regard for civil responsibility

With reference to our current litigious society, the church needs to keep her ears to the ground and eyes on the law, while seeking every opportunity to be well informed of its members' rights and privileges. Like never before, she must engage in social and civil dialogue on matters that affect both church and state. And this conversation must not any longer ignore the current ethical and social dialogue taking place in our nation. Not least of all, as to the question whether a church must conform to civil legal practices in issues not relating to its doctrine, the *Gatherer* v *Gomez* case of June 1992, confirms that the Diocese of Barbados and the Church generally, are not free to act outside the boundaries of civil law. Hence, there is also the need for regular and proactive discussion on civil law and church practices (ethical and ecclesiastical), especially where it impacts at the points where members' lives revolve around issues of gender discrimination and equality, segregation, sexual abuse and orientation in church, just to name a few.

Abuse of the vulnerable

While the Anglican Church over the years has led the way in discrediting homophobia, enough has not been expressly done to stamp out sexual predation of vulnerable members, including the poor, the young generally, and particularly young males. Child sexual abuse involving offences in which an adult engages in sexual activity with, or exploits a minor for sexual gratification cannot be overlooked.[7]

Sexual predation involving widespread abuse comprising eph-ebophilia (sexual interest in mid-to-late adolescents, generally ages 15 to 19)[8] and paedophilia (sexual interest in prepubescent children generally those 13 years of age or younger) offenders,[9] have become topics of popular, but painful debate. The American Psychiatric Association states that "children cannot consent to sexual activity with adults", and condemns any such action by an adult as "a criminal and immoral act which can never be considered normal or socially acceptable behaviour".[10]

Psychiatrist Thomas Plante states that "approximately 4% of priests during the past half century (and mostly in the 1960s and 1970s) have had a sexual experience with a minor."[11] Having 4,392 church leaders accused of sexual abuse, representing 4% of the 109,694 ministering priests during that time, is a formidable, if not alarming, number.

In Barbados, we need to spread the net to include physical, emotional, and psychological abuse. We need to include abuse of the elderly, many of whom are being abandoned, while being exploited for their property and pension. Gender and class discrimination must not be ignored.

We need to return the church and public institutions to self-respecting places of trust that are staffed with people of trust. Incidents of abuse are devastating to all who are involved—the child, the family, the local church, society and its leaders. We need to make our institutions safe havens from abuse—especially all churches, without exception.

In the UK, paedophiles and other offenders are being duly prosecuted for crimes they commit, even after 40-odd years and longer. Thus, too, the church in Barbados should be aroused and be similarly prepared to prosecute offenders. Nothing but zero tolerance for heinous offences will suffice to protect our vulnerable members; and our church must do all within its power to demonstrate that it understands the enormity of crimes against the vulnerable and is willing to address them.

Call to Action

The Church must provide guidelines for reconciliation, healing, accountability, and prevention of acts of abuse; hence there is urgent need for it to:

1. Respond promptly and effectively to allegations.
2. Have a zero tolerance policy for abusers. Remove all offenders against whom a credible accusation is made, regardless of how long ago the offence occurred.
3. Press for prompt investigation and, if warranted, prosecution.
4. Cooperate with civil authorities.
5. Have a strong, articulated code of ethics.
6. Have thorough background checks.
7. Expose and speak up against wrongdoing by all offenders.
8. Promptly impose sanctions for impropriety and breach of code of conduct.
9. Encourage marriage and require fidelity by young clergy, **all clergy**.
10. Provide widespread education and discussion about the problem of abuse and its consequences at every level of society.
11. Screen and 'rescreen' all persons who work with children, youth, or vulnerable adults.
12. Screen and 'rescreen' institutions in which vulnerable people reside or that they frequent.

13. Fully publicise disclosure forms of workers as part of the screening routine.
14. Make references mandatory and check them thoroughly.

Jealousy, inferiority and ignorance

From sitting "In the Pew" it was regrettable to observe:

- A young person who had the right voice and was articulate, who excelled in drama and performance, but who was not allowed to offer her talent to the glory of God, and the pleasure and profit of the congregation.
- Persons who sacrificed time and money and received training in theology, but were not afforded opportunity to teach or help in the church.
- Leaders doing most of the work, most of the time, when many of the members could ably and better perform much of the work, most of the time.
- Several retired principals and senior teachers who had spent their lives training and equipping persons at all levels of society being left to sit idly by, listening to some leaders—who were either 'losing it', and others who never had it—preach and preside.
- Bright and highly qualified people being ignored, while others of far lesser ability and skills were being used repeatedly.
- Leaders who felt threatened, and who distanced themselves from people whom they perceived as a threat, or whom they think could easily replace them. Often these disturbed/neurotic people use persons whom they consider loyal, irrespective of how much less able the choice might be. And so, these self-serving leaders, who feel threatened, demonstrate little regard for the welfare of the organisation, often allowing it to suffer.

Unfortunately, the church, being a microcosm of society, suffers from too many of the above-mentioned ego-tripping/self-serving agendas.

Indeed, a well structured 'leaders-equipping' training programme can address many of the stated problems, which should significantly reduce the negative impact and suffering that churches experience.

A word to wise leadership should be helpful, and hopefully lead to timely intervention for the benefit of the church and all concerned.

Notes

1. Sylvan R. Catwell, "Passing On The Baton". *Pamphlet* distributed, 1 May 2008 at the 49th Anniversary Service of Ellerton Gospel Hall, Barbados.
2. "BENEDICTUS PP XVI. Declaratio", 11 February 2013 www.vatican.va/holy.../hf_ben-xvi_spe_20130211_declaratio_en.html Accessed 3 May 2014.
3. Bishop Drexel Gomez's Seventeenth Charge to the 1989 Annual Session of Synod, *Synod Journal* 1989.
4. King James Bible Version Online. http//www.biblestudytools.com/kjv/ Accessed 7 May 2013.
5. Wolfgang Simson. "Houses That Change the World", in Introduction to *Mega Shift: Igniting Spiritual Power* by James Rutz, 2nd Edition. USA: Empowerment Press, 2006.
6. Rutz *op. cit.* "The game has changed. Top-down society is dead". Back cover quote.
7. The Holy Bible, New International Version, 1973, 2011 by Biblica, Inc. online. Peter Addresses the Crowd, Acts 2:14-18 www.biblegateway.com/passage/?search=Acts Accessed 15 June 2013.
8. Child sexual abuse definition taken from the National Society for the Prevention of Cruelty to Children campaigning in Britain and the Channel Islands. - Wikipedia. . . en.wikipedia.org/. . ./National_Society_for_the_Prevention_of_Cruelty_to. . . . Accessed 13 March 2013.
9. Ray Blanchard, *et al.* (2009). "Pedophilia, Hebephilia, and the DSM-V" (pdf). *Archives of Sexual Behavior* 38 (3): 335–350. . . . . . Shields, 13837 (United States Federal Court 2008), as cited in Ewing, CP (2011). http://en.wikipedia.org/wiki/Hebephilia. Accessed 3 January 2013.
10. Peter Cimbolic and Pam Cartor. "Looking at Ephebophilia Through the Lens of Cleric Sexual Abuse". *The Journal of Treatment and Prevention* Volume 13, Issue 4, 2006. 347–359. www.ncjrs.gov/App/publications/Abstract.aspx?id=238978. Accessed 10 August 2011.
11. APA Letter to the Hon. Rep. Thomas Delay (R-Tx), "Catholic sex abuse cases" (Press release). *American Psychological Association*. June 9, 1999. en.wikipedia.org/wiki/Catholic_sex_abuse_cases. Accessed 13 March 2013.
12. Thomas G. Plante. "A Perspective on Clergy Sexual Abuse", in Michael Nielsen, ed., *Psychology of Religion*, database, updated April 7, 2010. (http://www.psychwww.com/psyrelig/plante.html). . . Accessed 13 March 2013.

CHAPTER FOURTEEN

And the work goes on (2011 and Beyond)

This closing chapter on the first six months of 2011, including Canon Gatherer's retirement, will be short. I had asked the new incumbent, Rev'd. Allan Jones, to share information about the Church and his plans. However, preferring to let his record speak over the next few years, he declined to share. Nevertheless, the new incumbent with his workers and congregation seem committed to rebuilding and consolidating the work as he endeavours to make his own mark. From the outside, one sees some rather happy committees committed to redeeming lost time and ground, if not to rewriting some lost pages of the St. Andrew's book.

As long as persons put their hands to the task with resolution, fidelity, unity, loyalty and commitment, positive results can be assured.

The time is ripe for St. Andrew's to be revived. Several members of the community who stood aside during the past 30-odd years, and others who wandered off, and still others who were forced to wander, have the opportunity to visit and become attached, or reattached, to this historic Church. In fact, many old hands have been taking the opportunity to visit at funerals, and occasionally at services, to observe and "feel the temperature" at the Church.

The Church needs a vision for rebirth and growth. One hopes that all concerned see the need for godly commitment and rededication, as the leaders and members resolve to be vessels and instruments through whom God will powerfully work in building St. Andrew's. One hopes that there will be openness to warmly embrace those seeking aid and fellowship.

The author cannot help but muse on an arresting mission statement taken from notes of a USA female Methodist leader who co-chaired a conference in Barbados in the 1990s, which was found useful and with some adaptation is being recommended for consideration at St. Andrew's:

> TO ALL WHO MOURN AND NEED COMFORT, TO ALL WHO ARE TIRED AND NEED REST, TO ALL WHO ARE FRIENDLESS AND WANT FRIENDSHIP, TO ALL WHO ARE LONELY AND WANT COMPANIONSHIP, TO ALL WHO ARE HOMELESS AND

WANT SHELTERING LOVE, TO ALL WHO ARE HUNGRY AND
NEED FOOD, TO ALL WHO SIN AND NEED FORGIVENESS,
THIS CHURCH OPENS WIDE ITS DOORS AND IN THE NAME
OF JESUS CHRIST THE LORD SAYS— *'WELCOME'*!

All life (include St. Andrew's) must be seen as a dynamic stage with exits and entrances, deaths and births. This is a logical cycle, reflecting that found in Nature. Situations are not meant to continue as they were forever. No matter how we comprehend the revolving activity of life through resurrection, reincarnation, or rapture, 'the scene goes on'. In the cyclical pattern of life, inevitably, day follows night and rejoicing follows sadness. So there's hope for St. Andrew's.

Leaders, members and friends of St. Andrew's Parish Church could pay no greater tribute to their Patron Saint and caring Evangelist than to emulate him in showing love in building relationships, in listening empathetically to others, helping them where need is greatest, and in witnessing to and bringing your 'kith and kin' to Christ.

To the leaders, members, lovers and friends of St. Andrew's: now is the time to cast in your lot. Like Nehemiah and his builders of old, put your hands to the plough, build the work, slack not your riding! Be steadfast as you commit to building a good work!

And finally, "Let go and let God! Stand still and see God's mighty work and salvation among you!" Always remember that the battle is God's and not ours. In earnest, it is not merely by or through our work and effort, but rather by His Spirit that exploits will be accomplished!

St. Andrew's: Unite, Work Smart! Always imploring God's help for successful rebuilding!

"Keep the flame ever burning brightly!"

Figure 54: Skit at St. Andrew's Mother's Union Concert, July 2011

Figure 55: What's a concert without a laugh?

And the work goes on (2011 and Beyond)

Figure 56: Congregation at Mother's Union Concert

Figure 57: Obsolete Rectory, Belleplaine, St. Andrew

Figure 58: Farewell from the Sunday school

Figure 59: Farewell from the St. Michael's and St. Andrew's Choirs

Figure 60: Friends at Fr. Gatherer's 92nd Birthday island tour

Figure 61: Canon Gatherer—"I fought the fight, ran the race and finished my course in St. Andrew's, March 2011"

Appendices

APPENDIX 1

Formalising Appointment of Anglican Church Leadership in the 18th century

It was not until the early eighteenth century that a comprehensive attempt was made to formalise the appointment of the leadership of the church.

From the Supplementary Information found in the catalogue of descriptions based on the Calendar compiled by Dr. W.W. Manross from the Fulham Papers, it was revealed that Bishop Edmund Gibson, in 1723, began to address the ordination process by requesting information from candidates aspiring to the priestly vocation. The following comprised some of the issues that required a response:

1. How long was it since you went over to the Plantations as a Missionary?
2. Have you overseen any other church, and if you have, what church was it, and how long have you been removed?
3. Have you been duly licensed by the Bishop of London to officiate as a Missionary in the diocese where you are serving?
4. How long have you been inducted into your living?
5. Are you resident in the parish to which you have been inducted?
6. How often is divine Service performed in your church? And what proportion of the parishioners attends?
7. How regularly is the Sacrament of the Lord's Supper administered? And what is the average number of communicants?
8. Have you a house and glebe? Is your glebe in lease, or let by the year? Or is it occupied by your self?
9. Have you more cures than one? If you have, what are they? And in what manner are they served?

It was not until after May 1724 that a detailed interview and an extensive list of questions had to be completed by priests or prospective candidates.

Obviously, Richard Grey, appearing on the scene almost 100 years earlier, did not have to face such rigorous examination, as the ordination protocol was not yet highly formalised.

Even though Bishop Beilby Porteus' predecessors began the trend toward formalising ordination, it was not until after 1748 that detailed documentation for the priesthood was required from candidates in the colonies.

The Fulham Papers comprise the archive of the Bishops of London, which were transferred from Fulham Palace, the former residence of the Bishops of London. The collection includes correspondence on the administration of the Diocese of London, and on the churches, particularly in America and the West Indies, that came under the Bishop's jurisdiction before the founding of separate episcopates in those countries.

APPENDIX 2

Hudson's Contribution to and the Impact of Church Music in Barbados

Gerald Hudson, of Southport, England, was born into a musical family. After completing his stint in the Royal Air Force and some studies in organ music, he became qualified as an associate of the Royal College of Organists.

Before age 24, he came to Barbados in April 1921 to be interviewed to be organist at St. Michael's Cathedral; he retired from the post 50 odd years later.

In giving his passion, full life, and dedication to organ music in Barbados, it was also reported that Gerald, through his recital at New York City's Carnegie Hall and numerous local performances, raised funds for refurbishing the old pipe organ of the Cathedral, and eventually acquired a new one. Under his leadership, the choir quickly grew from 14 to 30 members. With the backing of The Very Rev'd. Dean Shankland, he also founded the Barbados Choral Society in 1922, which eventually boasted 100 members and performed with the Cathedral choir on festive occasions.

Gerald loved people and was highly praised for his kindness to needy persons, especially his choir members. He was a brilliant composer ('There was War in Heaven' and a *Te Deum Laudamus*), and a prodigious sight reader.

Among his many honours, he was elected an Honorary Fellow by the Royal College of Organists in 1953, and for his contribution to music, the Queen made him an Officer of the British Empire (OBE).

Gerald Hudson is memorialised in Barbados for not only sharing his musical prowess in teaching music, singing, and music appreciation at several secondary schools, and in teaching piano, but also particularly for his willing and unselfish contribution in enhancing the capacity of numerous budding organists of his day. Some of these organists include: Neville King, Winston Hackett, Harold Rock, Bentley Callender, Merton McCarthy, Ernest Rocheford, father and son, Samuel and Lionel Burke, Cleopas "Lee" Drakes, Herberston "Herbie" Moore, brothers Lester and Charles Vaughan, and Dacosta Straker, Seymour Clarke, Ed. Carrington, Lionel

Gittens, Byron Reeves, Victor Pilgrim, and both Curtis Bailey and Merton McCarthy (the latter persons were also tutored by Rev'd. William E. Hopkins).

Visually impaired organists

Special mention is due to Mrs. Ione Kirton (member of an organist family and organist of St. Ambrose for over 40 years) and Don Johnson (organist of St. Peter and St. James), who continued playing the organ for many years even after they lost their sight. Unlike Mrs. Kirton, Don had reportedly memorised all of the Psalms and pointing (i.e., fitting the words to the music), and so he occasionally assisted Ione.[1]

Singers who moved into prominence

The above-mentioned and many other persons passed through the Cathedral as musicians, organists and choristers, while others moved into prominence as leaders in our nation—Sir Branford Taitt and Sir Frank Worrell. An inexhaustive list of persons connected with the Cathedral would include: Dr. Donnie Archer and Dr. Belfield Brathwaite, brothers Festus and Chesterfield Thompson and Rudolph and Basil Hinds, Christopher "Christie" Smith, Bruce St. John, Harold Brewster, Neville Grosvenor, Lionel Crawford, and Basil Forbes and soloists Marjorie Moore and Norma Bowen.

Many artistes made their debut in the Church

In referring to the impact of church music broadly (not necessarily under Hudson) on the Barbadian society and Barbadians in general, mention must be made of the fact that several singers, artists and performers made their debut in singing and performance in our churches. Richard Stoute sang in St. Leonard's Choir under Harold Rock. Dr. Anthony "Mighty Gabby" Carter, a legendary Barbadian, calypsonian and a Cultural Ambassador of Barbados, sang as a youngster at the Berean Baptist, St. Leonard's and St. Mary's churches. He has composed over 1200 songs. Mark Lord, formerly sang in St. Leonard's choir.

Harold Rock and the Choir for the Animation of the Sick and Incapacitated

Harold Rock, organist and school teacher of Federal High School, formed the Animation Choir for the Sick and Incapacitated, many of its members drawn from various church choirs. Later, "Joy" Edwards followed this with the Junior Choir for the Sick and Incapacitated, from which the St. Andrew's Glee Club (Choir)

---

1. Much of the information contained in this Appendix was graciously volunteered by Rev'd. Laurence Small, MBE. Other contributors included Canon Lionel Burke, Neville King, Ronald Stoute, Dr. Anthony "Mighty Gabby" Carter, Andrew Allman and Norma Bowen.

was formed. Many of the members also came from church choirs. Under Harold Rock, these choirs sang in institutions, the 11 infirmaries, the hospitals (The Queen Elizabeth, Mental Hospital, Lazaretto), the prison, and correctional centres for young people at Dodds and Summerville, St. Philip.[2] Singer Norma Bowen reported how, in the 1960s, these choirs comprising a large cross section of Barbadians, including performers/soloists—Norma herself, May Ramdin and Sylvester Cave—sopranos, Andy field—treble, Colin Norville—tenor, Christopher Headley—violinist, Allister Williams—tenor, Alfred Burrowes—bass, Daryl Speede and Hilton Springer—tap dancers, Ben Gibson on the saw, Lester Vaughan on the bottles, Irvine Brathwaite often assisted by his brother Winston Brathwaite on the organ, all assisted the Choirs for the Animation of the Sick and Incapacitated.

Bowen also indicated that at Easter and Christmas, one of the choirs would often start the day's concert from St. Lucy's Infirmary, while the other choir would start from the Infirmary in St. Philip or at Oistin, Christ Church. The choirs would perform at all of the Infirmaries (government geriatric residential centres at the time), after which they met later in the day for a picnic. Joseph Niles and the Consolers would appear as guest performers with the choirs.

The choirs not only sang in the institutions across Barbados, but also in the churches. In the summer, the choirs toured many West Indian facilitated by the popular Federal Palm and Federal Maple inter-island ships. Thus the choristers and performers received training and valuable local and regional exposure which stood them in good stead for future.

Persons of national, international and world-wide repute

A few persons (the list is by no means exhaustive), who serve in the local and international musical arena include Soloist Grace Haggatt, mezzo-soprano, who started singing in the Junior Choir at Calvary Moravian Church under organist Arthur Maynard, after which she did formal training in singing with Doris Provencal. Nell Wycherley (Archer) also sang in many musical performances in the Cathedral (under organist Dr. John Fletcher) and in local productions, in addition to having sung in numerous other Anglican churches from childhood.

Barbados proudly celebrates world-renowned singer Rihanna (Robyn Rihanna Fenty), who reportedly had an early affiliation with the New Testament Church of God, 4th Avenue Parish Gap, Westbury Road, St. Michael. As a little girl Rihanna sang in her Church choir as well as the New Testament Mass Choir.[3] Rihanna has done exceedingly well, currently being one of the most famous women in the world, the holder of 7 albums, releasing 39 singles with 24 hitting the top ten, and achieving not less than 88 awards. She is unstoppable.

---

2. Interview with Norma Bowen, 25 May 2013.
3. Interview with Clare Phillip, 23 January 2014.

As a boy, Errol Barrow, who later became Prime Minister of Barbados, also sang in the St. Michael's choir under Hudson.

Other persons worthy of mention and who also seriously contributed to music in Barbados around the mid-1900s and onwards included: organist and composer Rev. William Edmond Hopkins, Vicar of St. Jude's, St. George, during the 1930s, who was also reputed to be the fifth best organist in the world.

Hudson "The Boss"

In his day, organist and composer Gerald Hudson, "The Boss", was regarded as 'one of the best organists in the West'.

At 78, Gerald Hudson OBE, FRCO (hons.), ARCM, LRSM who served in Barbados for 53 years, died in January 1975.

APPENDIX 3

List of Anglican Clergy 1989, According to Date of Ordination

Ullyett, B.C.	1932	Gill, F.E.	1975
Hazewood, G.V.E.	1932	Harewood, I.H.	1975
Simmons, A.E.	1934	Dixon, W. StC.	1975
Walcott, S.A.	1935	Gooding, G.S.	1976
Curry, C.W.	1936	Rogers, R.P.	1976
Brathwaite, W.B.	1936	Sinclair, S.G.	1976
Jones, I. McK.	1941	Lorde, S.O.	1977
Tudor, H. StC.	1942	Mayers, C. DeC.	1977
Payne, E.L.	1951	Murrell, DeV. B.	1977
Maxwell, M.A.	1951	Darlington, C.A.	1978
Gatherer, E.G.	1952	Harewood, G.A.	1978
Hatch, G.A.	1953	Rochester, W.O.	1978
Burke, L. DeC.	1955	Williams, M.T.	1978
Clarke, L.G.	1955	Goodridge, C.S.R.	1978
Hennis, J.G.L.	1957	Isaacs, W.E.	1978
Crichlow, H.E.	1960	Small, L.G.	1979
Springer, J.L.	1960	Beckles, W.A.	1980
Lett, L.A.	1960	Carrington, A. DeL.	1980
Brome, R.T.	1961	Lyte, E.S.	1980
Crawford, L.A.	1962	Massiah, F.E.	1980
Goodridge, S.S.	1963	Wiltshire, E.C.	1980
Titus, N.F.	1963	Fields, S.D.	1981
Worrell, T.C.	1965	Goddard, C.C.	1981
Lashley, P.H.	1966	Haynes, P.H.	1981
Stapleton, D.A.	1967	Gibson, J.D.	1983

Knight, G.W.	1968	Lynch, E.E.	1983
Gaskin, W.	1968	Clarke, M.A.	1984
Marshall, F.B.H.	1969	Burke, N.A.	1985
Nicholls, P. DeL.	1969	Walcott, F.A.	1935
Guy, H.B.	1971	Norville, I.A.	1985
Small, S. DaC.	1972	Morris, C.M.	1985
Holder, J.W.	1974	Alleyne, E.T.	1988
Layne, W.F.	1975	Lashley, M.G.	1988
Belle, C.V.S.	1975	Watson, V.E.	1988
Fenty, P. DeC.	1975	Drayton, E.F.	1988

Extracted from the 1989 Diocesan Synod Report, page 6.

APPENDIX 4

"Only in St. Andrew"—Story of the Green Giant and the Shepherd Boy

Fr. Gatherer was a person who seemed to enjoy the pleasure of writing. He also had a beautiful handwriting. Even in his seventies he exhibited a keen sense of humour and a sharp mind, enjoyed a wicked bit of satire and could not conceal his piercing and poignant rhetoric, even beneath an impish, but endearing smile and soft-spoken voice.

I was advised that Fr. Gatherer kept voluminous notes. He scribbled; rather, he wrote everything. It is a pity that the notes, sermons and memoirs of a person who led such an outstanding ecclesiastical life are not available for the benefit of the public. The photocopy of his handwritten compilation was obtained on 25 December 2009. The author does not vouch for the validity or veracity of the account, and accepts no responsibility for the claims therein.

Following is a copy of the actual text:

Resume: or The Story of the Green Giant and the Shepherd Boy
 " " " " - Light-weight champion
 and the Old man.

Sad & Tragic were the events which resulted in
The Expulsion from office of the Rector of St Andrew the Rev. Edward Lathrone
After nearly 33 years as rector of St Andrew

Jan 1987: Says the Bishop The Rev Drexel Wellington Gomez:
The Constitution Canon Regulation Say you go at 65 yrs.
Says the Rector: O No, The Law says I go on
for ever.

Jan 1989: Says the Bishop: I have appointed your Successor
Leave by end of Jan. or else Legal proceedings
upon you without further notice and without delay.

Says the Rector O No. Not So. This Injunction says Neither
you nor your agents must interfere until it is heard.

Dec 1989 Mr. Justice W.D. declares: The Law is on Rector's
Side, he is absolutely right - he goes on for ever.
Bishop, your regulations are a nullity. Pay costs only.

Feb 1990 Says the Bishop: I appeal
April 1990 The C.J. and The other Two declare: Appeal
upheld, reasons later. Rector must pay.

Apl 1990   Says the Rector: O. No. Not so. To the R' Privy Council
           I go.
           And they all said: You must be kidding! O.K.
           You may go where you wish: But out! out! of St Andrew
           at once you go
           And also goes the house where you have lived for 33 yrs.

Apl 1992   The Five Law Lords of Her Majesty's Privy Council
           hear the matter
18th June 1992   The Judgment declares — Fr Gatherer is right
           The Judgment of Court of Appeal in Barbados is
           Set Aside: Mr Justice Woodbine Davis' judgment
           is restored: Bishop must pay Costs and
           damages.

18th July 1992   Rev. Edward Gatherer, age 70 yrs, resumed his work
           at St Andrew and awaits a settlement from the
           Court

17th Sept 1992   Bishop Drexel Wellington Gomez age 55
           completely demoralised, throws in the towel, declaring
           he has an job offer, - not in writing - too good to refuse.
           and furthermore says he: I will be better off financially

Resume of the Sad & tragic events which resulted in the Expulsion of the Rector Rev. Edward Fitherer from Office for Two Years & Two months before he was reinstated as the rightful Rector of St Andrew by the Judgment of Her Majesty's Privy Council and the Command of Her majesty on the . . . of June 1992. "This is the Lord's doing: It is marvellous in our Eyes:" Fr Edward Gatherer at age of 70 yrs 5mth, on 1st July 1992 Resumed his office as Rector of St Andrew for as long as he wishes to remain in that office. The Bishop. the Rt Revd Drexel Wellington Gomez, at age 55, unable to bear loss of face and embarrassment, resigns. Returns to his homeland to a Secular job which he Says was so attractive that he could·nt resist and furthermore says he: "I will be better off financially." The good Shepherd lays down his life for the Sheep The hireling runs away and goes after better pay.

APPENDIX 5

Copies of Articles from the Media

The Development and Impact of St. Andrew's Parish Church, Barbados

4, MONDAY, FEBRUARY 13, 1989. DAILY NATION.

FOCUS/ St. Andrew's Parish Church celebrates harvest

STRANGER IN THE PEW
by Arthur Gay

Gatherer's flock offers up first fruits

GIRLS OUTNUMBER boys in the congregation by as much as three to one.

INCENSE floated to the heavens like the prayers of the saints. A heady atmosphere of scent and satisfaction filled the church at St. Andrew, where a large congregation gathered for an early morning harvest and thanksgiving service, yesterday.

The priest, Father Edward Gatherer, strolled down the main aisle to greet this stranger and photographer Charles Grant. His warm smile paved the way for a morning of pleasant greetings and exchanges of good words.

Since our last visit to this church much has been happening. The repairs to the building have not been completed, but it is comfortable. The sound system goes a long way to improving the acoustics, and a steady band of worshippers do their best to maintain the dignity that is associated with the Anglican church throughout the nation.

Part of the morning's service involved a procession; a female crucifier, robed in red and white, led the way. Indeed most of the congregation is female. They lead the intercessions; they bring the cruets of wine to the altar; in other words, they are very much involved.

If rumour were true, we would have expected to note some disaffection with the priest. After all, they say half the congregation has walked out on him. But, if the other half had indeed stayed away, then their presence would have needed another church of similar space to accommodate them!

A thanksgiving and harvest service in Lent, which season began last Wednesday, means the mixing of celebration with solemnity.

For, as Father Gatherer reminded us, the lesson for the day would have dealt with the temptations of Christ. Rather, he chose Deuteronomy: 26, 1-6, where Moses instructs his people to take the first fruits of the land as a thanksgiving to the Lord, who took them out of a strange land and let them prosper.

The priest took as the text verses 10 and 11. The more familiar authorised version has it:

"And now, behold I have brought the first fruits of the land which Thou, O Lord, hast given me. And thou shalt set it before the Lord thy God, and worship before the Lord thy God.

"And thou shalt rejoice in every good thing which the Lord thy God hath given unto thee, and unto thine house, thou, and the Levite, and the stranger that is among you."

The priest said, although Lent is a solemn season which should be spent preparing for a spiritual journey with Christ; instead "we are celebrating the harvest (which is) a very joyful time."

Father Gatherer was "very happy" to see the goodies which the people were offering to God. He noted, from the time of creation people felt it was their duty and common sense to offer something to God.

He recalled the story of Cain and Abel, the former a farmer, the latter a husbandman. They both offered the fruits of their labour but God found Abel's gift of the first lamb of his flock acceptable. Cain's gift did not find favour with God.

According to the priest, there must have been something wrong with Cain's gift. Perhaps it was not the best of his produce; for, says Reverend Gatherer, if one offers one's best, it will be acceptable to the Lord.

He related, as a result of sin, the world became very evil; and God destroyed the world by a great flood. After the flood, Noah and family were saved.

FATHER EDWARD GATHERER bids a smiling member of his congregation farewell after the service. (Photo: Charles Grant)

and Noah offered thanksgiving to God, sacrificing some of the animals that were with him in the Ark.

"Then God made a promise there would be a time for planting, a time for harvest, a time for heat and a time for cold, winter and summer, day and night.

So, Noah instructed the people, after they had occupied the land which God gave them, they should offer thanks to God and make offerings, in the presence of the priest, as in the chapter of the text.

Just as the Israelites were slaves, so were our ancestors in these parts, the parson said. He added, one should not only give thanks for the harvest but one should look back at the place from which God has brought us.

For, said Father Gatherer, people forget the past... forget where they have come from... forgot the hardships; but the Israelites were told to remember the lashes the slavemasters gave them. The parallel with us Barbadians is that our ancestors were slaves and God brought them to this "fat land with the valleys so thick with cane that we should sing!"

He repeated: "Offer only the best, otherwise it would be sinful. Don't wait until you are ready to die to give God the dregs of your life. Give him the best part!" Although, he said, we must thank God for the latecomers.

So, said the priest, as we offer the fruits and things made with our hands, the cakes, the goodies, the handiwork, we offer them with thanksgiving in our hearts filled with gratitude.

The preacher reminded his congregation that we must not be worried about food or clothes. For, as the Bible says, "look at the birds! Look at the flowers! Even Solomon in all his glory was not arrayed like one of them."

He said: "If God takes care of the earth and the birds, wouldn't He care about you? Seek first the kingdom of God and all things will be added.

Offer to God the harvest of the land and the sea and the things we create with our hands. Thank him for the gift of His Son."

Throughout the service we sang harvest hymns from the book Ancient and Modern: Onward Christian Soldiers, We Plough the Fields, Fair Waved the Golden Corn, Now Thank We All Our God.

But, during the communion

BREAD AND CAKES formed part of the thanksgiving offerings at St. Andrew's Parish Church yesterday.

YOUNG LADY SERVERS taking the cruets of wine and other elements for the communion service to the celebrant.

best part of the service, the songs were Lenten hymns, such as Forty Days and Forty Nights.

The organ tended to swamp the singing, but when the congregation and choir could be heard, the quality was excellent. Pity so much was missed by the enthusiastic playing on a modern piece of equipment.

In the main we all enjoyed being with the folk of St. Andrew once again. In spite of the inhospitable roads, it was an adventure which rewarded us spiritually and gladdened our hearts.

It is not ours to resolve a matter of contention, of which there has been much rumour, speculation, fact and fiction.

Suffice to say we found a congregation that displayed no emotion other than being glad to be in the house of the Lord on the Lord's day, even if some of them seemed distant. We share good sentiments and wish them all the best for the future.

STAR AWARDS, with a maximum of four in each category, were:

Atmosphere .... ***
Brotherhood .... ***
Praise in Song .... **
Sermon .... ***

Copies of Articles from the Media

6. FRIDAY, NOVEMBER 3, 1989, WEEKEND NATION.

Court

THE RECTOR OF ST. ANDREW VS THE BISHOP

THE NO. 1 SUPREME COURT took on the air of an Anglican Church diocesan meeting yesterday.

Rector of St. Andrew's Parish Church, the Reverend Father Edward Gatherer is asking Acting Mr. Justice Woodbine Davis, QC, to declare that he is the duly appointed rector of the parish and to award him damages and costs.

The Bishop of Barbados Drexel Gomez is counter-claiming that Father Gatherer refused to obey his instructions to vacate the St. Andrew's Church rectory.

At yesterday's hearing, the plaintiff was examined by his counsel Chesley Boyce.

He was subsequently cross-examined by Jack Dear, QC, assisted by Ms. Dorothy Williams.

Dean Harold Crichlow of the St. Michael's Cathedral was giving evidence for the plaintiff when the matter was adjourned until today at 9:30 a.m.

Bishop refused case in 'private court'

THE BISHOP of Barbados bluntly refused to appoint an ecclesiastical court to hear the complaints being made by the Rector of St. Andrew.

Father Gatherer, rector and plaintiff, made this charge yesterday in the No. 1 Supreme Court when being cross-examined by Jack Dear, QC, counsel for Bishop Drexel Gomez, the defendant.

The plaintiff said the suggestion for an ecclesiastical court was first made to him by Sir Frederick Smith who was particularly concerned that the church problem "should not be publicly aired".

The plaintiff said that when he put this suggestion to the Bishop, he bluntly refused. He said he was amazed because "I did not want to go through with this sort of thing."

He is asking Acting Mr. Justice Woodbine Davis, QC, to declare that he is the duly appointed rector of St. Andrew's Parish Church, and is seeking damages and costs.

He said he had reached the age of 65 in 1987, but did not retire because he felt the diocesan regulations stipulating the age of retirement did not apply to him.

He quoted from the Constitution, Canons and Regulations of the Anglican Church Diocese of Barbados at Page 10, which read: "Any person who at the date of disestablishment holds an ecclesiastical office affected by this Act shall continue in that office until he is appointed to another ecclesiastical office or until he retires or resigns or is removed or until he dies without having retired or resigned or without having been removed."

Responding to his counsel Chesley Boyce, the plaintiff stated that he had not agreed to any changes in the terms and conditions of his appointment and considered himself bound by the Anglican Church Act as far as it dealt with the preservation of existing interests.

Dean of St. Michael's Cathedral, the Very Reverend Harold Crichlow, was giving evidence when the adjournment was taken until

The right of a rector

Father Gatherer states his case as Rector of St Andrew

REVEREND Father Edward Gatherer said he has the right to remain as Rector of St. Andrew "until I retire or die".

The plaintiff priest was replying to Jack Dear QC, counsel for the Bishop of Barbados Drexel Gomez, the defendant in a law suit engaging the attention of Acting Mr. Justice Woodbine Davis in the No. 1 Supreme Court.

Father Gatherer is asking the court to declare that he is still the substantive Rector of St. Andrew, a post he has held since 1957 when he went through the process of institution and induction.

He is represented by attorney-at-law Chesley Boyce.

The Bishop is counter-claiming that Father Gatherer refused to obey the instructions to vacate the rectory at St. Andrew.

Father Gatherer, in evidence, agreed he had assented to the 39 articles of the Anglican Church and took a canonical oath of obedience in all things lawful. But he disagreed that he ever disobeyed the Bishop in terms of service.

The plaintiff said he was appointed Rector of St. Andrew on May 1, 1957, by an appointments board of the Anglican Church under the 1911 Anglican Church Act when it was made absolutely clear that a person appointed under the act would not terminate office at any limited age. Furthermore, it was clearly understood that a person would work as long as he wanted or until he died.

The plaintiff said when he was appointed rector, there were no rules in place for dismissal of rectors and absolutely no rules for retirement. The rectors, who were mostly English,

FATHER EDWARD GATHERER and Bishop Drexel Gomez: on opposing sides in the courts.

packed up and went away when they became tired.

He produced in evidence several pieces of correspondence between himself and Bishop Gomez, and told the Court he felt embarrassed when he was referred to publicly as the priest in charge of St. Andrew.

He was saddened by the term by which the Bishop had addressed him, but heartened by another paragraph in the letter in which the Bishop had praised his "zeal and devotion" to his pastoral work.

The plaintiff maintained there were no changes in his terms of appointment and he did not agree to any change before or after 1969.

Daily Nation, Thursday, December 21, 1989

PRIEST REMAINS AT ST. ANDREW'S
Gatherer wins case against Bishop

FATHER GATHERER

REVEREND EDWARD GATHERER is still the rightful rector of St. Andrew's Parish Church.

This judgment was handed down yesterday by Acting Justice Woodbine Davis, in the case of Gatherer against the Bishop of Barbados, Drexel Gomez.

The plaintiff priest had asked the court to declare that he was still the substantive rector of St Andrew, a post he has held since 1957 when he went through the process of institution and induction.

Davis further ruled that the constitution, canons and regulations governing the Anglican Church in Barbados are invalid and that they do not comply with the Interpretation Act of the Laws of Barbados.

Gatherer contended he was appointed rector on May 1, by an appointments board of the Anglican Church under the 1911 Anglican Church Act and did not agree to any change before or after 1969 when the new constitution, canons and regulations were alleged to be in force.

The plaintiff's case rested on the section of the constitution, canons and regulations of Diocese of Barbados, which reads: "Any person who at the date of disestablishment holds an ecclesiastical office affected by this act shall continue in that office until he is appointed to another ecclesiastical office or until he retires or resigns or is removed or until he dies without having retired or resigned or having been removed."

Justice Davis awarded costs for the plaintiff's counsel Chesley Boyce, but did not award damages.

Counsel for the defendant Jack Dear, QC, applied for a stay of execution for a period of six weeks.

The court ruled that Fr. Gatherer's status "remains intact and that he is entitled to continue in office under the terms and conditions set out in the 1911 Anglican Church Act and re-enacted under Section 9 of Cap 375 of the Laws of Barbados.

"Fr. Gatherer will continue to receive all the emoluments of his office together with the rights, rents and profits of the glebe attached thereto and to occupy the rectory at St. Andrew," Davis further ruled.

Davis said the constitution, canons and regulations should have been published in the Official Gazette for them to have the effect of law.

A number of the Anglican clergy, including the Bishop, Dean Harold Crichlow and members of the church's laity were in the No. 1 Supreme Court to hear the judgment.

After shaking hands with his counsel, Gatherer went over to greet and shake hands with Gomez, Crichlow and some of the priests and well-wishers.

Gatherer said he felt very much relieved "after all the pressures of the past years".

April 15, 1990   BARBADOS   BDS $1

OVER TO THE DPP

Not a very Good Friday at St. Andrew's Church

by Arthur Gay
SUNDAY SUN

A GROUP of people, including a priest, armed with a crowbar and a hammer, broke a window and entered St. Andrew's Parish Church on Good Friday.

They were not thieves, though, but worshippers who just wanted to give praise to their Lord on that most holy of days on the Christian calendar.

They went to church not knowing what to expect, against the background of litigation and confrontation surrounding church rector the Rev. Edward Gatherer.

A new priest was appointed to the church in January 1989, but Gatherer refused to vacate the pulpit to which he said he was legally entitled. Court cases followed in which he was restored as rector but the ruling was overturned in the Appeals Court recently.

In spite of that ruling, Gatherer preached at the church last Sunday (Palm Sunday).

The Anglican Church then sought and obtained an injunction from the High Court ordering Gatherer to stop preaching at the church immediately and vacate the rectory.

Radio announcements gave credence to the rumour that Anglican Bishop Drexel Gomez would himself conduct the traditional Good Friday services.

But at mid-day Good Friday, Father Rogers, rector of St. Saviour's and St. Simon's, arrived to say Gomez told him to conduct the services.

He then attempted to enter the church, but it had been locked and bolted from inside, the sexton could not be found and no one knew where the keys were.

One parishioner suggested she drive the parson over to the rectory, hoping Gatherer would hand the keys over so services could be held.

But at the rectory, Gatherer was nowhere in sight and people dressed in Sunday best were milling around. None had knowledge of the lock-out at the church.

In the end, Father Rogers and his group returned to the church. They approached the north side of the building and, armed with a hammer and crowbar, removed a pane of glass from a window, thus gaining entry to the church.

Inside it was discovered that a small altar had been placed up against the west door. There were two pews, capable of seating about eight persons, placed there facing each other, north and south. Before a small prayer desk was a priest's chair.

The setting was that of a miniature chapel, situated at the west end of the church.

With a little help, Father Rogers removed the altar to the side. The main doors were opened and he invited the faithful to join him for "a short service".

A police sergeant and constable who appeared on the scene later returned to their other duties.

▲ PEOPLE dressed in Sunday best were locked out of the Church. (top pix)

▲ FATHER ROGERS and his group, armed with a hammer and crowbar, removed a pane of glass from a window.

► THE window opened, this parishioner proceeded to enter the Church.

Photos by Charles Grant

REV. EDWARD GATHERER, accompanied by some parishioners, gives the "V" victory sign after yesterday's hearing.

Gatherer decision tomorrow

ACTING CHIEF JUSTICE Clifford Husbands will hand down his decision tomorrow morning, as to whether to grant Rev. Edward Gatherer leave to appeal to the Privy Council.

He heard submissions by Rev. Gatherer's attorney Chezley Boyce, seeking leave to appeal to Her Majesty-in—Council the decision earlier this month of the Appeal Court headed by Chief Justice Denys Williams and comprising Justices Clifford Husbands and Elliott Belgrave.

The Appeal Court then upheld an appeal by Bishop Drexel Gomez against a recent High Court decision favouring Fr. Gatherer and given by Acting Judge Mr. Justice Woodbine Davis on December 20, last year.

Mr. Justice Davis had allowed the priest to remain as rector of St. Andrew's Parish Church.

While the Appeal Court accepted the grounds presented by Jack Dear, Q.C., on behalf of the Anglican Church, no reasons were given and a written judgement will be given at a later date.

Boyce, associated with Herbert Arthur, had contended that the Constitution, Canons and Regulations, a document set out by the Anglican Church Synod, was null and void.

Copies of Articles from the Media

REPORTS ON THE MURDER CASES
PAGE 4

THURSDAY, APRIL 26, 1990.   BARBADOS, W.I.   CIRCULATED COPIES: 30 410   BDS. 60c

NEXT STEP THE PRIVY COUNCIL
But Gatherer must leave rectory

FATHER EDWARD Gatherer's fight to remain rector of St. Andrew's Church may now be taken to the Privy Council.

In the meantime, he must gather his belongings and vacate St. Andrew's Rectory, where he has lived for the past 32 years.

Acting Chief Justice Mr. Justice Clifford Husbands yesterday upheld an April 5 Court of Appeal decision that ordered Gatherer from the rectory. But the judge granted "conditional leave (for Gatherer) to appeal to Her Majesty in Council..."

One condition is that Gatherer must, within the next 42 days, pay the Barbados equivalent of £500 (£1: $3.25) "as security for the due prosecution of the appeal".

The money also covers "the payment of all such costs as may become payable by the applicant".

Meanwhile, Anglican Bishop Drexel Gomes, the respondent in the civil suit, has been ordered to post a bond of $40 000 with the Registrar of the Supreme Court. The money must be in place before any steps are taken to evict Gatherer or before he leaves as ordered by the court.

The judge ruled the sum of money to be "good and sufficient security for the due performance of such Order as Her Majesty in Council shall think fit to make thereon".

Mr. Justice Husbands also gave the 67-year-old priest 90 days to take the necessary steps for procuring and preparing the necessary records to be sent to England and ordered that the Registrar of the Supreme Court notify both Gatherer and Bishop Gomez of the date when the records are sent.

The matter, heard in the No 1 Supreme Court, was the latest chapter in a story that goes back over a year. Anglican Bishop Drexel Gomez wrote Gatherer advising him his period as priest-in-charge of St. Andrew's would conclude at the end of 1988 and that a new appointment would be made.

Gatherer's appointment was extended until the end of January 1989, at which point the priest served a writ on the bishop seeking to remain as rector of the church.

Mr. Justice Woodbine Davis found in favour of Gatherer, basing his decision of the invalidity of the Canons and Regulations of the Anglican Diocese.

That decision was overturned by the Appeal Court on April 5 this year.

And last night CBC-TV reported in its late news telecast that Bishop Gomes had withdrawn Gatherer's licence, a move that means he cannot preach in any church in the Anglican diocese and bars him from weddings, funerals or baptisms.

The Development and Impact of St. Andrew's Parish Church, Barbados

---

DAILY NATION

MONDAY, JULY 6, 1992. BARBADOS, CIRCULATED COPIES: 28 951 BDS. 75c

The Popular Choice For Crop-Over

A FUN RIDE IT WAS — ALL THE WAY CENTRE PAGE

UNIQUE SWEEP BY BRC CYCLIST PAGE 28

UNTOUCHABLE!
Gatherer vows to stay on until 'I expire'

by Marva Cossy
DAILY NATION

FOR THE past 20 years, Bishop Drexel Gomez has been trying to move Father Edward Gatherer from St. Andrew's Anglican Church, the rector told his congregation yesterday.

But he assured his flock that he would not leave until God took his last breath.

Referring to May 1990 when he was dismissed from the church and evicted from its rectory, Gatherer said: "They thought they had me.

"But you can't stop the unstoppable, you can't touch, the untouchable, you can't dismiss the undismissible."

And he told his congregation he was looking for a lot of holy water to wash away the many wrongs that had been done at St. Andrew's.

Yesterday he was back in his pulpit as decreed by the Privy Council, and in his first sermon he preached of loving his enemies and being chosen by God.

Preaching "from the heart", the balding priest reminded the attentive 133 parishioners that he had described himself two years ago as chosen by God.

"I feel more strongly today that I'm one of God's chosen people and I hope you are one of God's chosen children too," he added.

Gatherer drew attention to his middle name "Godson" — admitted that once he could not understand why his mother selected it, but now he stressed son-of-God on mention of it.

"That is why I can never retire until I expire..." he said as the congregation burst into spontaneous clapping, drowning out a few voices crying "thank you".

The tall, smiling rector reaffirmed his belief that God sent him to the parish 35 years ago. Gesticulating and occasionally bending over the pulpit, as if reaching out to his audience, he emotionally related the events leading to his selection and introduction to the church by Bishop Lisle Mandeville.

"I came reluctantly, I didn't like the hills. Now I love them... and I love every person in St. Andrew," he confessed.

Recalling aspects of his problems with Bishop Gomez, Gatherer said: "My conscience is right, and so I don't care who try to prosecute me. Blessed are you when people shall prosecute you..."

He said that just as Job and Joseph were tested by God, his recent problem was a test. "I took my licks and God is pleased..."

Gatherer referred to the eviction notice at the start of the dispute which gave him two weeks to leave the rectory as not the way to speak to a poor man". He recalled being so hurt that he cried, but after praying, God told him to see a man call Chez-ny Boyce, who became his lawyer.

Gatherer said he still had some fond memories of the past, for instance, being warned about his possible arrest, which gave him the chance to hide in order to avoid spending a night at Glendairy Prison.

Receiving nice letters was also a bright spot in those days, he told his congregation. But he added that the nicest one came from the Privy Council.

Gatherer recalled the negative things too. For example, the taunting remarks of "Belle-plaine boys" shouting "Gatherer, you are clean bowled".

"But here's Gatherer batting and bowling," he said as the congregation erupted into applause.

FATHER EDWARD GATHERER yesterday: 'They thought they had me. But you can't stop the unstoppable ... and you can't dismiss the undismissible.'

Rectory no more — just a wreckery

FATHER Edward Gatherer wants a home.

The St. Andrew's Parish Church rector, back from a two-year absence, has found the church rectory in a state of disrepair.

"...even the prodigal son had a better reception than I had — no welcome party, no ring for my finger, no shoes, no robe, no feast, no rejoicing; only a very dirty church, padlocked and stuffy.

"A house which was once a haven of joy and happiness, a shelter for many, where one could sit and admire the beautiful hills and enjoy the salubrious air — what was once the rectory is now the 'wreckery'," he told his congregation in his first pastoral letter.

"They have done a splendid demolition job on the people of St. Andrew," he added.

The two-storey four-bedroom, two-bathroom home located near Belleplaine is now a pitiful sight. The yard is overgrown with weeds and shrubs.

Inside the building is worse. Piles of debris — books, papers and card — are heaped in the corners of some rooms.

Cupboards seemed to be missing, glass panes on windows and doors are broken, rotting wood is all around, while the plumbing and electrical systems need major repairs, the rector pointed out.

Gatherer does not think vandalism is responsible for the disrepair. He told the Press that he had been away from the house many times and there had never being any vandalism.

However, Gatherer said he had been promised recently by Bishop Drexel Gomez that the house would be rebuilt.

IT'S joy all around as Father Edward Gatherer is reunited with his flock.

Sun on Sunday, July 27, 1996

Case adjourned

FATHER EDWARD GATHERER will have to wait until December to know how much money he will get from the Anglican Church.

When his exemplary damages claim came before Mr. Justice Garvey Husbands in chambers yesterday, it was adjourned until December 11.

Gatherer, 72, was prohibited from preaching at St. Andrew's Parish Church in 1989 because he had reached 65 years of age. That decision was overturned by the Privy Council in June 1992 and sent back to local courts for the priest to be awarded damages.

Chezley Boyce appeared for Gatherer and Sir Jack Dear for the Anglican Church.

FATHER EDWARD GATHERER

The Development and Impact of St. Andrew's Parish Church, Barbados

Sunday Sun, January 4, 2009

Till death do us part!

Gatherer still going strong at St Andrew church

by MARIA BRADSHAW

"I AM GOING ON until the Almighty stops me. Not my people!"

These words flowed softly from the lips of Anglican priest Edward Gatherer, 86, who sued the Anglican Church about 20 years ago after then Bishop Drexel Gomez attempted to retire him compulsorily when he reached the age of 65.

Today, as rector of St Andrew's Parish Church, Father Gatherer is probably the oldest practising Anglican priest in the diocese.

In a brief exclusive interview with the SUNDAY SUN yesterday he maintained that his long tenure at the church was proof that he was still able to continue despite his age.

"That is what I was fighting for. That was my own belief," he said as his caretaker Cherie Hurst – the woman he calls his right hand – stood at his side.

His seven-year battle with the church started back in 1988 when he received a letter ordering him to vacate the church. He challenged the decision and the court ruled that he was the rightful rector of St Andrew's Church.

The Anglican church in turn challenged that decision in 1990 in the Court of Appeal and won and Gatherer was evicted from the rectory.

However, he appealed to the Privy Council and in 1992 it ruled that there was no legal requirement compelling the church to retire priests at age 65.

Gatherer returned to the church after a two-year absence, saying he would not leave until God took his last breath.

Gatherer sued the church for $12 million but was awarded only $200 000 by the court.

53 years at church

Still going strong, Gatherer, who will be celebrating 53 years this year at St Andrew, explained that he spends his time preparing for two services a week at the church – Sunday mass and Wednesday morning services – as well as performing other duties such as weddings, christenings and funerals.

"I have two weddings and four funerals coming up. I am trying to hold on and do whatever I can," he said, after taking a stroll around the manicured grounds of the church.

Asked about his relationship with the hierarchy and other priests of the Anglican Church, he simply said that he carried his fight alone, but that the young priests may not be aware of his historic fight.

However, he quickly pointed out that Bishop John Holder attended confirmation at the church last Sunday.

But a sore point for Father Gatherer seems to be the fact that he has been without a rectory for the past two years.

He explained that it was destroyed by fire.

"This is about two years and two months that I have been without a rectory, but let them do what they want to do. They told me faithfully that they will repair it and then it went up in flames . . . ."

Faithful supporter

Questioned about a reportedly dwindling congregation at the church, Gatherer said there were still reasonable numbers of parishioners who attended.

But Hurst, who has stood faithfully by his side over the years, interjected that some people who had left the church during those tumultuous years returned while others chose to stay away.

She said Gatherer was wrongly portrayed as a power-hungry priest who was not willing to let go.

"What people don't understand is that [the Anglican Church] was trying to make a point but it got into personalities and that wasn't the case, and that is what people are still holding on to."

Asked to explain further, she said Gatherer was portrayed as an "old, dying person" but she pointed out "that wasn't true and that was how the majority of people saw him and most of them did not know him and that wasn't fair".

She said there were hundreds of people who came up under Father Gatherer's priesthood.

"The church is rebuilt. We are all getting older, and he still has the church and at least he has shown us a good example."

Hurst also expressed the belief which was supported by Gatherer that all he has ever wanted was an apology.

"I believe that unless we can say we are sorry we will never move on and it is not a good example for the young ones," she said, as Gatherer nodded in agreement.

• mariabradshaw @nationnews.com

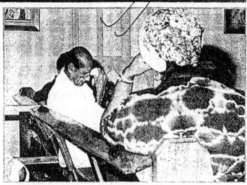

FLASHBACK: two days later Father Edward Gatherer weeping openly during a prayer service at St Andrew's Church. (FP)

STILL GOING STONG: at 86, Father Edward Gatherer is the oldest practising priest in the local Anglican Church. (Picture by Maria Bradshaw.)

BACK IN 1990, surrounded by parishioners, Father Edward Gatherer gave the victory sign after the court granted him leave to take his case to the Privy Council. (FP)

Daily Nation Monday, March 28, 2011

Gatherer 'fought good fight'

REVEREND CANON EDWARD GATHERER, rector of the St Andrew's Parish Church, "has fought the good fight, finished the race and kept the faith".

This description was used by Gatherer's long-standing friend the Rev. Canon Wilborne Austin as he addressed members of the Anglican communion in Barbados, Government officials and Gatherer's family during a retirement church service at the St Andrew's Parish Church, where Gatherer served as rector for 34 years.

Austin, priest of the St Stephen's Episcopal Church in Bloomfield, Connecticut, in the United States, said that his friend had touched the lives of thousands of people in one capacity or another during his 60-year service to the Anglican Church and would be remembered for being resolute in what he believed to be right.

"You have shown all of us how necessary, especially in the days in which we are living, [it is] to stand for something or we will fall for anything. You have fought not just any fight; you have fought the good fight. You have fought to lead people to Christ. We all know the song **Will There Be Any Stars In My Crown**. Well, I heard a preacher say once that there will be no starless crowns in heaven. I know that your crown will be star-studded."

Austin indicated his friend came to Barbados,

and specifically to Codrington College, to be trained in the priesthood, and upon becoming a priest he opted to remain in Barbados. He said that he was unaware of Gatherer's intention when he left his home in St Vincent, but based on the work he had accomplished in Barbados, and specifically in the parish of St Andrew, "I would say that God led him here".

"He did not jump and come, in my humble but accurate opinion. I believe that he was called by God to this part of God's vineyard."

As tears streamed down

KATHLEEN PILGRIM and Roger Hutson were two of the many individuals who signed a congratulatory card to be presented to Reverend Canon Gatherer (inset).
(Pictures by Nigel Browne.)

his face, an emotional Gatherer thanked the congregation for assembling to give him a "very spiritual and moving-send-off".

"My tenure at St Andrew has been long, very eventful but very fulfilling. I am grateful to have served in this parish. The Lord is my rock, my fortress and my deliverer; my God is my rock in whom I take refuge. The Lord is faithful to all his promises and loving toward all he has made. I bid you farewell," said the 87-year-old. **(AH)**

The Development and Impact of St. Andrew's Parish Church, Barbados

DAILY Nation

MONDAY, MARCH 28, 2011 — BARBADOS, WI — www.nationnews.com

BL&P: We can handle tsunami – Page 5

The face behind that football voice – Page 16

Bajans end with a fass – Page 22

Gatherer retires after 60 years

YESTERDAY IT WAS TIME to say goodbye to a man who gave 60 years of his life to the Anglican Church.

The Reverend Canon Edward Gatherer was wished farewell by members of the Anglican Communion in Barbados, Government officials and family members during a retirement church service at the St Andrew's Parish Church, where he served as rector for 34 years.

After listening to complimentary speeches about his life in and contribution to the church, an emotional Gatherer acknowledged: "All of you gathered here today to recognize my retirement, I thank you. I thank you for a very spiritual and very moving send-off." (AH)

Here, 87-year-old Gatherer (right) gratefully accepting a gift from long-standing friend the Reverend Canon Wilborne Austin, priest of the St Stephen's Episcopal Church in Bloomfield, Connecticut, in the United States.

■ Please see also Page 4.
(Picture by Nigel Browne.)

APPENDIX 6

Oldest Anglican priest to retire: The Church of England Newspaper, March 18, 2011, p 8.

Posted by geoconger in <u>Church of England Newspaper</u>, <u>Church of the Province of the West Indies</u>. <u>trackback</u>

The Rev. Edward Gatherer

First published in <u>The Church of England Newspaper</u>.

The oldest stipendiary priest in the Anglican Communion, the Rev. Edward Gatherer (89), will retire on March 27 after serving 55 years as the incumbent of St Andrew's Parish Church in Barbados.

While the Church of the Province of the West Indies, like all other Anglican provinces, has a mandatory retirement age, Fr. Gatherer took the Diocese of Barbados to court when its bishop, Drexel Gomez—later to become Archbishop of the West Indies—attempted to force him to retire when he turned 65.

The case of <u>Gomez v Gatherer</u> eventually came before the Privy Council in London which in 1992 held the failure of a Church to follow its rules of procedure served as a bar to enforcement of acts not properly enacted.

The <u>Gomez</u> case centered round the issue of whether a church was required to conform to civil legal practices in issues not touching upon doctrine. In 1969 the Church of England in Barbados was disestablished and the 1947 Anglican Church Act governing the clergy and church was rescinded. New regulations were made by the church, in its new capacity as a non-established religious body that provided for retirement of clergy upon reaching 65 years of age.

However, the church failed to publish the new regulations in the Official Gazette as was required by law. The Privy Council held the Diocese of Barbados was not free to act outside the boundaries of civil law.

After a two year suspension, Fr. Gatherer was returned to St Andrew's by the court and awarded $200,000 in damages. He vowed to remain at St. Andrew's until he had to be carried out dead.

---

4 "Oldest Anglican priest to retire". George Conger (geoconger) in *The Church of England Newspaper*, Church of the Province of the West Indies, 18 March 2011. http://www.google.com/#hl=en&sugexp. Accessed 20 January 2013.

Archbishop John Holder of Barbados announced last week that he had named Fr. Gatherer an honorary canon of St Michael's Cathedral in Bridgetown "in appreciation of his 60 years of ministry in the diocese."

"I think that he has made a contribution to the diocese and he takes his ministry and his priesthood very seriously," the archbishop said.

While there are older priests at work in the Anglican Communion, the introduction of mandatory retirement rules has seen older active clergy take up honorary or non-stipendiary work.

A spokesman for the Church of England told *The Church of England Newspaper* that there were "about a dozen Church of England incumbents still in stipendiary ministry because they are not caught by the mandatory retirement legislation" and are still working past the age of 70.

"However, we can't find anyone still in post older than Mr. Gatherer in Barbados," the church spokesman noted.

APPENDIX 7

Copies of Correspondence and Notes

BARBADOS DIOCESAN TRUSTEES

TEL: 426-2761

DIOCESAN OFFICE
"MANDEVILLE HOUSE"
HENRY'S LANE
ST. MICHAEL

January 13, 1987

Brian H. Claxton Associates Ltd.
Consulting Supervisory Services
P.O. Box 31B
Brittons Hill
St. Michael

Dear Sirs,

St. Andrew's Church

Thank you for your letter of 10th November 1986.

The Trustees wish to thank you for your help and assistance in stabilising the foundations to the Church and have placed on record the contributions which have been made by Mr. Claxton, his fellow professionals and other members of the building industry.

In view of the need to carry out the remedial works expeditiously, especially inside the Church, the Trustees request an indication of the cost of the remaining work to be completed.

Yours faithfully,

H.L.V. Griffith
Secretary

c.c. The Lord Bishop
Rev. E.G. Gatherer, Rector
The Secretary, St. Andrew's Church Council

HLVG:mm

```
NOTE FOR FILE                                          1981-02-12


                       ST. ANDREW'S CHURCH


     I visited the Church with Mr. Brian Claxton, structural
engineer, today, after first calling at the Rectory and inform-
ing Fr. Gatherer of our intentions.  He told us the Church (and
vestry) would be open.

     We found the Church and vestry open.  The tap of the vestry
handbasin was turned fully on and there was a strong flow of
water; we turned it off.

     We did not go up to the main roof or into the Bell Tower,
as Mr. Claxton had recently broken his wrist, which has not yet
healed and is still in bandages.

     We found the report and recommendations of the de Jongs, the
Peace Corps Volunteers, made in early 1979, appropriate.

     The roof appears to be in good shape as evidenced by the
main ceiling which bears no stains and seems to be in good con-
dition.

     The vestry is an addition and has cracks; these should be
ignored at least until the movement, due to water seepage in to
the sub-soil round the foundations, has been arrested, and the
sub-soil has had a chance to dry out and stabilise.

     The main problem is with the south-west corner of the main
structure.  Here water off the bell tower roof, and possibly
water running down the slope on the west of the church as well,
is seeping into the sub-soil around the foundations; the sub-
soil alternatively swells with water and shrinks as it dries out,
causing movement in the foundations, which is transferred up
the main structure.

     The foundations are similarly affected on the north, east
and south by water off the roof seeping through cracked drains
into the sub-soil; however on all these three sides the land
slopes away and the problem is not serious or urgent.

     The recommended remedies are:-

1.   Bell Tower:  Replace roof, guttering and down pipes.  This
     work is as shown at item D in Sydney Moore's unfulfilled
     contract ($4,200).

2.   Main Roof Guttering:  Clean out behind parapet and renew
```

guttering. (NOTE - The copper guttering obtained under the supervision of the de Jongs for this purpose is still held and available).

3. West Side Exterior Concrete Slab: Remove, fill and relay the concrete slab along the length of the west side of the main structure of the Church forming an open drain alongside the existing garden retaining wall, using three inch concrete reinforced with BRC and sealed to the main structure. (NOTE - the objects of this measure are to carry the water from the roof as far from the main structure as possible.). It will be necessary to relay this concrete slab because:-

   (a) It is cracked and broken.
   (b) The levels are not correct.
   (c) The open drain is near the main structure instead of being as far away as possible.

   The new levels incorporating a broad shallow drain will carry the water at the south-west corner of the main structure to the south and then down the driveway.

4. West Side Exterior: As we feel water from the slope to the west may be backing up against the garden retaining wall and then seeping under the wall into the sub-soil surrounding the foundations, weep holes should be made in that wall. Any water flowing through the weep holes will drop into the new drain, which will be as far from the main structure as possible.

5. Down Pipes: All down pipes should be angled, some twenty to thirty inches above ground level, to throw the water from the roof as far from the main structure as possible. A more costly alternative is to run the roof water through down pipes into tanks a few feet above ground level. The overflow from these tanks can then be taken further away from the main structure than can be done with the angled down pipes.

(NOTE - The use of tanks is not thought necessary at this time, but should be borne in mind if water is found to be seeping into the sub-soil surrounding the foundations).

When the foregoing works have been completed there should be a halt to all work for an interim period of several weeks or months. This will allow the sub-soil to dry out and the effect of these measures can be determined. Thereafter the position can be re-assessed and other less urgent and important work can be embarked on).

It should be noted that the wooden stairway to the Bell Tower is rotten and should be replaced or repaired soon.

After leaving the Church we returned to the Rectory and reported our findings to Fr. Gatherer.

T.N.H. Wells
1981-02-12

Bibliography

BIBLE / HYMN BOOK
English Standard Version Bible (ESV). Wheaton Illinois: Good News Publishers, 2001.
King James Bible (KJV) Online. http//www.biblestudytools.com/kjv/
New International Version (NIV). Colorado Springs: Biblica, Inc., 1973 (latest update 2011).
Hymns Ancient and Modern. Norwich, UK: Canterbury Press, 1988.

BOOKS
Anson, Sir William R. *The Law and Custom of the Constitution,* (3rd ed.). Oxford: Clarendon Press, 1908.
Campbell, P. F. *The Church in Barbados in the Seventeenth Century*. Barbados: Barbados Museum and Historical Society, 1982.
Catwell, Sylvan, *The Brethren in Barbados: Gospel Hall Assemblies, 1889–1994*. USA, Michigan: McNaughton & Gunn, 1995.
Harlow, Vincent T. H. *A History of Barbados 1625–1685*. Oxford: Clarendon Press, 1926.
Henson, Herbert H. *The Church of England*. Cambridge University Press, 1939.
Hill, Barbara. *Historic Churches of Barbados*. Barbados: Art Heritage Publications, 1984.
Hoyos, F. A. *Grantley Adams and the Social Revolution*. London: Macmillan, 1974.
Lawrence-Archer, J. H. (James Henry), 1823–1889. *Monumental inscriptions of the British West Indies*. London: Chatto and Windus, 1875.
Oliver, Vere L. *Monumental Inscriptions: Tombstones of the Island of Barbadoes*. Three Rivers, Mass.: Van Volumes, Ltd. 1989.
Reece, J. E. and C. G. Clark-Hunt, *Barbados Diocesan History*. In Commemoration of the First Centenary of the Diocese of Barbados, 1825–1925. London: West India Committee, 1925.
Rutz, James. *Mega Shift: Igniting Spiritual Power* (2nd ed). Colorado Springs, USA: Empowerment Press, 2006.
Schomburgk, Robert H. *The History of Barbados*. London: Frank Cass Publishers, 1971 (copy of 1848 original).

Wilkinson, Audine. *Anglican Ministry in Barbados. Anglicanism in Barbados 1627–2002. A bibliographical Portrait. A Commemorative Portrait in Celebration of 375 years of Anglican Ministry in Barbados*. Bridgetown: Church of Christ the King, 2001. Unpublished.

INTERVIEWS

Alleyne, Winston. 12 December 2009.
Beckles, George. 26 July 2011.
Belgrave, Simeon. 9 February 2013; 17 March 2013.
Bovell, Everton. 26 July 2011; 2 August 2011; 11 October 2011.
Bovell, Newton. 19 January 2010.
Bowen, Norma. 25 May 2013.
Brome, Bishop Rufus, GCM. 12 October 2011.
Burke, Canon Lionel. 11 October 2011.
Campbell, Pastor Andrew. 30 October 2011.
Catwell, Dolores. 18 February 2010.
Catwell, Henderson. 8 November 2012.
Clarke, Rev'd. Dr. Michael. 21 January 2013.
Clarke, Patrick. 18 July 2011.
Claxton, Brian. 20 December 2009.
Cumberbatch, Emeline. 18 February 2010; 12 September 2011; 29 September 2011.
___ and George Beckles. 26 July 2011.
Crichlow, Dean Emeritus Harold, GCM. 20 December 2009; 15 March 2013.
Drakes, Hutson and organ builder David Burke. 21 January 2013.
Foster, John. Retired Chief Public Health Inspector, 26 November 2013.
Goring, David. 19 February 2013.
Grecia, Gwendolyn and Gwendolyn Gibbons. 21 January 2010.
Griffith, Stephen. 7 September 2012;
Harding, Cyrillene. 16 March 2010; 26 September 2011; 29 September 2011.
Hoad, Richard. 15 March 2013.
Hurst, Cheryl and Cyrillene Harding. 16 March 2010.
King, Neville, Harriet Lowe, Canon Lionel Burke and Fr. Laurence Small. 20 November 2012.
Knight, Berkeley and Bertram Murray. 21 January 2010.
Luke, Doug. 28 October 2009.
Mahon, Daphnie. 26 July 2011; 21 August 2011.
Marshall, Dean Frank, CBE. 3 March 2010.
Maxwell, Patrick and Stanton Jordan. 20 October 2012.
Maynard, Jennifer. 8 November 2012.
Phillip, Clare. 23 January 2014.
Roett, Anthony. 15 March 2013.
Sandiford, Rev'd. Hugh. 1 October 2011.
Sandiford, Melba. 24 September 2011; 7 September 2012.
Simon, Dr. Bromley. 17 March 2013.

Small, Erma. 23 July 2011; 2 August 2011; 24 September 2011.
Small, Rev'd. Laurence, MBE. 4 December 2012; 8 March 2013; 13 March 2013; 4 April 2013, 20 November 2013, 22 November 2013.
Smith, Hersie. 31 October 2011.
Smith, Joan. 12 December 2009.
Smith, McDonald. 8 April 2010.
Solomon, Oliver. 26 September 2011.
Tucker, Michael. 27 October 2011.
Turney, Deborah. 29 August 2011.
Watkins, Perometta. 27 July 2011.
Williams, Nigel. 1 October 2011.
Wood, Bishop Wilfred, KA. 12 October 2011, 28 November 2013.

JOURNALS

2011 Journal of the One Hundred and Forty-First Annual Meeting of the Synod of the Church of Jamaica and the Cayman Islands in the Province of the West Indies.

Cimbolic, Peter and Pam Cartor. "Looking at Ephebophilia Through the Lens of Cleric Sexual Abuse". *The Journal of Treatment and Prevention,* Volume 13, Issue 4, 2006.

Handler, Jerome S. "A Rare Eighteenth-Century Tract in Defence of the Slaves in Barbados: The Thoughts of the Rev. John Duke, Curate of St. Michael". From the *Barbados Gazette,* or *General Intelligencer,* 15–19 March 1788, and recorded in the *Journal of the Barbados Museum and Historical Society,* Vol. LI, 2005.

Harrison, J. B and A. J. Jukes-Browne. "The Geology of Barbados, 1890", in Alfred Senn *Paleogene of Barbados, AAPG Bulletin,* Vol. 24, Issue 9, 1940.

Holder, John. "Religious Trends in Barbados during the last Sixty Years". *The Journal of the Barbados Museum and Historical Society.* Volume XLII, 1994:59.

Yeo, Jeffrey. "A Case without Parallel: The Bishops of London and the Anglican Churches Overseas, 1660–1748". *Journal of Ecclesiastical History,* Vol. 44, No. 3, July 1993. Cambridge University Press.

LAWS / ACTS / REGULATIONS / GAZETTE

Anglican Church Act 1969, CAP 375.
Constitution, Canons and Regulations of the Diocese of Barbados, S.I. 1992, No. 77, Regulation C3.
Official Gazette, 19 May 1938.
Official Gazette. 26 June 1941.
Official Gazette, 29 June 1949.
Saint Andrew's Parish (Barbados) Loan Act, 1893.
Saint Andrew's Parish (Barbados) Loan Act, 1925.
Saint Andrew's Parish (Barbados) Loan Act, 1949.
Saint Andrew's Parish (Barbados) Loan Act, 1950.
Saint Andrew's Rectory Act, 1937.

LECTURES
Globe Event Planners. "Financial Instruments". Lecture held at the Grand Salle, Bridgetown, Barbados, January 2013.

Goodman, Marcia. "Financial Stewardship and Prudent Investment". Lecture held at Ellerton Gospel Hall, St. George, Barbados, 29 January 2013.

LETTERS / MAGAZINES / PAMPHLETS / TRACTS
APA Letter to the Hon. Rep. Thomas Delay (R-Tx), "Catholic sex abuse cases" (Press release). *American Psychological Association*. June 9, 1999. en.wikipedia.org/wiki/Catholic_sex_abuse_cases

Blanchard, Ray, *et al.* (2009). "Pedophilia, Hebephilia, and the DSM-5" (pdf). *Archives of Sexual Behavior* 38 (3). . . . . . Shields, 13837 (United States Federal Court 2008), as cited in Ewing, CP (2011). http://en.wikipedia.org/wiki/Hebephilia

Catwell, Sylvan R. "Passing On The Baton". Pamphlet distributed 1 May 2008 at the 49th Anniversary Service of Ellerton Gospel Hall, Barbados.

Evans, Bishop E. L. quoting from R. J. Phillimore in an article addressed to the Church in the *Barbados Diocesan Magazine*, May 1967.

MAPS

The following Maps are a few that indicated St. Andrew's Parish Church on an apparently different location from, and south of where it is presently situated:

Phillip Lea, London, 1695

Surveyor William Mayo's Map of 1717–1721 engraved by John Senex, 1722

H. Moll, London, 1739; and

Thomas Jeffers, London, 1775.

NEWSPAPERS / VESTRY MINUTES
Ally, Terry. "Can Barbados be hit"? *Sunday Sun,* page 16A. Sunday, 5 September 1999.

Evans, Bishop E. Lewis. "What It Means to Be Established". *The Barbados Advocate*, 31 March 1967.

Hutchinson, W. G. Vicar of St. Philip-the-Less Church, Boscobel, St. Andrew. "Terrible Landslides in Boscobel. Hundreds of acres silently disappear". *Barbados Advocate Parish Publication—St. Andrew. The Barbados Advocate* newspaper, 4 October 1901 (reprinted in issue of 15 December 1996).

Hutt, Maurice. "Need for Conservation". *Sunday Advocate News*, 10 August 1980.

"Disestablishment. The Anglican Church Bill 1969 Explained". *The Barbados Advocate,* 3 March 1969.

"The Anglican Church Bill Explained, Part II. Proposed Basis of Settlement". *The Barbados Advocate,* 4 March 1969.

"Repeal of 1911 Act Ends Church-State Link". *The Barbados Advocate,* 5 March 1969.

"UWI honorary degree for Archbishop Woodroffe". *Sunday Sun*, 1 February 1981.

"Road Project Ends November". *Daily Nation,* 22 April 1998.

"Priest Remains at St. Andrew". *Daily Nation*, 21 December 1998.

Bibliography

"Shaping Barbados—The Role of the Anglican Church". *The Anglican*, December 2006:23.

"Oldest Anglican priest to retire". George Conger (geoconger) in *The Church of England Newspaper*, Church of the Province of the West Indies, 18 March 2011.

The Bajan, July–August 1989.

The Barbadian, 2 December 1846.

The Barbadian, Volume XXIV, 1846.

The Barbadian, 7 November 1857.

The Barbados Advocate, Saturday, 14 March 1946.

The Barbados Advocate, Friday, 25 August 1950.

The Barbados Advocate, Wednesday, 23 December 1959.

The Barbados Advocate, Friday, 25 February 2000.

The Visitor, 15–18 June 1987.

The Visitor, June 15–28, 1987.

Vestry Minutes, 10 May 1911.

Vestry Minutes, May 1912.

Vestry Minutes, 1 September 1938.

Vestry Minutes, 29 September 1955.

Vestry Minutes, 11 November 1955.

NOTES / DIARIES

Beckles, George. Unedited and unpublished notes. Accessed 26 July 2011.

David Burke and Sons, Organ Builder. Edited and unpublished notes. Accessed 20 October 2010.

Gatherer, Canon Edward. Diary. Accessed 24 December 2009.

Mahon, Daphnie. Unpublished and undated notes. Accessed 21 August 2011.

Small, Rev'd. Laurence, MBE. Unpublished and undated notes. Accessed 13 March 2013.

Springer, Senator The Rev'd. Canon James Levi, GCM, unpublished, undated typewritten copy of Springer's Résumé, Accessed 22 November 2013.

Stoute, Ronald A. Undated and unprinted typewritten copy of notes. Accessed 2 March 2010.

Warren, Larry. Undated typewritten note. Accessed 5 November 2013.

Whittaker, Undine. Unpublished notes. Accessed 9 December 2009.

_____. "Anglicanism in Barbados 1627–2001". Unpublished notes. Accessed 3 March 2011.

_____ and Vanessa Knight. "Selected Writings of the Clergy in the Diocese of Barbados, 1969–2009". Unpublished notes. Accessed 9 March 2011.

PAPERS

Brathwaite, Herman. "An Examination of the Way the Anglican Church in Barbados Functions—Its Structure and Actual Operations". Diploma in Theology (External). Final Year Essay, Codrington College, 1983.

Fulham Papers (Official papers of bishops of London). Volume 15, 16 July 1724; Volume 16, December 1772.

Norville, Ian. "Some Outstanding Events in the Anglican Church of Barbados 1955–1980". Diploma in Theology, Codrington College, 1980.

REPORTS / SPEECHES / SERMONS / TRIBUTES

Belgrave, Simeon. Speech given at Canon Gatherer's 91st birthday party. January 2013.

Brome, Bishop Rufus, GCM. Charge given to the 1996 Annual Session of Synod, *Synod Journal 1996*.

Crichlow, Dean Emeritus Harold, GCM. 1992 Sermon at the Commemoration Service for Rector Gatherer's 35 Years' Service at St. Andrew's Parish Church.

Gomez, Bishop Drexel. Seventeenth Charge to the 1989 Annual Session of Synod, *Synod Journal* 1989.

_____. April 1990 radio broadcast.

_____. Report to the Annual Session of Synod, *Synod Journal 1991*.

_____. Report to the Annual Session of Synod, "Barbados Diocesan Trustees – 1991, St. Andrew's Rectory", *Synod Journal 1991*.

Small, Canon Seibert. "A Tribute To Father Gatherer" in the booklet, *The Holy Eucharist and Commemoration of the Ministry of The Reverend Edward Godson Gatherer*. Sunday 27 March 2011.

Wood, Bishop Wilfred KA. Speech given at Canon Gatherer's 91st birthday party. January 2013.

THESIS

Ellis, Suzanne L. "Disestablishment and the Challenge of Finance for the Anglican Church in Barbados (1969–1999)". M.A. thesis, University of the West Indies, Cave Hill, 2008.

Fields, Stephen. "A Decade of Disestablishment 1969–1979". B.A. Thesis, Caribbean Studies, UC 300, University of the West Indies, Cave Hill, 1980.

Lucas, Betty. "The State and the Disestablishment of the Anglican Church in Barbados". B.A. thesis, University of the West Indies, Cave Hill, 2008.

WEBSITES / INTERNET

"Andrew the Apostle"—*Wikipedia, the free encyclopaedia*. en.wikipedia.org/wiki/Saint_Andrew, Barbados.

"Archbishop Cuthbert Woodroffe Passes". *The Vincentian*. The National Newspaper of St. Vincent and the Grenadines. thevincentian.com/arch-bishop-cuthbert-woodroffe-passes-p1743-10.

"BENEDICTUS PP XVI. Declaratio", 11 February 2013. www.vatican.va/holy.../hf_ben-vi_spe_20130211_declaratio_en.html

"Caribbean Elections". Sir Hugh Worrell Springer. "www.caribbeanelections.com/knowledge/.../bios/springer_hugh.asp.

"Colony in English America", published in http://www.jstor.org/pss/1922291.

"Cuthbert Woodroffe". en.wikipedia.org/wiki/Wilfred_Wood_(bishop).

Bibliography

"Cuthbert Woodroffe". *Wikipedia, the free encyclopaedia* en.wikipedia.org/wiki/George_Cuthbert_Manning_Woodroffe.

Davies, Tony, Ven. Archdeacon of Croydon. ". . .Inexhaustible faith in the promise of Christ". *The Bridge*, Vol. 7 No 7—September 2002. Southwark People: The Diocese pays tribute to Bishop Wood. www.southwark.anglican.org/thebridge/0209/page11.htm

DeGraff, J. V. *et al*. 1989. Transcribed by Nicholas DeGraff, University of California at Santa Cruz. "Landslides: Their extent and significance in the Caribbean", in E. E. Brabb and B. L. Harrod (eds.), *Landslides: Extent and Economic Significance*. Rotterdam: A. A. Balkema, 1989.

Dunn, R.S. 1969. "The Barbados Census of 1680: Profile of the Richest Colony in English America". http://www.jstor.org/stable/1922291.

"1831 Barbados Hurricane". *Wikipedia, the free encyclopaedia*, http://en.wikipedia.org/wiki/1831_Barbados_hurricane.

Ellis, J.B. "The Diocese of Jamaica". Project Canterbury: Society for Promoting Christian Knowledge, 1913. anglicanhistory.org/wi/jm/ellis1913/10.html

Gill, Joy-Ann. "Renaming Of St. Andrew's Primary School". *BGISMedia*; published June 15, 2011. http://www.gisbarbados.gov.bb/index.php?

Government of Barbados, UNDP and GEF "Capacity Building and Mainstreaming of Sustainable Land Management in Barbados". PMS 3408 – Atlas Project ID 00046566. http://asia-pacific.undp.org/practices/energy.

Hawn, C. Michael, UMR Columnist. "HISTORY OF HYMNS" *The United Methodist Reporter*. www.umportal.org/article.asp?id=8634

"Historical Development of Education In Barbados 1686—2000", booklet. Planning Research and Development Unit, Ministry of Education, Youth Affairs and Culture November 2000. http://www.mes.gov.bb/UserFiles/File/Historical_Developments.pdf.

"History of the Anglican Church in Barbados". *Email Webmaster*. Last Modified: 13 August 2007. http//www.anglican.bb/hist.

"History of the Anglican Diocese of Barbados". http://www.anglican.bb/hist.

"Jesus Calls Us". http://homeschoolblogger.com/hymnstudies/564962/

List of Governors of Barbados (1627–1833). *Wikipedia, the free encyclopaedia*. http://en.wikipedia.org/wiki/List_of_Governors_of_Barbados.

'List of sovereign states and dependent territories". *Wikipedia, the Free Encyclopaedia*. 2011. http://en.wikipedia.org/wiki/

"Loop Barbados: A North-Eastern Sight to See in Barbados" – St. Andrew Parish Church, ...loopbarbados.blogspot.com/2011/12/northern-sight-to-see-in-barbados-s.

"National Heroes of Barbados", published by The Barbados Government Information Service. http//www.oas.org/children/heroes/Barba.Heroes/springer.htm.

"Order of Barbados". *Wikipedia, the free encyclopaedia* en.wikipedia.org/wiki/

Plante, Thomas G. "A Perspective on Clergy Sexual Abuse", in Michael Nielsen, ed., *Psychology of Religion,* database, updated April 7, 2010. http://www.psychwww.com/psyrelig/plante.html. . .

artha B. Sawant. "Theme of Child sexual abuse in Mahesh Dattani's play Thirty Days in September". Vol. 2, Issue. III / April 2012. pp. 1-4 *Indian Streams Research Journal* http://www.google.com/#output=search&sclient=psy-

Stephen A. Nelson. "Slope Stability, Triggering Events, Mass Movement Hazards" - Tulane University. Jul 9, 2012. Natural Disasters–EENS 3050. http://www.tulane.edu/~sanelson/Natural_Disasters/slopestability.

Sir Hugh Worrell Springer". 1913–1994. . . In 1998, Springer was named one of Barbados' National Heroes thus. . .

http://www.independent.co.uk/news/people/obituary-sir-hugh-springer-1433334.html.

"Saint Andrew, Barbados" - Wikipedia, the free encyclopedia http://en.wikipedia.org/wiki/Saint_Andrew,_Barbados Viewed on 29 August 2011.

"ST. ANDREW (Thorne)"—"Calvin Institute of Christian Worship". http://www.hymnary.org/tune/st_andrew_thorne.

"St. Andrew's Primary School Renamed". *Nation News*, 22 June 2011. http://www.nationnews.com/articles/view/st-andrew.

"St. James Church, Barbados". *Wikipedia, the free encyclopaedia.* http://en.wikipedia.org/wiki/St._James_Church,_Barbados.

"The History of the Barbados Railway". http://www.enuii.org/vulcan_foundryRailway.pdf.

"The Mothers' Union of Barbados, 1998–2000". http://www.cariblife.com/pub/mothersunion/default.

"The National Archives". http://www.nationalarchives.gov.uk/

"Vestry". *Wikipedia, the free encyclopaedia.* http://en.wikipedia.org/wiki/Vestry.

"Wilfred Wood (bishop)"—*Wikipedia, the free encyclopaedia.* en.wikipedia.org/wiki/Wilfred_Wood_(bishop).

CPSIA information can be obtained at www.ICGtesting.com
Printed in the USA
LVOW02s0012280714

396234LV00001B/1/P